RAPE SPEAKOUT

Organized by New York Radical Feminists in January, 1971, this was the first time women began to tell their stories publicly. One woman remembered the "depantsing" ritual where grade-school boys forcibly removed the underpants of little girls; another was raped by a gynecologist; another recalled being forced to masturbate in front of her psychiatrist as part of her "treatment." There were women raped by their husbands, on the street by strangers, on dates, by house-breakers. One woman, a near victim, suggested castration as an appropriate punishment for the rapist, and her suggestion was greeted with wild applause by the almost all-female audience. Had all these women been raped on the street by strangers, or was there something in their relationships with men that gave them a gut understanding of the meaning of rape?

Rape can happen to any woman: And here is the first book that explores the reasons for rape, tells women what they must do to protect themselves, and how they can work together toward a solution.

ABOUT THE EDITORS: NOREEN CONNELL was born and raised in Mexico City. After graduating from high school, she came to the United States to study sociology and became involved in teaching remedial reading, anthropology, and Spanish to women convicts. She holds master's degrees in sociology and film criticism, and has worked at a halfway house for ex-mental patients and as a caseworker in a day-care center.

CASSANDRA WILSON studied modern dance at Juilliard and Sarah Lawrence. In her varied career, she has been a vacuum-cleaner saleswoman, a long-distance operator, a lawyer's representative, and a price marker. Currently, Cassandra is involved in film production and the feminist movement.

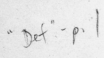

RAPE:
THE
FIRST SOURCEBOOK
FOR WOMEN

RAPE:

THE
FIRST SOURCEBOOK
FOR WOMEN

BY

New York
Radical Feminists

EDITORS

Noreen Connell
and Cassandra Wilson

A PLUME BOOK
NEW AMERICAN LIBRARY
TIMES MIRROR
NEW YORK, AND SCARBOROUGH, ONTARIO

Library of Congress Catalog Card Number: 74-79402

PLUME TRADEMARK REG. U.S. PAT. OFF. AND FOREIGN COUNTRIES
REGISTERED TRADEMARK—MARCA REGISTRADA
HECHO EN CLINTON, MASS., U.S.A.

SIGNET, SIGNET CLASSICS, MENTOR, PLUME and MERIDIAN
BOOKS are published *in the United States* by The New American Library,
Inc., 1301 Avenue of the Americas, New York, New York 10019, *in Canada*
by The New American Library of Canada Limited, 81 Mack Avenue,
Scarborough, 704 Ontario

First Printing, October, 1974

2 3 4 5 6 7 8 9

PRINTED IN THE UNITED STATES OF AMERICA

We gratefully acknowledge the contribution of the following people who made this book possible: Brighid Donahue, Winifred Ingalsbee, Leo Lerman, Cyrilly Abels, Mari Foss, the New York Foundation, Brendan Connell, and Evan Morley.

To Hanna

Contents

RAPE:

THE
FIRST SOURCEBOOK
FOR WOMEN

New York Radical Feminists Manifesto

It is no accident that the New York Radical Feminists, through the technique of consciousness-raising, discovered that rape is not a personal misfortune but an experience shared by all women in one form or another. When more than two people have suffered the same oppression the problem is no longer personal but political—and rape is a political matter.

In January, 1971, at the Rape Speak-out organized by the Radical Feminists, women began to tell their stories publicly. One woman remembered the "depantsing" ritual where grade-school boys forcibly removed the underpants of little girls; another woman was raped by a gynecologist who was, incidentally, a close friend of the victim's mother; another was told by her psychiatrist to masturbate in front of him as part of her "treatment," and still another had sexual intercourse with her therapist, his way of curing her neurosis. There were women raped by their husbands, on the street by strangers, on dates, by housebreakers, etc. One woman, a near victim, suggested castration as an appropriate punishment for the rapist, and her suggestion was greeted with wild applause by the almost all-female audience. Had all these women been raped on the street by strangers, or was there something in their relationships with men that gave them a gut understanding of the meaning of rape? Is it possible that the *average* male is programmed to be a rapist?

When the Radical Feminists held the rape conference in April, 1971, a body of information that dealt with rape from the political, social, and psychological point of view of its victims began to be developed. The central revelation was that the violent rapist and the boyfriend/husband are one. The friend and lover commits rape every bit as much as the "fiend" prowling the street.

Man has invented standards of superiority (male) and inferiority (female). Unsupported by reality as this idea is, man is always uneasy and threatened by the possibility that woman will one day claim her full right to human existence, so he has found ways to enslave her. He has married her, and through the family, binds her to him as wife and mother to his children. He has kept her helpless and dependent, forcing her to work when he needed her labor, isolating her, beating her (physically or psychologically), and as a final proof of his power and her debasement as a possession, a thing, a chunk of meat, he has raped her. The act of rape is the logical expression of the essential relationship now existing between men and women.

It is a matter to be dealt with in feminist terms for female liberation.

MARY ANN MANHART
July, 1971 FLORENCE RUSH

ONE

Consciousness-Raising: Rape Is Sexism Carried to its Logical Conclusion

Introduction

Rape, as an issue, did not arise because certain feminist leaders viewed it as "the issue" nor did it arise because it was a designated topic on a consciousness-raising list. Instead, rape became an issue when women began to compare their experiences as children, teen-agers, students, workers, and wives and to realize that sexual assault, in one form or another, was common. Conditioned to believe that the rapist was sick and a social aberration, while at the same time held accountable for attracting and precipitating the sexual violence we often experienced, many women repressed their memories of rape. It was either an incident unrelated to their "normal" lives as women or a situation that they had let "get out of hand." In her first sessions of consciousness-raising a woman would "admit" that she had been a "seductive child" or that she had made the "mistake" of drinking too heavily at a party or that she must have given her date "the wrong idea." But as women compared their experiences they began to come to some understanding of the anger they had kept hidden even from themselves. The pattern that emerged from their individual experiences was not a common pattern of assault—some had been brutally raped by a stranger while others had been psychologically assaulted by a lover—but a common pattern of responses that they encountered—"You're lying," "It was your fault," "You should have been more careful," "You're exaggerating." Through the process of consciousness-raising, women moved on from the discovery that sexual assault was not just an individual and unique experience to the realization that rape, as an issue, was a means of analyzing the psychological and political structures of oppression in our society.

We begin our book on rape where most feminist activity begins—with consciousness-raising. As the manifesto states, consciousness-raising is and has been a very important analytical tool for the women's movement. Our book is a direct result of discussions on rape in New York Radical Feminists consciousness-raising groups which, in 1971, led to the New York Radical Feminists Speak-Out on Rape and, later, the New York Radical Feminists Rape Conference. These two historical feminist events are the sources of much of the material in our book. The New York

Radical Feminists was organized in 1969 as a women's group committed to feminist principles as well as feminist process.* Because we feel so strongly about the importance of this feminist process, we have organized this book so that it approximates what most often is experienced by those of us in the movement. The initial step in the process is consciousness-raising. Out of the consciousness-raising experience comes speaking-out, then theory and research, and finally political action. But in reality these are not separate steps at all, but a complex experience of growing awareness and involvement. We are radicalized not only intellectually and politically, but emotionally as well.

We must make it clear that rape is one feminist issue among many. It does not encómpass our experience as women nor reveal every form of oppression. The very concreteness and immediacy of its nature makes it an issue that is easy to understand and to support, but that does not mean that other issues, sometimes less tangible, are less important. Nor do we mean to suggest that a consciousness-raising group must inevitably deal with the experience of rape. Our lives as women are varied and complex. There is no narrow standard of a raised consciousness nor specified issues that all feminists must deal with. This book, then, is structured so that other women can follow a process of political awareness in which issues, such as rape, develop. We have outlined the techniques of consciousness-raising and traced the development of our political awareness through it because we want to demystify the process of becoming radicalized. Ideas and social movements do not emerge mysteriously through some sort of vague osmosis; instead history is created by individuals. And in this era, history is being created by women. We want to reveal the sources of our ideas and political organization—we do not want any issue to be an abstraction that has been removed from the day-to-day lives of women. We also want to show other women, no matter where they are, that they can form their own consciousness-raising groups and that through this process other issues may develop which at this stage we can have no awareness of.

Organizing a Consciousness-Raising Group

Consciousness-raising is a process through which women come to their own conclusions about themselves and society. Here is a brief outline of how a consciousness raising group can be organized:**

Start with your friends. It is not necessary to have a large number to start a consciousness-raising group. Anywhere from five to ten is a good

*See Appendix I.
**See Appendix II.

start, not more than fifteen. You can advertise in your local newspaper, at your church, or school. Word-of-mouth is most effective.

Meetings are usually held weekly—each at another member's house. It is helpful to have a chairwoman and a secretary, rotated on a weekly basis. People can be encouraged to keep some notes on the work done in the group and to write short pieces; these can be collected and published for the movement. The chairwoman's main function is to help keep minimal order and to help the group stay on the consciousness-raising topic.

It is very important to have sufficient copies of membership lists so that every member has one. In this way group communication and later intergroup communication is facilitated simply by one person calling the next person on the list after her own name. When your area has many groups, some effort should be made to consolidate the membership lists. It is also helpful if someone in the area is willing to have her phone number available for incoming and outgoing information about groups that are forming or open for new members; this is a great help in organizing.

Consciousness-Raising

We work from the concrete experience of our personal lives in order to see a pattern—the pattern of the oppression of women. It is not group therapy. The basic assumption of the therapy situation is that there is an ideal feminine nature and psychology and that unhappy women are sick. We say our personal problems are political and should have political solutions. In consciousness-raising meetings we go around in a circle speaking in turn. This is very helpful in giving each member a chance to compose herself and her thoughts. It also helps us to listen to each other and breaks down feelings of competitiveness among women. Questions and responses to specific ideas and experiences may be answered at any time during this period. However, it is important to stay on the topic and get as much out of it as possible. Only when you have gone all around the circle and everyone has spoken should the group analyze what has been said and draw its own conclusions about its relevance to the positions of women. It is not always necessary to use the form of the circle but it is good self-discipline. The more concrete, specific, and personal the group can be, the more information it will have to work with. This body of experience will lead to your own feminist politics.

Things to Remember about Consciousness-Raising

Consciousness-raising does not work when people talk abstractly, theorize, talk political "lines," talk about others. In consciousness-raising we do not challenge another woman's experience. No one's experience has to "fit" into a preconceived pattern of oppression, so that it never becomes a matter of "who is more oppressed." ALL women are! So, let's use consciousness-raising to become strong and proud. Allow for diversity— women's liberation can never mean conformity.

Suggested Topics for Consciousness-Raising

It is helpful at the first meeting to have each person introduce herself and tell a little about her life before starting the topics. One or, at most, two

1. How I came to this meeting. What it means to me now.
2. First awareness of your role as a woman.
3. Childhood training for this role.
4. Early childhood sexual experiences.
5. Puberty.
6. Dating and social life with girls as well as boys.
7. Adult sexual experiences.
8. Work.
9. Education.
10. Marriage.
11. Pregnancy and childbearing.
12. Motherhood.
13. Aging.
14. Family.
15. Fashion.
16. Politics.
17. The media.
18. Women.
19. Homosexuality.

The final consideration is, of course, what the movement means to you now. What do you want it to do for you? Where do you think it is going?[1]

The consciousness-raising process does not limit women to a discussion of themselves, but through comparing their own experiences they begin to explore ever-widening territories of their physical/emotional makeup, and ultimately, the societal norms and institutions which shape all women's experience. Juliet Mitchell describes consciousness-raising as "The process of transforming the hidden, individual fears of women into a shared awareness of the meaning of them as social problems, the release of anger, anxiety, the struggle of proclaiming the painful and transforming it into the political . . . "[2] But how does this happen? How do women move from the realm of their private worlds, each unique and complex, to a feminist analysis of society? It may be that the simple act of communication among women becomes a radicalizing process. Susan Brownmiller describes what occurred in the first consciousness-raising groups in New York City, "Few topics, the women found, were unfruitful. Humiliations that each of them suffered privately—from being turned down for a job with the comment, 'We were looking for a man,' to catcalls and wolf whistles on the street—turned out to be universal agonies."[3]

It must be remembered that women are oppressed in ways that are very different from other forms of oppression. We are not physically isolated, but nevertheless, we are psychologically isolated from the larger society and its main avenues of power by an inbred sense of our worthlessness. It is only when women begin to communicate and to compare their pain that its origins are exposed. Through consciousness-raising we begin to recognize that our private humiliations are universal and part of a larger pattern. In a society where all the major institutions protect male prerogatives, women have only themselves to turn to. Conditioned to view males as our protectors and every other woman as a potential rival, the act of communication among women allows us to discover not only the hypocrisy of male protection in all its forms, from chivalry to "special" legislation, but also to discover that a common bond exists between all women. We also find new emotional strength.

In many respects when the feminist movement emerged in the late sixties it was a rejection of the male establishment and the male-dominated Left. It is only now in reviewing our recent history that we are beginning to realize that we must also learn how to relate to each other in new ways. Consciousness-raising is not an automatic solution to the problem of political organization or how we can set up new patterns of relating to each other. Nor is it suited to developing a deep understanding of oppression that women do not directly experience. Women learn from each other in consciousness-raising, and if the group is composed of women from the same economic and racial backgrounds, it may be difficult to see the different ways in which women are exploited. Thus while consciousness-raising avoids the pitfalls of rhetoric and abstract discussions, it can also narrow the scope of our newfound knowledge to what we know firsthand. When rape first became an issue, white women realized how it had affected them. They also began to discover how certain ideas, such as the racist image of black men as rapists, had been used against not only black men but white women to keep both of them obedient. But because there were so few black women in consciousness-raising at that time, white women did not realize that for black women rape is even more of a constant fear, since they already know that the police will be hostile and skeptical. Now that more black women are becoming part of the women's movement and are forming their own consciousness-raising groups, new lines of communication and awareness are opening up between white and Third World women. And now in New York City women from working-class communities are beginning to form their own groups.

Another drawback of consciousness-raising is that a group can lose the sense of its purpose and evolve into something else. There is a tendency to make consciousness-raising into a therapy group that seeks out latent motivations in our actions or that makes collective decisions as to what is the "best" way to solve a personal problem. Another tendency is to view the group and the supportive relationships that develop as a final goal of consciousness-raising. Often close friendships are formed and the weekly meetings become social events. While one of the purposes of consciousness-raising is to create warmth and acceptance among women, the consciousness-raising group should not become a closed circle where the sense of a larger feminist community is lost. And it must be remembered that our ideas can only be tested and expanded through action. Consciousness-raising is a method of communicating and through it women have discovered their common oppression, but the discovery of our oppression is only an initial stage in ending our oppression, it is not a solution. Just as consciousness-raising groups began to form in the 1960's, women's abolitionist societies formed in the 1840's, and both have led to a national feminist movement. In 1840 Lucy Stone wrote in a letter, "It was decided in our Literary Society the other day that ladies ought to mingle in politics, go to Congress, etc., etc. . . . What do you think of that?"[4] It took eighty years of organizing, public speaking, and campaigning before that decision was realized. We can have no way of knowing when sexual assault and exploitation of women will end, but the discovery of rape is a beginning. We do not have written records of the first consciousness-raising discussions on rape, but what follows is an account of a consciousness-raising workshop that took place at the New York Radical Feminists Rape Conference. —N.C.

NOTES

1. From "An Introduction to the New York Radical Feminists," 1970.
2. *Woman's Estate,* Vintage Books, 1973, p. 61.
3. "Sisterhood Is Powerful," *Women's Liberation,* ed. Sookie Stampler, Ace Books, 1970, p. 145.
4. Eleanor Flexner, *Century of Struggle,* Atheneum, 1970, p. 42.

Consciousness-Raising on Rape*

Helen: Would you report a rape?

Rita: Not really. If there's one conviction in a thousand, why go through all that torment and go through whatever personal things would be involved? Like having your name on the docket.

Marge: You have to change the laws before a lot of women will tell.

Leslie: I think it's more than the law, now that I think about it; first of all there's a certain amount of guilt among all women who are men's sexual fulfillment, and I think women don't want to go talk to other men about rape. I remember I saw an exhibitionist in The Boston Museum so I ran to the guards at the desk on the floor and I said, "There's an exhibitionist standing there." And they said, "What do you mean?", kind of smirking. I said, "He's got his pants open and he's got his penis hanging out," because I was a loudmouth kid. They were shocked and they had to do something about it. I guess they hoped I would say, "Uh, well, never mind," and forget it.

Gladys: I think the police report and the guilt (why do people say things to you on the street and all that) is because you're betraying something. I read a police report from the Housing Police about a seventeen-year-old girl who got raped in the hallway; it was two pages long and it stated exactly in the girl's words everything, down to "and then he put his penis in me and then he . . . " You know they got the report from her right there in the hallway. That's enough not to report it, two pages long from a seventeen-year-old girl. Without the guilt, which I think is extra.

Helen: What do you think the police attitude is toward a woman who comes in?

Connie: My cousin called me last night and I was telling her that I was going to a conference on rape, and she said, "Oh, my boyfriend, he's a policeman, and he told me there's no such thing and that a woman is

From the NYRF Rape Conference Workshop on Psychology of the Rapist, His Victim and Rape Fantasies.

asking for it subconsciously; she's probably being seductive or enticing in some way." This is the police attitude; and I wouldn't go to a policeman and tell him that, because you'd be in a back room and he'd say, "Show me what happened."

Gladys: I think that this is where the guilt comes in. Also women have been taught to be attractive since they're young children and they're involved in a whole seductive thing and are told men can't restrain their sexual impulses. When I was a teen-ager, I believed—it was a complete miseducation, a complete naïveté—that men simply couldn't stop themselves and you couldn't just neck or whatever because it was painful.

Helen: What's it called?

Sue: Love nuts.

Gladys: Blue balls.

Diana: I came here because a young friend of mine, twenty-one, was raped about a month ago. Somebody climbed into her bedroom window and raped her at two or three o'clock in the morning. She was so terrified she couldn't move until the next day. A friend of hers came and got her over to the police department. They said they couldn't do anything about it but they had to find out all the details, because right next door was a place that sells drugs and they have the payoff. She went to Bellevue, and I say the mentality of the police department and the doctors should be investigated; they should not be allowed to take over any case of rape; they have no integrity. She had to wait three hours to get shots against infection; she had to give all kinds of details; she had to go through one string of doctors after another. And they wrote on her paper that she claims, she *claims* to have been raped. And the poor girl called me last night; she has moved into another apartment, and she is in the most terrible terror; she can't go to sleep.

Connie: I think the police just generally use this opportunity, particularly around the sexual thing, to intimidate and humiliate women. They also use it politically. I have a friend who was kidnapped by two men; she was hitchhiking with a man; they separated them, told them a lot of lies, and kept her locked up in the small compartment of their truck for thirty-six hours. Her friend called her father, who called the FBI, unfortunately, because what happened was she pointed out the man; the FBI spoke to the man and said that because they didn't have a weapon or something like that or because she didn't physically fight them, there was nothing that she could do; they proceeded to give her a political interrogation for three hours, asking her what kind of political things she read, did she know any Weathermen, why was she wearing pants, what kind of woman was she? She had been thirty-six hours without sleep, most of the time without any place to go to the bathroom and they just gave her the third degree for three hours, all of it oriented towards politics. In addition to the insulting things like what did they do to you, did they put their hands here and there, and at that point she hadn't slept in several days and she was at the point of going crazy. It was in Chicago, and they wanted anything they could get on political things going on. I think generally the police just use the opportunity to humiliate and downgrade, and I think that's what they want to do.

Pam: When I went to the hospital after being raped, two nurses came in; both of them bullied me, two female nurses, because there had been a barroom brawl in my approximate neighborhood at the same time. A man was knocked down and his head had been beat up; he was knocked out; he was brought into emergency at the same time I was, and the nurses were very upset with me because I was hysterical and taking their attention away from this man *who really needed help.* Some cops came to get me after I called them, because I was waiting for my boyfriend to come back; he was out walking my watchdog and it happened in those fifteen minutes. The cop didn't tell me I needed medical attention and a medical examination to determine legal rape, and so they very carefully let my boyfriend go down to the police station with me, but when I was breaking up while they interviewed me, every time he came over and put his hand on my shoulder or told me to cool it, they threatened to throw him out because he was interfering with their interview. And finally after I had been down there for about five hours, somebody said but how do you know that you've been raped? I was there, that's how. They said I had to go to a hospital, and by that time it was maybe six hours afterward! I had to go to the hospital, for a medical examination to prove it, and when I went back three weeks later I had to have shots for syphilis and they had lost all my records. Roosevelt Hospital. It's a very bad place for rape; don't go to Roosevelt Hospital. They had no record I had ever been there except my bill.

Diana: I have never been raped. I was once working at a small bookstore, and a very big man came in. I was trapped behind the desk, and he said, "This is a stickup, give me all the money out of the drawer." There was eight dollars altogether; it was not a successful bookstore. As soon as he left, I called the cops, and when they came, I gave them the description and so forth, and they said to me, "Did he touch you?" I said, "No, he stood with his hands in his pockets." They said, "Oh, did you see that he had a weapon?" "No." "You mean he just asked you for the money and you gave it to him?" "Yes." That's not a robbery." It's as if the guy said, May I have some money, and I said, Certainly. Apparently that's not a robbery. It seemed to me that they thought I should say, No! My money or my life. And that I should fight this man off. What am I, crazy? For eight dollars? They seemed to think it was just like if a beggar comes up to me on the street and says, Ya got a dime? I say,

Yeah sure, here's a dime. I can't very well tell the police that I was robbed of ten cents. They seemed to think there isn't much of a distinction between that and somebody coming in and saying, Give me your money, and not show a weapon and not threaten violence.

Helen: What about women? Are we psychologically victims? Are we ready-made victims that make us good objects for threats and violence? You know that rape is not primarily sexual. All this talk about evidence, a lot of rapists can't even get an erection and they can't keep it, and they don't ejaculate. In some states the mere touch of the penis is rape. One guy, a judge by the name of Ploscow, made the comment that that's an unjust law, unjust to the man. That there should be full penetration. No one talks about how deep you have to be stabbed, how shot do you have to be shot, but boy, how deep do you have to be penetrated to be raped?

Marge: A hospital examination must require a certain amount of penetration.

Sue: You're lucky if you got a sadist, because if he rips your vagina—

Gladys: Most psychiatrists say that all women have fantasies of being raped and that psychologically deep down they want to be raped.

Sue: We don't need the fantasies; it's real enough. Rape is real enough; what do we talk about fantasies for? That's for something that's unreal; it's real; you walk down the street, you go to get a newspaper, and in most cities something can happen to you.

Gladys: Women are so ashamed and paranoid about their own sexuality that if they are brutalized sexually they somehow assume responsibility; a woman feels responsible and guilty if she's assaulted sexually and that's why women usually keep this kind of thing to themselves. They feel guilty about the event.

Diana: I happen to be sixty-two years old, and I remember as a child the different characters that used to follow me and molest me; then I got married, trying to escape some of this, and then I tried to escape my husband and went through the divorce, and I climbed over more benches and back chairs trying to get away from lawyers and judges and so forth. It was always we who are to blame; and then I stopped smiling, stopped talking, dressed funny; but if you wore a gunny sack, they came after you and you were still to blame. To hell with that, honey, *they* are to blame. They tell every young girl, from Eve on, that she was to blame and she must have done something. My brother said, "It must be the way you walk." And then I tried to go to work. And you run away from life because of this guilt. We have to bring this into the schools and everywhere for little girls and break down this myth of guilt.

Gladys: But I think more important or just as important is what you said before. I married a man, I married my husband to protect me; that's the kind of relationship between men and women in this whole society, married or not, and that's the kind of sanction that brings us to this sort of relationship. What I'm trying to say is that it's a psychological predisposition; I mean it's society-determined.

Rita: Yes, the whole thing is that you're taught that life without a man is naught; without a man, who'll protect you? Nobody. Yourself. Unless you do it yourself, don't ask for protection, not legal, religious, medical.

Helen: Why do we need protection? I know we need it—but why? What's going on in our man-woman relationship that down through the centuries we have to be protected from men.

Diana: I'll tell you, we try to get support—arch supports, corset supports, the man as support, and all of them are pieces of bondage, and we're taught that until it's so engrained it takes many years to break these crazy habits.

Pam: A lot of men are bigger and stronger and they know how to fight, and they really get down to it; we've been brought up not to fight, not to defend ourselves; violence is very scary to me.

Helen: How many of you had rape attempts that you didn't know were rape attempts? I'm thinking of this in connection with my own life. I only realized working on the rape conference that someone did try to rape me, a drunk whom I was driving home because he was the friend of a friend; he grabbed me in my own Volkswagen on Hudson Street. I regarded it as a joke, brainwashed as I was; I had a stiff neck, I had bruises, scratches, but it was a joke, it was funny; it was ludicrous. I had to laugh at it, because I didn't know how to fight. It occurs to me that maybe since I was five, I don't think I've ever hit anyone or even begun to. I don't even know if I would know how to hit anyone. What about the rest of you? How about the tremendous anger we all feel?

Marge: I've hit some men. Well, one guy came up in the escalator, in Gimbels, going up, and as he went past he grabbed my rear end, so I let him pass ahead of me and as he was going into the door I slammed it on his arm. I hurt him pretty bad and I smiled at him, and he looked like he thought I was crazy. It was really weird, looking at you like you're really nuts. After all, he only grabbed my ass, and now I'm trying to break his arm. But sometimes you can't get back at them. It so happens I saw the opportunity, his arm was there, and the door was swinging out.

Rita: When I think of not being able to fight, I think we're afraid to swing and have them make a comment and miss them and how humiliating it would be. They're big men; how could I miss?

Gladys: What about retaliation? To me, that's the terror.

Connie: I don't think it matters, knowing how to fight; most men I've known don't know how to fight; they don't really know how to, like judo, karate. I think they're used to being confronted with violence since they were little kids, like they've had the experiences of a friend coming at them wildly or men treating them gruffly; we're not taught; it's not in our experience and the fear is not knowing what to do, paralyzed in a situation because we just haven't faced it.

Gladys: I think for me the fear of retaliation is very strong. I've sort of been hitting back. I was in the Port Authority and I was going up the elevator and some drunk put his hand on me and I hit him and there were a lot of people in the elevator and I don't know how it happened but he said he was going to kill me and we got out on the top floor and I walked out and found some policemen. He walked away; but he said he was going to kill me and he was drunk and walking away and I got two policemen and they walked over and took him away. They were actually very kind, unusually. I was terrified; it was an instinctive reaction when I hit him; keep your hands off me; it is frightening to think that if you do hit somebody, they're going to kill you.

Rita: They ignore it; people ignore it.

Gladys: Yeah, but I'm saying that when you do feel, it's such an incredibly violent type of situation, and it's so—I can hardly think about it. It was so long ago too, but I think that there's so much terror involved I think that I don't ever remember hitting anyone in my life and I think in that situation you don't know how you'll react until you've been in it.

Leslie: But that should produce a response; that kind of feeling should produce a response; it's like we've all been cut, like a big nerve in us has been cut.

Helen: It's not only a question of being cut, but women have been taught to turn their response inward.

Gladys: Right, we internalize.

Helen: The psychology of rapists . . . it's almost as if they're a normal person, isn't it, because what do these people think of themselves? I mean, do they think they're normal and I'm asking for it, even though they have to take me behind a building and show me a knife and tell me they're going to kill me if I don't cooperate in some way.

Sue: It's like rape's completely normal; except if you can prove it completely, they might go to jail; otherwise—Are husbands and boyfriends walking around buildings half the time? They're normal people.

Rita: It's very complex because I think that the sexual assault is a paradox; it is somewhat of an aberration, and at the same time the so-called pattern of sexuality follows the exact same course as the aberrations.

Leslie: They're just extreme examples; it's like going one step further.

Helen: Overpowering the female is acceptable; you'll find people saying, "Oh, well, all females protest." The experienced male has learned to ignore her minor protestations; the man is expected to overpower, to be the actor and the aggressor, and so rape is a slight exaggeration of the normal pattern.

Marge: We can't fight these rapists, and if we're afraid to go to the police, then they're going to keep on doing it. I don't think going to the police is such a terrible idea. Once I had the experience of being assaulted, shortly after I had taken a jujitsu course and could throw two two-hundred pound marines against the wall. I was feeling very, very confident that this would never happen to me and then suddenly this idiot came from behind a building like a streak of lightning and he had me down on the cement floor before I knew what was happening. Before I could say a word, he put his hand over my mouth, etc., and he was going to rape me, and at that instant, like in the comic books, along came some cop with a gun and he stopped him. If it hadn't been for that, I would surely have been raped. Well, I didn't have to do much work, because the cop was there and he saw the whole thing; he just happened to see it, I was darned lucky. When they took this guy in, I had to say I was willing to press charges and of course I was. It was discovered that he had done the same thing to five, six other women, and it had some effect, because this one wasn't going to do it anymore. I was lucky because it didn't happen in my home or his home or some vaguely compromising situation. It was a clear case of assault in a city street, which was lucky because it could be reported. I understand the shame about not being able to go to the precinct, but I didn't encounter any of it. Something was done, and I think that as women we have to get together and not think policemen are kind and loving and gentle individuals, most of the time they are a bunch of liars and sadists, but we have to go to them when these things happen. We have to report it and press charges, because this at least gets some of them off the streets. Not every man is a rapist; I'm sure very few of them are, and those few just have to be locked up.

Pam: Well, you have to be believed.

Diana: That's a different matter. I keep finding consistently, in every discussion of rape that rape is the easiest charge to make and that hell hath no fury like a woman scorned. Men believe, and it's a very widespread belief, that every woman is just waiting to get them; have a quarrel with a man and she runs right down to the police station.

Helen: Do a lot of women bring false charges of rape?

Sue: I believe it's a mistake to talk just about criminal rape, the guy who comes out of nowhere and grabs you. I think you've also got to talk about your supers, your acquaintances, your boyfriends, your husbands. We've only been talking about criminal rapists, which is where we get into trouble with talking about how many women go in and say they've been raped. Well, maybe they have been; maybe the whole relationship that they had with a man was a continuous rape. I'm not sure how many times I've gone to bed with a man I really wanted to, how many times I've done it because he wants it and I don't feel I have the right to say no. I try saying no, but I don't really know how to say no, how to assert myself sexually, and I'm rather an assertive woman in every area except sex, where I become a masochist. I feel that I have not accepted society's role; I didn't get married or have children; I don't want to live in a house; I want my own life, so I become super passive in sexual relationships. I'm sick, sick, but it isn't just my problem. And I submit. I have never asked a man to go to bed with me who didn't want to; it's always me who goes to bed without wanting to. Yes, there have been times when I wanted to, but if one of us didn't want it, it was me. And how many guys have I been with who are really turned on by a quarrel; that's when they want me the most, and it's when I feel nothing, nothing, but I want to keep the relationship. This should come into our category of rape and we should see it ties in with that guy in the street, who perhaps grabs you.

Helen: Is there a difference in sexuality between men and women? Our sexuality isn't as strong we tell ourselves; we should compromise ourselves and help this poor man with his drives and we're being masochistic; we've been taught to be raped, in a very broad sense of the word, not in the sense of walking down the street.

Rita: "You're cute when you're mad."

Gladys: In psychiatric literature, struggle is a component of the sex act.

Leslie: I think in college I must have met fifteen men in my senior year who were really into that. The more you protested, the more determined they were to make love to you in the Sig Ep house parking lot. What do you do? Do you get out and run away at two o'clock in the morning? Yes, if you're smart. But a lot of girls can't.

Rita: Think of pornography. It's full of penises becoming weapons, swords; he rams it into her, and she's a virgin; the harder her hymen is, the more exciting it is for him. He batters away and then, triumphant, pulls out a bloody trophy. She begs for more, after all the screaming.

Pam: A sexually agressive woman is kind of frowned upon by men too, and I don't know how other women feel about it, but I prefer men who do take aggression. I had thought when I've been with a man that I want a man not to rape me but to be aggressive sexually.

Sue: How do you know what you prefer? You haven't been given a choice.

Pam: Well, I would like to be aggressive, but I'm terrified, because I'm really scared of men.

Helen: Is it a projection that we would like to be able to assert our sexual drives, our sexual desires?

Connie: The woman has to wait around for the man to initiate the sex act. I lived with a man for three years, and we had sex when he wanted it, period. There was no question about it. I don't think it's fair.

Gladys: I don't think you can talk about sex and rape together, for some reason. I identify rape in my own head with an act of violence; I can't relate it to sex because that would become very painful for me. If I related rape to the sexual act, it would really warp me for a long time about sex, so if I think of rape in terms of myself, I think of it in terms of violence. It comes into my life, and then it's over, and that's where it would stop. I think part of the problem with rape is that women who are raped cannot, most of the time, accept that kind of violence in their own life. It happens to other people. I had a sense that it's there, but what do you do with it if it's not real?

Leslie: A movie that really impressed me . . . it was about a highschool girl coming home from school on a train with a boy and girl holding hands; they were obviously a couple . . . Romantic love, arms around each other. This girl was walking home, and she was thinking all these pleasant thoughts about love and romance, the way it was going to be when she fell in love. She was walking through the park in broad daylight. She was raped. The next scene is when she wakes up. She goes home and the whole process is to destroy all her clothes; she burns everything, she takes a bath, scrubs herself clean. Then she leaves home and wanders around the city. She gets a job, she tries to pick up her life. One act altered her whole life. She allowed the reality of that to completely change her own way of living, and it was not the act, not that she couldn't fight back. She couldn't accept that this even happened to her; she just couldn't understand why men could do that. The interesting thing about that film is that the girl de-classed herself after that. She had been studying for a career, and she took menial jobs after that, wound up in a menial sort of job and considered herself a skunk.

Diana: She tried to commit suicide.

Pam: So how can you prepare your daughter for such a thing?

Helen: Well, we were talking about when violence enters your life—do you drop dead at that point psychologically?

Sue: One of the causes of so much emotional damage and humiliation around sexual abuse is what does a grown woman or adolescent do with the rage she feels, the humiliation? You can't have recourse to the law, very, very little. We heard about corroborative laws: you have to have proof of this and that. You're not very good at retaliation. How do you vindicate yourself? If a woman could really lash out and get revenge and justice somehow, the experience itself would be less destructive because there would be some kind of rationality in the whole world, but it just seems to point up, to blow up the whole injustice of your whole life, the whole situation that is so frustrating and circular.

Rita: I was raped when I was eighteen. I had just left home, and I was also pregnant at the time and very ashamed, and my whole self-image was already terrifically undermined. As usual I couldn't have any redress in law because the situation looked as though I had enticed the man, which is the part of the law I think one ought to attack. He had asked to speak to me—he said he was in trouble. He was a good Catholic boy from a very good school, just the kind of guy my mother would have wanted me to marry. And he looked perfectly all right, but there was something strange about his manner, but I sort of put the feeling down because one is embarrassed about one's neurotic fear of rape, which is even sillier than the realistic fear of rape. So I went out to the garden with him, quite by mistake, and he said, "Let's walk along here," and I thought, Well all right. He said, "Let's get into this car," and I thought, Oh hell, and I got in. He put me on the driver's seat; there was no handle on the door. Then he asked me to kill him. Rapes are probably very different. This one was a battle of wills. In a curious way, he didn't want me to want him—he wanted me not to want him and to have to submit to him all the same. I was too dumb to figure the play and work out another one. I guess I was being panicky as well. He said, Kiss me, I said, No; and he said, Kill me, and I said, No, and put my mouth up in a very insulting way. He wasn't satisfied with that so he hit me across the face. I made the mistake of fighting him, which was what his particular type of neurosis needed and so I got completely bashed up. I tried to get out of the car, I got the door open, and then he slammed the door shut on my head and at this point I began to get very confused. I didn't really understand what was going on. I used to belong to the school of thought that you wouldn't really be raped unless you wanted to and that there was always a way out. He weighed fifty-seven pounds more than me, and he kneeled on my thighs and broke all the tissues, sort of ripped them off. All I remember saying is, Please be quick, which of course he was. And the curious thing was I couldn't move, because I had been so bashed around the head. There was no abdominal damage, unfortunately, because there was nothing I wanted more than a miscarriage. There was the added drama of trying to find someone to give me an abortion at the same time. I remember he pulled me out of the car. I couldn't stand up; I fell on my face in the grass, and he asked what was the matter with me. This boy was really psychopathic—there was nothing that could be done. Finally he managed to pull me to my feet, and he put me in a car, another car, and he said, "I'll get someone to help you." So I sat in the car and nothing happened. I went into shock and got pretty shivery and began to retch, and I finally went back to the party. Everyone was either too drunk or too far out. I didn't look very beaten up or anything, so no one would take me home. I went back into the street and just hailed a passerby who took me home. And the curious thing was that the punishment was then exacted from this boy by the other boys in my own community. In a sort of Puerto Rican way, they drove him out of all areas of social contact. I never had a chance to revenge myself; the curious thing was I didn't really want to, because what I was really most appalled by was the fact that my will had been overborne. That was all. Physically I wasn't awfully hurt. I couldn't go to the beach, it was summertime, because those bruises were really obscene and sort of, I guess, turned on sadistic people. I was very aware of sadistic people at this stage. But I gave up all idea of revenge; it never really worried me. What appalled me most was this, the fact that I was a kind of tree or dog or a pillow that he had decided to beat up on, except that he needed me to fight back, which is something I didn't understand. As you can see from my story, I couldn't ever have brought a case against him, because I had gone out of the party with him, and they would have found witnesses to say I was lascivious or something . . . The fact is that this boy was in terrible trouble. If I'm not mistaken, I'm very confused about it, I think he was weeping some of the time. When he said to me, "I'm in trouble, I'm in real trouble," he really meant it. And that real trouble was something to do with the diabolic pattern his sexuality had taken, which he could do nothing about. That's why I didn't feel vindictive; I felt more horrified, and I had too much on my mind then, with the abortion— that was worse—and I guess of course other relationships and other kinds of men kind of balance out the picture. I saw him much later and became ill when I saw him, a reflex. And he committed a crime again. And in that case I said I would go to court, regardless of the fact that my evidence wouldn't be much good. He raped an engaged girl, and her fiancé took out an action against him, but the action was dropped because her fiancé said she couldn't possibly bear to give evidence, because they ask specific questions. They say, Was he erect, did he expose himself, did he do this, did you allow that, and so forth. And her fiancé said, No thanks, living through it once was quite enough. I think that's the whole point; it's that we consider that rape is demeaning and diminishing to us. There is no way in which we can face the problem, and I have to say to myself that I wasn't demeaned or diminished by this situation.

Helen: Aren't we talking about a power relationship here also?

Diana: During the war, 1942-45, the German women, some of whom escaped over here, lived in the most terrible fear of being raped by Russians. Some that I have met went to any extremes—some gave up all their industry, their home, everything, to get out of Germany before the Russians got in. And their sole fear was of being raped.

Helen: It is very dangerous to feel you have been diminished or degraded in any way.

Gladys: I think women have to stop looking at it as a sexual thing, because then they get messed up.

Rita: It has to be suggested that rape doesn't have to be violent; it's not necessarily the violence that's the most harmful aspect. If your sexual will, your sexual dignity is imposed on, why is that so much less terrible to you than if you are beaten by some violent and brutal person? You are assigning away your dignity, which women have too frequently sacrificed.

Gladys: One of the reasons women do not report rape and do not react to rape is because they internalize it. It is a matter of taking things out of proportion and not being able to answer questions as to whether he was erect or not. When a man is stabbed or violence comes into men's lives, they're able to report it and give an account in most cases. What I'm saying is that until women start reacting to rape in terms of violence and of legality, in terms of you being presumed upon in that way, they will react with internalized rage rather than with a kind of rage that will enable them to act by dissociating it from psychology.

Leslie: I don't think conditions necessarily have to be violent; I think that you can be just as outraged by . . .

Diana: . . . The threat of violence.

Helen: I would like to make the point here that rape is violence but it's not necessarily physical violence.

Rita: Maybe the term "violation" . . .

Connie: It can simply be sexual exploitation and aggression, not necessarily violence.

Helen: I think some people here are saying that rape is violence that takes sexual form.

Pam: Hostility, perhaps.

Gladys: Sexual hostility . . . Therefore one should not be any more a-shamed than you would be in reporting that you were beaten and stabbed. Rape is sexual, but I think the violence aspect, the threat of violence or the overpowering psychology of the victim, has a whole lot more to do with it than true sexuality.

Helen: I think looking at rapists in the extended view of rape shows they are after all to some extent normal people. The old view is that you can sort of excuse a person for this nocturnal bout because this person is sick. Whether your friend or some stranger in the street grabs you, there's no excuse, no matter how sick a person is or how normal they are.

Leslie: Because we blame it on ourselves.

Rita: That's because it's more acceptable, completely acceptable in our culture.

Sue: You hear all this crap that the rapist doesn't repeat. That's just not proven. Like I was reading through *The New York Times* and came across these scattered articles, which no one puts together. You read about a man, twenty-two, arrested and twenty women identify him as a rapist. That's twenty women who came forward, in three years. I call that repeating.

Rita: The authoritarian society is our enemy. It's what oppressed us, and I think it's the authoritarian society that's distorted sexuality to this extent, making it an instrument of power. If we begin to adopt the same flaw in treating rape in punitive terms, then we can only deal with it symptomatically as it turns up bit by bit. There will still be new rapists, because rape is the psychology of sex in our whole culture.

Leslie: When I asked him why he raped me, he said, "Because I love you." That was the message of the whole thing. A rapist will obviously not be reacting to the personality of his victim. He may be reacting to the stereotype of chicks or booze.

Helen: The rapist in rape situations takes all kinds of forms. Until I began reading, it was very unclear to me. Rapes by convicted rapists frequently do not occur in the streets; they follow you home. Many take place indoors. There are the rapes by one rapist, by two, the gang rape. Then there's the interesting variant, which is not uncommon, where the rapist wants a woman who is with a man because they're taking property. The power thing is very clear there, where they go to a car and pick a couple. They take the woman from the man; they rob the man, lock him up, and then they rape the woman.

Diana: Yeah, there's also another variant where a rapist at gunpoint forces a man and a woman to have intercourse. I have a friend who was forced to do something to another woman while the rapist watched at gunpoint. He locked one of them in the closet, raped one of them, locked the other one in the closet and raped the other one.

Gladys: It's interesting that in many studies I read most rapists, if they can finish coitus, it's once; but where it's a gang thing, where other men are watching, then you get a higher percentage of one individual who rapes a woman two or three times.

Leslie: In connection with the gun and rape, I had a friend who was a policeman, and we had a date when he was going off duty. He took off his gun. I didn't pay any attention—he wanted to put it away somewhere. He said to me, "You know, some girls think this is a very phallic symbol." So I said, "Well, it looks small enough." Was he angry! I insulted his gun.

Sue: Can I say something to you? I think we are falling into the parlor bag of this-guy-needs-help. A lot of people make speeches, but with their lousy contempt for women and their supremacy, don't think these bastards need help. When they're married, they go to their wives, but they'd rather go to their daughters. I don't think that they're so much sick as subject to this whole male supremacy and power thing; they're frightened. Because I fought back in a rape case, I would have been up for manslaughter; I was at the Rape Speak-out, and I brought out the

fact that I did kick a guy in the lower extremity and put him in the
hospital; now I was brought up for manslaughter because I fought
back—*if that guy died*. And it was just this type of woman who said,
The poor man, because a block later when I finally caught him and
started to kick his balls in, they thought I was crazy. They thought that
if he did this, he was sick, but I was even sicker because I really
attacked him. So I want us to get out of the bag of "poor guy." Shit on it,
we are so sick from what happens to us because of this fucking male
who causes us to have maybe an illegitimate child when maybe later on,
the state won't even let us have an abortion. I would like to bring up
that I was brought up Catholic, so I'm not prejudiced. The Catholic
Church is notorious for this whole system of go out and screw a woman
rather than plant your seed in the street; don't masturbate, that will
drive you insane, but instead of throwing your seed away, they tell guys
it's better to plant the seed in the belly of a whore—it's a regular quote
from the Bible. It hurts me when I hear women say these guys are sick,
because I get very upset, because I was not sick when I kicked that
bastard's balls and at the time I was only seventeen. At the time I
hoped he would die, but now I'm glad he didn't because I wouldn't be
around now. God knows where I'd be. They told me I couldn't leave
the state; it would have been manslaughter, not self-defense. They said
a month later that I was a crazy, hostile hippie. I was treated like a
criminal. I had to be a criminal.

Helen: Wouldn't you hate the system for that?

Sue: Shit with that, he was a pig.

Pam: I'm not ready to hate all men.

Marge: It's not that you hate all men, you can hate what they do to you.

Pam: I know what all of them do to me, I hate that one, but . . .

Sue: The point is that you can't tolerate saying they're sick and make any
more excuses because you heard what Phyllis Chesler said today, you
heard what Florence Rush said, no matter what, it's the woman's fault,
and that's why we have to get out of the bag ourselves.

Connie: Well, I agree with that, that's it's not the woman's fault.

Sue: The priests who told the kid in school, rather than masturbate and go
insane, to plant his fucking seed in somebody's womb and then the
priest turns around and says to the woman—and I was in a Catholic
school—you have to be a virgin and be chaste. It's going to be rape,
because if you're going to be chaste and a virgin and going to say No-no
and he's going to say Yes-yes, I have to plant my seed, it's going to be
rape. On 42nd Street they're selling buttons; it says, "Avoid rape, say
yes." These men aren't sick, they're contemptuous, and until we can be
a little contemptuous back, regardless of what we're called, I don't care
what they call me, a man-hater, a lesbian, whatever they want to call
me, groovy, baby, because I've been called worse. We have to start

getting a little contemptuous back, and it just really hurts me to hear women say men are sick.

Helen: I think the point should be made here that study after study shows that women do not fight back, that the most the man has is a scratch and . . .

Sue: Oh, come on, if a big . . .

Diana: They're very vulnerable.

Marge: You try to get a guy in the balls.

Sue: Then they get you in the eyes and they break your eyes and you're dead. And you'd rather be raped than dead, so you make a choice.

Gladys: You have to know how to do it, you really do.

Marge: That's right. You practice at home so you know how to do it.

Connie: I have a friend who as a child was brought up as a little boy. It gave her troubles when she became a woman, of course, but she was trained by her father to aim for the balls and he made her practice. When a guy did try to rape her, she pretended to be compliant, and when he got into a position where she could get him, she did. She leaped out of the car with the car keys, which she threw into the bushes, and ran like hell.

Pam: How come she got into the situation?

Connie: It was a date, a normal situation—it's a very likely or plausible setting. This is blaming the woman.

Diana: I wish we could have a seminar for people who have been raped or who have had an abortion. Women should not think of themselves as damaged goods. It's just an incident, it happened, and don't attach any important emotion to it.

Gladys: Maybe there should be some place where a woman who has been raped can go to other women.

Diana: There's no disgrace.

Pam: I was ashamed to tell my friends. They knew I had been assaulted, but I was unable to say that the assault was successful. They knew I had been beaten up on, but I couldn't bring myself to say that he had actually ejaculated inside my vagina. It was too terrible to say. I had to bear it on my own.

Diana: Even if in New York we can do this, how about the girl who lives in the Italian village or lives in the country towns or the Midwest? Here in New York a woman can lose her virginity and have sixteen happy love affairs; she can marry or not as she sees fit. We're not in a typical situation. But you get to the Florida towns and a girl who has been raped is the talk of the town for the next six years.

Gladys: It hurts me that we're talking and thereby thinking on two levels. I'm a little bit off this small town and do you tell or don't you? I was thinking that I have remembered reports of cases in which the gal who was raped is thought of as an object of shame—no man will want her—and the feeling is why? This was something done against her will, why then is she an object of shame? And I think before we were talking about, Does the attack have to be violent, well, what I think we're really talking about is violations. I don't know whether I can make a clear connection, but I feel that there is a connection, that the men who say that the woman is shamed and no longer desirable if she's been raped are talking about the violation of her purity, which is this lovely abstract thing that all women are supposed to adhere to. Whether women feel it consciously, they feel violation in the sex act. Whether out of marriage or in, even the expected sex is for many women a violation because she is not genuinely a part of it, nor is she on equal level with a man in the performance of the act. It's a question of responding to, being the answer to his prayers . . .

Leslie: It's also a question of being the man's property. It seems to me to get the man on two levels in response to the woman who has been raped. His property has been damaged and this in turn affects him. Also his role is to protect the woman, she takes care of the home, provides the sex, the food, she cleans the toilet bowl, and he provides all the security and safety. If she gets raped, he has not protected her, in other words, he has failed in his role. Her presence is a constant reproach to him because he has not been a real man.

Pam: I think that's why men are so much more active about punishment for rape. My father used to think rape should be punishable by death.

Marge: I think if we get that heavy in punishment we're going to get murdered as well as raped because they've got nothing to lose and at least we can't tell about it if we're dead.

Helen: I think that's why ultimately we get down to the primary cause, which is the power relationship in our society. It's also "Sex is dirty." And I think you can connect them and that's what it's about.

TWO

Speaking-Out: An Open Act of Rebellion

Introduction

If communication between women can become a radicalizing process, the act of speaking-out is an open act of rebellion. It is a declaration of one's right to speak, but it is also an attempt to define one's own experience, sometimes in the face of a male definition of that experience, one which serves to support male supremacy. In New York in 1971 women who had been raped "spoke out" about it to tell other women their experiences. They did so to counter the myths that (1) women cannot be raped against their will, (2) women really want to be raped, and (3) women make false accusations. These myths are not only sustained by the popular media, not to mention the pornographic media, but by the academic and professional establishment as well. As Ralph Slovenko points out in his survey of sexual behavior and the law, there is an assumption supported by psychiatrists and criminologists that women's underlying masochism makes them participants in their own victimization. He goes on to suggest a parallel between this myth and the myth of the passivity of Jews under Hitler: "These incredible events in Germany, it is said, happened because of some deficiency in the people who suffered from them; the victims themselves were allegedly at fault and contributed to their own destruction . . . Thus, under this logic, responsibility for the catastrophe falls not on the Nazi, but wholly or partly, on the victims. In one sense, it is quite logical: aggressive people are usually the "top dogs" in society and have the power to place the blame on the vanquished."[1]

Speaking-out about rape is an attempt to destroy the power of the "top dogs" to place the blame on women for crimes committed solely by men. It is an act that hopes to combat self-serving rationalizations with the truth of firsthand experience. Self-definition is a crucial step, because as women we live in a world where we are defined by others. The value placed on our appearance only indicates that women are a class of human beings who are observed, but not the observers. Psychiatrists tell us what our subconscious drives are, gynecologists tell us how to have babies, psychologists tell us how to bring up our children, dress designers tell us how to dress—and if we do not perform our supportive, submissive, and decorative roles, then a battery of "experts" are called upon to interpret our "deviant" behavior. Their pronouncements, no matter how complex and subtle, do not go beyond the popular attitudes toward women who refuse to toe the line—"castrating bitch," "spoiled brat," "overbearing mother." The "experts" are not as interested in the "deviant" behavior of men, because, of course, the "experts" are men. The Don Juan complex, the drunken father, or the habitué of prostitutes do not inspire the same interest as the promiscuous woman, the neglectful mother, or the prostitute unless they are the traits of poor or black males, another class of human beings who can be observed and analyzed. Though we are interviewed, tested, and written about, our opinions are recorded but not listened to, for they are data to be interpreted and categorized. If we complain about our economic dependence and our emotional vulnerability, we are told that we are maladjusted and neurotic. If we say that we do not enjoy being sexually assaulted and victimized, we are told that we are essentially masochistic. Speaking-out, in many ways, is simply the act of speaking, of doing away with out "interpreters" and "translators."

Speaking-out is first and foremost not an exercise in rhetoric and propaganda, but a personal and factual testimony by women about themselves. However politically and emotionally involved one woman may be in an issue—whether it is rape, abortion, or marriage—she does not speak "for" her sisters but only out of her own experience. It is a way of cutting away at male supremacist myths without creating new and equally false myths. Speaking-out may lead to a feminist analysis of an issue, but its immediate objective is the much more modest one of describing the real-life situation of women. As a political act, it developed from the model of the public hearing: "Redstockings made its first public appearance at the New York legislative hearing on abortion law reform in February, 1969, when several women sought to gain the microphone to testify about their own abortions. The hearing, set up to take testimony from fifteen medical and psychiatric 'experts'—fourteen were men—was hastily adjourned. The following month, Redstockings held its *own* abortion hearing at the Washington Square Methodist Church. Using the consciousness-raising technique, twelve women 'testified' about abortion, from their own personal experience, before an audience of three hundred men and women. The political message of the emotion-charged evening was that *women* were the only true experts on unwanted pregnancy and abortion, and that every woman has an inalienable right to decide whether or not she wishes to bear a child."[2]

It is the philosophy of radical feminism that consciousness-raising prepares women for participation in the women's movement. The women in the preceding consciousness-raising discussion on rape cry out for action. But history as we have known it is a history of men, their actions and ideals. If women entered into it to try and shape it, they did so often at great personal risk or sacrifice. When women dared to speak publicly they were either chastized for their unseemly behavior or punished. Anne Hutchinson, one hundred years before the American Revolution, was imprisoned, excommunicated, and exiled from the colony of Massachusetts for making the "unprecedented demand that she, a woman, be permitted to think for herself about God and provoke others, women included, into doing the same."[3] While religious tolerance may have been one of the principles established by the American Revolution, the right of women to comment on moral matters was not. When the Grimké sisters began to make abolitionist speeches in the 1830's, the Council of Congregationalist Ministers of Massachusetts formulated a Pastoral Letter which stated in part, "We appreciate the unostentatious prayers of women in advancing the cause of religion at home and abroad; in Sabbath-schools; in leading religious inquireres to the pastors for instruction; and in all such associated efforts as become the modesty of her sex . . . But when she assumes the place and tone of man as a public reformer . . she yields the power which God has given her for her protection, and her character becomes unnatural. If the vine, whose strength and beauty is to lean on the trelliswork, and half-conceal its cluster thinks to assume the independence and the overshadowing nature of the elm, it will not only cease to bear fruit, but fall in shame and dishonor into the dust."[4] After several years of fighting the standards of appropriate behavior, Angelina Grimké refused to speak in public after 1838.

To the women who gave the testimonies that are recorded on the following pages, the act of speaking-out was more than getting up in front of an audience or in front of a video recorder. To many it was a difficult and uncomfortable experience, but it also meant breaking the male myths that have defined their situation as women and that have kept them silent. There are no "unimportant" issues for a speak-out—women can testify about their experiences with abortion, marriage, job hunting, street-harassment, motherhood, childbirth, sexuality, housekeeping, illegitimacy, work, prostitution, divorce—the issues are limitless. The need to testify comes out of consciousness-raising, whether from a consciousness-raising group or from more informal contact with women friends. This is a vital precondition, because without this support, both emotional and intellectual, the speak-out may lack focus and direction. It must be remembered that while the speak-out itself should be without rhetoric and sloganeering, it is essentially a political act. There is no level of feminist consciousness that must be attained nor is there a mold that all women's experiences must fit into, but speaking-out demands a certain degree of understanding, both of oneself and the reasons why one is testifying.

The rape testimonies that follow come from three sources, the New York Radical Feminists Rape Speak-Out, the NYRF Rape Conference speak-out, and a video tape made by four women who had been raped. At the first speak-out, forty women gave personal testimony before three hundred women of the community, whose interest and support made us realize the importance of having a conference. At the conference another speak-out was held so that the participants in it would be reminded that they were dealing with the lives of women and not abstractions—this is another important function of speaking-out. The video tape is a unique way to combine consciousness-raising with speaking-out and it has the additional advantage that it can be viewed by people in a different location and time. This particular tape has been seen by women's groups, law students and lawyers, psychology groups, college classes on sexuality and women's studies, and general audiences of women and men. It has also been shown to other rape victims. Since the women are not speaking before a large group but among themselves before a video recorder, they are more at ease and they can respond to one another.

—N.C.

NOTES

1. "A Panoramic View: Sexual Behavior and the Law," *Sexual Behavior and the Law,* ed. Ralph Slovenko, Charles C. Thomas, 1965, p. 55.
2. Brownmiller, pp. 149-50.
3. Flexner, pp. 9-10.
4. Flexner, p. 46.

Personal Testimony

I

All the girls in my neighborhood went through a ritual between the first and third grades known as pantsing. It was a symbolic rape. If we tried to fight back, we were beaten. All the girls were frightened; we knew we had crossed some boundary after pantsing and had been subjected to ridicule. We were grabbed and dragged into a vacant lot. The boys tore off our pants, spread our legs, and looked. We couldn't avoid it. Even if a girl tried to walk home with another girl, there was some day when she had to stay late after school or couldn't find someone to walk with her. We couldn't tell our parents. We would be punished and it would be called protection. We would be kept in. Also the boys threatened to hurt us if we told.

II

I was eleven. Looking back, I'm amazed I was so naïve. I was coming home from the dentist with my sister at four in the afternoon. I was aware of a man behind me; I was wary. He followed us into the building. I felt guilty afterward for not having taken it seriously. We took the stairs instead of the elevator. Suddenly there was a knife at my sister's throat. He said, "Pull up your dress and pull down your pants, or I'll kill your sister." I was afraid, I thought he'd kill her, but I screamed to her to run. She ran, he ran after her, and I followed, yelling, thinking he was going to kill her, but he ran away. People in the neighborhood took the incident seriously—a child had been molested. The police rode me around looking for him. I felt it was my fault. I thought my dress was enticing, or my walk. I had done something to make him follow me. I was ashamed for a long time.

III

My father was having a nervous breakdown. He and my mother committed me to a home for delinquent boys and girls. I hadn't done anything
wrong. They just wanted to get me out of the house. They left me there
for five years, from the ages of twelve to seventeen. All the others had
sentences which they served, then they were released. I had to stay. When
I was fourteen, I was raped. I had just begun menstruation. I never
menstruated again until I was twenty-one. Another time I was raped by
the porter. It later came out that he had a long history of molesting and
raping the girls at the various institutions where he'd worked. When I was
fifteen I had a job working in a hospital off the grounds. One winter night,
coming home, six boy inmates of the home surrounded me, holding
knives. I was forced to have intercourse with all of them. The next day I
found a boyfriend who became my protector. When I was without a
boyfriend, I was public property. Once I got a boyfriend, I was never
molested or raped again.

IV

I was figuratively raped by my analyst. I was eighteen and came from a
strict Roman Catholic family. At the age of sixteen I was reading Simone
de Beauvoir. The more militant I became, the more isolated I became.
There was pressure from my family to marry. I refused to be an object. I
knew I would have to pay my dues some day for my independence. A
friend suggested I try therapy because I was becoming very withdrawn. I
was ignorant then about psychiatry—I went to a lay analyst. I could reject
my family, but I believed him. I was a virgin, repressed. He asked, Do you
masturbate? To a Catholic this is a sin of self-abuse. I said, No. He insisted,
Do you know how? I said, Yes. He said, Do it here. In front of me. I
couldn't. My whole therapy was like that. I was having homosexual
fantasies. He said, Get a lover. I was interested in my studies. He said I
couldn't do well in school if I wasn't having intercourse with someone, if I
didn't have a lover. I told him I was thinking of suicide. He said I was too
chicken. I tried five times, I told him, I really tried. He said, You're still
living, aren't you, baby? I couldn't pursue my studies as I should have. I
had been a very good student. I began doing badly. I tried other analysts
afterward. It was always my fault, I did these things to myself. I would
like feminists to look into analysis. How many women have been seduced
by their analysts?

V

In 1955, when I was nineteen, I went to a Harvard weekend to visit a friend of mine and spend the weekend with him. I took the bus back to _____ and in _____ I found that I had missed my connection. Desperate to get back to school Monday, I went to a parking lot and tried to hitch a ride. The attendant told me that he was going to visit an uncle in _____ after work and would I wait. I waited the hour. We went for coffee and doughnuts so that I could get an idea of who he was. He seemed okay.

He took me by car to "get some clothes" for himself. While I waited for him, he dispatched a man to guard me in the car. Shortly thereafter, three men joined us and the guard left. They told me they were going to take me somewhere and I'd better cooperate. I knew there was no getting out of this since there were three of them and one of me, and it was about 1 A.M. and no people were around.

Shortly, we came to a park. I was told to be quiet or I'd be buried here and no one would know. Since I chose to save my life, I decided to cooperate, all along beating myself for the idiocy of buying such a classic story. I decided to find out more about each of them since it seemed like such a polished operation. They told me that they do this regularly, usually with more guys. They get the girls from other guys, parties, or clubs, and then they all use this "catch." If a guy doesn't participate, he's thought to be weak, unmasculine. He needs to save face whether he wants to screw or not. One of the guys thought poorly of this practice and his lack of enthusiasm with me would corroborate this. However, he would in no way pretend to screw me lest he lose face. It just was not done. I found out that two had prison records for other charges and were awaiting trial, one of these was also on probation. One was a criminal, but uncaught yet.

Finally, as dawn broke, they took me to an apartment. One stood guard over me and attempted to rape me again. I played "passed out" and he gave up. When his head was turned, I sprang up and ran out. I found a milkman who told me where the police station was. I ran in and reported it.

When I reported the rape, I was coherent, and the police said, "You're so clear, are you a sociologist? How come you can tell us everything?" The police didn't believe me; they treated me like a criminal. I got disgusted with their questions and slow typing and asked to type my version of the report. They permitted this. I wanted to see these people indicted. I typed the report and said I wanted to be there for the trial. The police said I would have to pay for my own expenses; there were no funds for this situation. They went to the apartment and arrested the one guy there. He said, "The landlady won't let me back in because of you."

The police asked me personal questions especially geared toward my part in the "seduction" or my academic ambition. There was no sympathy for my ordeal, my fear—only the questions pointing to accusations at me which I already felt because of the mistake of hitching and buying such a classic story. It was unreal.

The trial was put off several times. I couldn't afford to go to it. At the trial, all of them were given suspended sentences. They were all twenty years old.

VI

I was depressed and went to a bar for drinks. I knew the bartender, who knew two men and a woman at the bar. The woman invited me up for drinks. We were high and kissing. I got bored and got up to leave. The man said he would walk me to the elevator. He got on with me, but we got off at the wrong floor. He pushed me to the roof. He said, "Take off your clothes." I didn't fight because I was too scared. So I started to unbotton my blouse. Then I tried to talk him out of it while I was buttoning up my blouse—but he noticed that and reached over and with one pull ripped my slacks. Then he gave me a big shove and I fell down on the concrete. He got on me, but kept asking me to help him. I kept saying, Let's go somewhere comfortable. My head was hurting. He apologized for that and raised me and put my head on a step. Then he asked if I were more comfortable. He didn't have enough of an erection and I didn't help him get one. I kept telling him that I was a virgin. "I never do this," I kept saying. But he said, "I can fuck that other woman any time I want. So don't you see I'm doing you a favor?" Finally he stopped, and said that he believed me when I said I was a virgin. I said, "But that's what I've been telling you all along." He said, "Women lie, but I believe you." I thanked him because I was scared and didn't want to get him angry.

He brought me to the door leading to the top floor, opened the door for me, and said, "Maybe we should try later? May I call you tomorrow?" I wanted to kill him, but I had to say, "Please do." He then walked me to the elevator and held the door, he being a gentleman. He called twice the next day. I felt guilty and ashamed and didn't report it.

VII

When I got married, my husband and I moved to the South. He was a radical, working with poor people. I could tell from the way he treated me that he was trying to decide whether to copy the mores of the people we lived among. Sometimes he treated me like a lower-class woman and sometimes like the middle-class woman I had been. After we had been married nine months I no longer had any feeling for him, yet I felt that I couldn't refuse to have intercourse with him. He expected it, even though we were completely alienated by this time. I finally got to the point where there was no feeling in my body when we had relations, yet he insisted on his "marital" rights. This is a part of the marriage contract, that a wife must be ready to have sex on demand, no matter what her feelings are. Withholding it is grounds for divorce, yet the reverse is not true. The husband does not *have* to provide sex for his wife.

VIII

Mother's Day I realized I hadn't talked with my sixteen-year-old brother since I visited my parents' house six months before. I went to his room, sat on my twenty-five-year-old brother's bed, and asked him how school was, etc. I was concerned about his possible use of drugs, but he seemed okay there. He still hadn't gone out with any girls and, when he wasn't working, hung around with his boyfriends. Like them, he was chiefly concerned with sports, cars, and fishing.

I was eager to see if his macho attitudes, which made him eager to want to volunteer for Vietnam, had changed. His description of a movie he had seen the night before led me to believe they hadn't. The film featured a John Wayne type sheriff who killed this guy, busted that guy's head, and shot holes in that guy's stomach. Central to the plot was a prostitution ring and, though I pointed out to him the situation of women in prostitution, his eyes still gleamed at the thought of their arrest and punishment.

He changed the subject to ask me for ideas for a school paper. As big sister, I kept generating topics which he considered, pacing the room with his head down. My mother called to him to change his clothes so he could help my father. I got up to leave the room.

As soon as I stood up, my brother quickly shut the door and lunged at me, saying, "I've got to do it." I found my baby-faced 180-pound six-foot brother pushing me into a prone position on the bed.

As he climbed on top of me, I realized what he "had to do." A year previously when I as big sister, was trying to educate him about women's feelings in sex (his sex education class had informed none of the students about the clitoris), he suggested that we "do it." I told him I had taught him a lot of things but that wouldn't be one of them and made it a point to stay away from him until this time. Apparently his wish had not gone away and I knew he wasn't wrestling with me when he started groping at the buttons of my pant-suit blouse.

I decided not to scream to alarm my parents downstairs but to handle it myself. With my free hand I pulled at his ears and hair. Before he put his sloppy mouth on my lips and breasts, I told him to get off. His reply, "You've probably done it with other men, so you could do it with me" (an echo of the movie from the night before), made him feel more justified to continue his angry, desperate groping of my body. I found a foot free and kicked his calves with all the force I could muster. Finally I was able to end the four or five minutes of horror.

I ran out of the room feeling very strange and nauseous. All my body feelings had been assaulted and activated against my wishes and I felt numb all over. I buttoned my blouse and went downstairs to the kitchen where my mother and grandmothers were making pastry. I played my guitar for them.

I couldn't keep up the facade and went into the living room to be by myself. My brother followed me to tell me he was sorry. I wanted to kill him. Being ten years older than he, I thought I should try to act more mature and helpful. After all, he was my baby brother.

I talked with him about getting to know girls his own age better. He said they wouldn't talk to him. I pointed out that he was so limited to sports and cars, the girls wouldn't have anything to talk with him about (apparently many young women nowadays have their own interests and don't get into things like sports just because boys are interested in them). I mentioned activities he could participate in to meet women as peers, but he rejected all my suggestions. I told him that I appreciated his apology, but I wouldn't be friends with him any more.

Back in New York I pondered if I had done anything to provoke him. I decided I had not. When I was fourteen and he was four, I had a fantasy about screwing him, and when he got into puberty I thought I might be attracted to him. Hashing it with my therapist, I realized I had more hostile feelings about his manhood and male privileges than sexual feelings.

I sought succor from an older friend. She said he was old enough to know better and we agreed that part of his behavior was that of a spoiled brat's. As the family baby who had everything he wanted all his life, why shouldn't he have me too? Obviously, he also thought I was a whore who should be available to him if I was willing to be with other men. The idea of a woman wanting sex of her own choosing, whenever she wanted it, hadn't reached him.

The next day I told the woman I share an office with what happened. She wondered how I was able to work that day.

I wanted my brother to talk with someone to reorient his confused and hostile attitudes toward women. Of course, none of his friends would be interested in men's consciousness-raising or even vaguely interested in developing new attitudes toward women. (Liberation often is an after-the-pain consideration.) I doubted if the average therapist would help; his behavior would be sloughed off in the psychiatric profession as part of his developing manhood.

I told his older brother (one year my junior) what happened and begged him to talk with our kid brother. He laughed and said he couldn't believe it, but my brother was so spoiled, he could do anything. The notion of my provocation entered his head; it left when I reminded him I'm a lesbian.

He laughed again when he told me that he had a lot of fantasies when we were teen-agers but he'd never act them out. He concluded that our brother was going through a phase. Of course, he felt bad for me, but he didn't think it worth his while to talk with him. When I suggested telling our father, we agreed that he'd kill _____ for defiling his daughter, his property, but his attitudes toward women were equally archaic and hostile.

I turned to my mother when she called to ask why I'd only be at their house for part of Father's Day and not the whole weekend. " _____ was fresh with me," I began and told her everything except his opening my blouse because I thought she'd be in rage about that. I told her he needed someone to talk to to reorient his attitudes about women, but I could feel her "Ho-hum, there she goes with her women's lib stuff, again" vibrate through the phone wires. She pointed out that one incident didn't make him a deviant and wasn't I overreacting? After all, her brother did that (and more) to her when she was a lot younger than I and she didn't tell her mother. She just made sure she locked her door if she was alone in her room and that's what I should do, too. Besides I shouldn't be alone in my room so much—it invited trouble.

I told her I felt I had a right to be alone in any part of the house without being molested. Didn't she feel she had that right, too? Apparently she didn't. Besides that was forty years ago and you didn't talk about those things then. She was too afraid her family and friends would accuse her of provoking him.

My mother was sure that her brother grew out of it and mine would too. After all, he was a healthy kid interested in sports. "Well," she breathed in relief, "at least we know he's not queer."

On Father's Day, my mother called me into her room. She had a talk with my brother after our conversation. He told her he was just wrestling with me—just fooling around. He wouldn't do anything like that. "After all, she's my sister," protested the wide-eyed innocent. He didn't know he had frightened me. (How would he know anything that a woman felt.) But he was sorry that he had.

Her tone made it clear that his story was right and mine was wrong; a sixteen-year-old boy was to be more believed that a twenty-six-year-old woman. My perceptions of reality were being so invalidated, I felt a little crazy.

My brother's apology, which came later that afternoon, made me feel crazier than ever. His patronizing, paternalistic manner suggested I was his younger sister, he was confident his one-line apology for "frightening me" would do the trick. All I could do was laugh. I never was frightened, but I *was* abused.

My women friends renewed my faith in my perceptions of reality and shared my anger. The whole story reminded us of a consciousness-raising testimony where you listen to the woman talk about her experience and laugh cynically at her naïve trust in people. But this all really happened to *me.*

My therapist put me in touch with all my anger. I wanted to kill my brother for violating my senses. She asked if anyone else in my family had made similar overtures to me. "Oh, yes," I remembered, "my grand-father." When I was fourteen, if we were alone when my mother and grandmother went shopping, he would "hug" me to him and get an erection. I wanted to kill him too, but he was already dead.

I blurted out, "But I thought families were supposed to protect you." Apparently it's not the case with me and many other women. I realize that one family can't counteract all the movies, books, and rock 'n' roll songs that nurture my brother's misogyny and machismo. But I know angrily that more women than I will be my baby brother's victims. Only a very few people will give these women any support or comfort.

IX

About five years ago, I awoke one night gagged, my hands pinned down by someone wearing leather gloves and holding a razor to my throat. I wasn't quite sure I was awake. The main thing I can remember wanting was the light. I remember thinking I could ask to turn the light on once I got the gag loosened enough. The rapist would loosen it up so I could make comments and then he tightened it again. I was able to notice the time. I had on a luminous-dial watch and this did help me in later time. But there was this terrible fear of being in the middle of a nightmare that seemed more realistic than ordinary and I couldn't break it up. I was trying to establish if there really was a person there. And then I did get my wrist cut slightly and realized that I was risking my life and that I'd better hold still and let the man have intercourse with me. He was very fast. He wasn't wearing any clothes on the bottom half of his body and he ran out the window in that position. Just like Romeo on the balcony, onto a tree and down!

I remember I got up and turned on the lights and took a bath in alcohol. I didn't have any douche around. I was living alone and I didn't have one (and I had never used one). I set off after forty-five minutes with a coat on and then I realized the man had gotten in my purse and had stolen some cash and left me without a penny and I wanted to get out of the place and I realized I had no money and also had a fear of going outside the building. I realized the man had also apparently been in the apartment for some time. He must have had a flashlight because he gagged me with my own dishtowel. It was then that I thought to call the police, not because I had been raped but because I wanted to get out of the place.

And I called them. I got a rather immediate response from about two or three cops. They must have started coming about three in the morning and they continually came. I had at least between twenty or thirty cops that night just coming in out of curiosity, just to see what the victim looked like. Most of them were extremely rude. They were talking about the mud on the streets . . . he certainly was a filthy son of a bitch, did you douche . . . the questions were very brutal at that time. I am not exactly sure who was supposed to have standing outside the emergency room. And then they all came back to my place and sat around my kitchen table until it was time for them to get off work, which was at six in the morning.

I had to go to the hospital for the police report. This was in the state of _____ . They have to take a semen count. They do nothing else to help a woman. They don't even offer a douche. You should have penicillin shots to prevent any possible syphilis and you should be given hormone shots to prevent any possible pregnancy. None of this was done. In fact, I paid a medical bill at that hospital for a lab report that was not done because they could not wake up the lab technician. But still I had to submit to the examination with the cops standing outside the emergency room. And then they all came back to my place because they weren't off duty yet.

At six o'clock they all decided to leave and I asked them to give me a ride to a friend's house. I was new in the city and had only one person I knew I could go to. They refused, but because I started to get noisy they agreed to take me with them. They were going to the area where my friend lived anyway.

They dropped me off at his place, I rang the bell, got him out of bed.

This friend's first thought was to get me to a near-by hospital which was Catholic and does give good care. However, it's not wise to go to a Catholic hospital if you've been raped because they don't usually take measures to prevent pregnancy. By this time it was getting rather late, I don't know, about nine in the morning, I guess. It seems that I had first gone to a drugstore, too. I'm a little confused about the time element here. I went to the hospital, the nurse asked me what time the incident had taken place. I told her. She said, "That's all right, dear, because a douche won't harm anything, so we can do that for you."

I left the hospital. I had to go back to the police station for questioning. I was trying to perform my duty as a good citizen and help the police catch this criminal. The questioning at the station was much more brutalizing than it had been in my apartment. They asked me, for instance, how long the man's penis was. I really didn't know. I had no idea.

After that session I then managed to find another doctor via a friend who was going to the dentist. This dentist recommended someone in his building. This was my first physical examination since having one once when I was twenty. I had heard sometime that there should be a nurse in the room with you, but it passed through my mind and I didn't think about it too intently. The doctor said I had to take all my clothes off in order to fill out a report. I don't know why I needed a report, by the way. I didn't go there for that reason. He said he had to examine me for bruises or cuts, etc. He then explained to me that it was impossible for me to have been raped as I wasn't *ripped* around the vaginal area. I had long since ceased to be a virgin and intercourse does not normally rip the vagina open, but men hold it is true that a woman cannot be raped against her will. I then had to get on the table and he said I had to have an examination, and *this* man tried to attack me. I cooled—I did need shots, I wanted to get those shots before I got out of there. I got up off the table and remained cool enough to get my penicillin and hormone shots. I was never billed by that doctor for professional services. I did give him cash at the time for the penicillin.

After this, I had to move from my apartment because it was dangerous to go back there. The police refused to give me any escort service to get my belongings out. And I needed simple things like a change of underwear and clothing, but they would give me no protection, they would not go up with me. Yet, if I went up alone they would not be responsible for anything that would happen. I stayed with a girl in a rooming house, a girl that I was working with. After a period of four or five days, when I decided I really had to have some of my belongings, I went back to the place with the girl. I entered through the back door as I had locked everything else up from the inside so that no one could get in there again. I saw I had just missed another break-in, by the same character, apparently. I could tell by glove marks on the windows. Only this time, there were two. There had to have been two because they entered through a transom and took out some hi-fi equipment which could not have been carried out by one person. I don't know if I had missed another attempted rape by him and his friend, but I can assume that that is true.

This time I called the police. It had only been a robbery. The place was ransacked—every drawer turned inside out. I couldn't get a policeman. I had to call them three times. They said that this was a case of robbery, and rape in the state of _____ was listed as homicide and so they just don't work together, not even in the same department. Eventually, after harassing the police department, I got a detective to come question. I later got a lawyer so that I could get some kind of help on this. I was getting goofed up with my lease on the apartment. I had to pay rent, but I wasn't allowed to live there. The lawyer was on the telephone forty-five minutes being transferred from one department to another in the police department. He had to threaten to get the mayor on the police department's head, to make a noise in the newspaper, etc., before I could get a detective to come and actually talk to me and try to help with this.

Their help consisted of taking me to the police station about one week later to identify the man when I had *repeatedly* told them that I had not seen his face. The room was dark, all I could see was a silhouette. I said I wouldn't convict a man I hadn't seen. The victim, the man that I considered a victim, the police brought me to see was a very large blond kid, a very young kid. The man who had raped me was extremely small. He had left his clothing outside and the shoe size was very tiny for a man, so the police knew he wasn't a football player type. He also left a fingerprint on the balcony window woodwork. They also knew he had black hair. He was Caucasian, but with black, straight hair. The kid they showed me was this huge blond boy and this was done obviously to pacify me.

I left the matter. Once I straighted out problems with my apartment, got the medication I needed, I was rather exhausted by the whole thing. It took approximately two days without sleep going through all this business. The last policeman that I saw was several months after I moved. He came with photographs, again of those whom I could not identify, and asked me for a date.

Sometime after the visit from the detective with the photographs, I was notified that a man had been caught who fit the descriptive evidence of the man who raped me. He had committed seven known rapes in the neighborhood that I had lived in. I feel it safe to assume that he would have raped many more women if I hadn't been an outraged and vocal victim.

X

I got raped three years ago about this time of year. At the time, I was living with a man in a dangerous part of _____. We were both Black Nationalists and we went to these meetings late at night. This man would be putting me down or ignoring me or just acting in a very oppressive way when we would go to these meetings. I felt really angry and humiliated by this, but I would submit and would go to meetings together with him. This particular night I couldn't stand it . . . the way he was acting toward me at this meeting. As a show of independence and because I was angry and instead of submitting to the way he was going to act on this night and just waiting for him to deign to notice me and go home, I left on my own. I decided like going home when I felt like going home. And this was at ten thirty at night.

So I left the meeting and I was still very angry. I was thinking about the way he was treating me. I was very preoccupied with that. I got on the train and I wasn't noticing anything around me. I was thinking about this whole situation and what I was going to do about it. I was preoccupied by that. So when I got off the train, I didn't notice the fact that a man—a white Puerto Rican man—was following me off the train. In this neighborhood where I was living with this man . . . it was like a poor ghetto neighborhood, it was very dark, no lighting and you never see any police. And I just got off the train and I was walking along with my head down and thinking and not noticing footsteps behind me until I got to the house. And I got to the house and went through the entrance door. This man suddenly appeared and slipped through the door behind me and he had a gun. At that point he said (he looked sort of excitable), "Do what I tell you, I won't hurt you."

He made me leave the building and took me down the block and across the street. While he was taking me there—with this gun on me—a car passed and there were people around the block and nobody noticed anything. With this excitable man with a gun I didn't appeal to anybody in the cars or the people I saw down the block because I had no confidence that anybody would help me anyway and that people would just mind their own business. I would end up getting shot and nobody would help me if I tried to call out to somebody.

This man made me go behind a building, and as we were going behind the building, there were people in lighted apartments with windows open and I didn't call out to them. But they could hear us going around the building, but nobody noticed or nobody decided to mind anybody else's business. And nobody came to investigate or anything.

And . . . um . . . he . . . um. So, the man . . . um. He forced me to take off my lower clothing, he forced me to have intercourse with him behind this building. Before the actual rape took place I was trying frantically to talk him out of it by saying things. "You don't want me." Like, you know, he was white ... "I'm ugly, I'm black and you don't want me." And he was responding with this stuff about how much he liked black people. He actually said to me that some of his best friends were Black Muslims. I'm not kidding you! The whole time we were behind this building, after he finally got me back there and he knew I wasn't going to call out or anything like that, he started volunteering his life story and talking about his black friends. He was like solicitous, like, "I'm not hurting you, am I?" He was talking like he considered himself like some kind of Third World Nationalist. And as long as he was solicitous about me he had a right to my "service," and as long as I went along with it everything was fine and we were still in solidarity, right? Really. That was the thing that got me the most. There was no contradiction between his friendship for blacks and his solicitous attitude about me and the fact that he was raping me!

And after the rape it was as though he was doing two contradictory things at the same time. He was asking me did I want a cigarette, was I all right and he didn't hurt me, did he? and continuing to tell me about his life. He volunteered the information that he had just gotten out of jail the day before and he hadn't had a woman for so long that he couldn't wait, like before the rape. I don't know ... I was trying all kinds of stuff. I was acting as though I was concerned for him because he had this gun, right? And he was excitable and I was saying, "Yeah, you want sex very badly but don't you think that you could find some girl who would willingly have intercourse with you instead of having to do this? Why are you doing this?" And he was saying that he couldn't wait and that no, he didn't expect to persuade a woman to have intercourse with him. So, of course, he was going to have to do this. He felt that this was going to be the only way he was going to have sex.

And, okay, we were having this discussion and the chummy thing about the cigarettes afterward, but every once in a while he would say, "Are you going to tell anybody?" and he still had the gun. "You're not going to tell anybody, are you?" and like these threats in between this friendly conversation. And so I said, "No, I'm not going to tell anybody. No, I'll certainly not." I still continued not to be angry and to be concerned for him and his welfare, I mean to ward off his killing, which he easily could have. I said I was married and I said no, I couldn't tell anybody. I wouldn't even tell my husband because my husband would kill me. And no, I wouldn't do that, I wouldn't tell anybody. And so he finally believed me and we got back onto the street and he disappeared.

It was really weird. It was like a delayed terror reaction. Like, when I started thinking how easily he could have just killed me behind the building. I was shaking, but I wasn't just shaking. I was telling this man I couldn't tell my husband because my husband would kill me. The way I was feeling after this happened, I was afraid to tell this man that I was living with when he showed up that night, because for me to take the initiative and do anything independent was forbidden anyway. And I had taken the initiative in leaving and this happened to me, so it was my fault for leaving the meeting by myself.

I told the man I was living with and his reaction was, like . . . he could see how shaken I was. To some extent he was angry with me, but his reaction was that he was supposed to be comforting me later, for what happened. But I could tell his reaction was first that I was dirty. Like, he pushed me into the bathroom and handed me a kind of douche thing. He gave me this tube and stuff and said to me, "Get clean." So he considered me dirty, but he was also excited by the fact that this had happened to me. After I had gotten clean, he was supposed to be comforting me, but he screwed me. It was kind of a fascination with the fact that another man had had me that night. I got the definite impression that what he felt he was doing was retaking possession of me and my body.

And I didn't report this to the police. Nationalism was all mixed up in this. It was partly being a Nationalist and the police were white. I felt I would be guilty in turning in another Third World person who had raped me. I felt I shouldn't do that, that it would be somehow wrong for me to do that. It was wrong for me to retaliate against abother Third World person. It was partly that and partly because I was just terrified and partly because I was sure that if I went to the police that (1) they weren't going to do anything and (2) they weren't going to protect me. We never see any policemen in that neighborhood and the man would just come back and get me for it if I turned him in. And (3) black women are supposed to be whores anyway. They wouldn't believe it and they would jeer and I would just be humiliated if I did that, and possibly physically injured by the man when the police told him that I turned him in.

So I didn't do anything. I just went into this whole terror thing. I was afraid to take that same subway and was just generally shaken. I was shaken for weeks afterward and on those political meeting things—I just stopped all political activity. I just couldn't stand to go and be humiliated with this man. I was terrified to go anywhere on my own. I just stopped going to meetings at all. I felt too defenseless and too afraid, and so I just stopped doing anything. Like, my entire political activity would stop for months after that and I would just stay home and I was just frightened.

The Rape Tape*

Jane: This is a tape about rape that we're making. It began because Nellie and I were once talking as we were waiting for the elevator. We were saying how we were so scared just to live alone, and we just had tremendous fear of anything happening at night and in the apartment. We discovered that the reason we were both scared was because we had both been raped and that being raped had long-lasting effects on us. We started to talk about how we felt about being raped. We decided that it would be really good to make a tape of women who had been raped talking about the effects, so that other women who had been raped can see the universal effects of rape and can deal with them better and realize that nothing's wrong with them. So Nellie and I called up the Women's Center and got in touch with Sandra. We're all here now and we're going to talk about it.

Sandra: I'm going to tell about my experience first. I've been part of the Women's Rape Squad at the Women's Center. I was raped several years ago when I was looking for an apartment. I had my daughter along with me. She was a very small child at the time. This fellow was showing me this large one-room with fireplace and sitting room and bed and all that whole jazz. Then he started showing me his prizefighter scrapbook and telling about his middleweight career and how he beat up his wife when she was in bed with another man and he wouldn't give her a divorce. He was getting crazier and crazier, and I was getting less and less fascinated by the prospect of looking at the apartment. I decided I wanted to go. My daughter had fallen asleep on the bed in the meantime and he locked the door, blocked it. He said, "You're not going anywhere. You're going to have sex with me, and if you don't, I'm going to beat you up." He was over six feet and I think even if I'd had any kind of weapon I wouldn't have put up a struggle because I was really stuck in there. I was afraid of getting beat up myself. I was afraid of the baby

---

*Note: This transcript is an edited version of "The Rape Tape." The original tape is a dialogue between four rape victims. See Appendix III.

waking up. I was afraid of her being beaten up too. So I did allow him
to rape me. The experience itself was—I felt it had this awful quality to
it because I did want more than anything else just to haul off and just
punch him in the teeth. I really wanted that. I was furious at him. I
don't see how anybody could possibly relax and enjoy rape when it's
actually happening. I was terrified because he just did seem like a real
sicky. And so I didn't—I was like lying low. I was not going to shake
him up any more. And he kept me there all night. He would fall asleep
and I would try to get out of bed and then he'd say, "No, no. Stay,"
and he'd reach over and grab me. My daughter didn't wake up at all,
fortunately. Finally, as dawn was breaking, I slid out of bed very
carefully and I got dressed and got the baby together. I very quietly
unlocked the door and, with all my stuff together, I said "Good-bye"
very casually, and I went out the door.

Then I went home. I was living in _____, this happened in
_____. I was just relieved to get out at first. I was just going to go
home and not press charges, not do anything about it. I told my
husband. He was embarrassed; he was all for my not reporting the rape
because it would reflect on him. Then I told some friends. A couple of
women that I knew said, "Oh, you should really throw the book at
him." They were very angry on my behalf. This was years before the
women's movement, but they sympathized with me. They were on my
side. Then a couple of men who heard about it insisted, as a matter of
pure justice and principle, that I should definitely report the rape.
Practically speaking, this fellow didn't know where I lived, but I had
fantasies of him coming to get me if I did report it because he was such
a nut. But I figured, well, he doesn't know where I live and so therefore
I'm going to go up and report the rape.

So I went to a police station in _____ and as I went to the desk,
I explained I wanted to report a rape. They said, "Whose?" and I said,
"Mine." The cop looked at me and said, "Aw. Who'd want to rape
you?" He wasn't being contemptuous. He was just being patronizing. I
said, "Well, apparently somebody did." And so they sent me up to a
detective with their usual, Oh boy, here comes another broad, and
everything. They were very, very cynical at first, even though I told
them the story of how I had had my daughter with me. If I'd wanted to
have a tryst with somebody, or just to go and tease some guy, or
whatever they thought I was doing, why the hell would I bring a small
child with me? But I told the story over and over again. Finally I did
get angry. Although by the time I told the story about seven times I
was really seriously wondering inside my head, "Do I have the right to
get angry?" That's what it does to you. Something about the police

station and the total attitude toward rape and the whole thing about women do not have a right to protest—I couldn't help myself—I lost my temper. I said, "God damn it. This guy threatened me with his fists, which are deadly weapons because he has been a prizefighter, and I want you to do something about it so he doesn't go and rape somebody else." They kept trying to put words in my mouth by telling me that I really must want to get even with him for some reason, although I had only known him two days, and that whole bit. But finally they took his name and address. I went home, and a few hours later they called me up and had me come up to the station to identify him.

They had a preliminary hearing the next day in the courtroom. The fellow was there. His lawyer was there. The rapist didn't speak at all, which is a constitutional right, of course. The lawyer spoke on his behalf. They were trying to build the case on—well, I didn't have much of a case, that was basically it. I was questioned. It was determined that nobody had witnessed the rape. And so they had to simply close it. No witnesses.

Jane: Is that the law?

Sandra: Yes. New York and Iowa, folks, have this law which requires corroboration.* And of course generally when a woman is raped, if there are witnesses, they're friends of the rapist holding her down. Or sometimes even if they do sympathize with the victim, they don't want to go to court because it's time-consuming, or they'll get their name in the papers, or their fear is also of retaliation or they don't want to rock their own personal boat. But anyway, I did not have any witnesses . . . After my case was thrown out, one of the cops was in the courtroom. He tried to be consoling and sympathetic, for whatever reason of his own he might have had. He said, "Oh, look, honey, at least we kept him overnight in jail. That ought to make you happy." I just felt like I was existing in this total vacuum where nobody really was aware of what my real motives might be. I am not a person to them and they are trying to tell me that I should be happy by doing something vindictive, that I must have had some kind of unconscious vibes that I sent off to provoke the rapist or that I wanted to get this guy in trouble. They threw this whole big pile of garbage and mickeymouse at me.

Even after the trial was over, all my sympathizers who were my friends congratulated me on being so courageous as to report the rape. The women remained angry at the rapist. The men started to put me on the grill themselves, like, you know, "Are you sure you didn't encourage him subtly?" and this kind of shit.

*See Chapter IV.

Jane: Do you think they really believe that?

Sandra: No, I don't. I think it was what everybody did, what I did, maybe everybody except the cops who were very callous and used to this kind of thing. What they all did was attempt to get some kind of control over the situation, to get some feeling of being able to cope, you know. The women got angry. This is something which women are allowed to get angry about if it's somebody else who is raped and if it's their friend whom they sympathize with. The men became the DA and became terribly intellectual about it. They were trying to be objective, to see which hole is there to seal up so this never ever happens again. I felt that I was in a very repressive situation, even with my men friends who were asking me about this.

I was thinking back—when I was asked to do this tape—about what were my personal feelings about this. I think that I felt that if I were going to be protected I would have to invent something myself. I would have to build my own protection because there were very few people who were really able to help me or to give a shit about me. Obviously, the law itself was not structured to help me very much. I think that because I am a moody person and my moods shift rapidly, I would occasionally get these wonderful feelings of euphoria—like the DA really is not as nasty as I thought he was. They really are not trying to convict everybody in the world, as I thought they were, because they had shown this sympathy for the rapist and were not eager to get a conviction. But, you know, it was years before I was able to put this together and see that it was not any kind of humanitarian sympathy on the part of the DA. It was simply they don't know from rape, they *just don't know*. I think personally I was afraid, not of being alone—I had vague fantasies of the guy coming to get me and things—but I think I became more defensive. I also became more sensitive to pain. This is just something that I remembered. I was never a Spartan to begin with, but I did have uptight feelings about things like going to the dentist or getting shots or also the emotional pain of being able to reveal myself and open up to people and simply be friendly. I don't know, I had a lot of feelings. I was more aware of my vulnerability and lack of protection. I never told my parents about it because I just felt they wouldn't understand. They would think that either I had brought it on myself or they just didn't want to know from it because it was an unpleasant thing. They're the type of people who like to have as pleasant a life as possible and this means, if necessary, to turn your back on unpleasant things, to have your own enclave which you can be in and feel protected and secure. . . .

Another thing, he was white. He was an Italian from Rome and quite a presentable, neat, and well-dressed person. That was another reason I was urged to report the rape. I was told only the blacks were ever turned in and here you've got this white rapist who raped you and you should really do something for civil rights. They loaded the whole Lady Bountiful shuck on my back in addition to the urge for justice. They said I should do something for civil rights by reporting a white rapist. I suppose that when you do have something like that happen in your circle or to yourself, you do tend to pull out some of the justifications which are already on the books to rationalize it because there was and is so little consciousness about this whole thing. It's like either it doesn't happen, or if it does happen, the woman is damaged goods, she's defiled, you know, the whole thing. The only degrading thing that I can recall about it is simply not being able to hit the guy. I just really wanted to sock him in the teeth. But there are circumstances in which it would be stupid to struggle because it would make things worse. I can see that there might be certain fellows who might try to rape a woman and you could just turn around and say, "Look, you don't want this," or "I just remembered, I have an appointment at Western Union," or some kind of thing, and get away from it. Or some even you might be able to struggle with. But most of the time the guy's got a knife or a prizefighter's fists or some kind of weapon. Rapists don't walk around unarmed and just overpower women by their magnetism or sheer physical strength. It doesn't happen that way. Anyway, I have spoken to my daughter about rape. I've explained what she should do about it if she's ever threatened with it. It would depend on the circumstances, whether the guy had a weapon, whether he seemed all there. And, you know, I think she understands this.

Jane: Well, with me the worst effect came afterward. The rape wasn't half as bad as what came afterward. I've been raped in the past more than once, but the first time was about five years ago when I was seventeen. I had come to New York with two girl friends. We were going to stay at the house of one girl's cousin. It was getting late and we were walking around the Village—we had been in New York about a month before. We had met this guy on the street. He had invited us up to see his paintings and he said he was a painter. When we went up, we found he was sort of weird. His paintings were very sort of negative. And we left. But while we were in his apartment, one of the girls had been sort of nervous and she had picked up this piece of jewelry which was something special to him. Well, when we came again to the Village she wanted to return it to him. But she was afraid to go up. So I said, "Allright, I'll go up and return it, and you two wait right here downstairs." And I ran up and returned it. And just as soon as I got there, the buzzer started ringing crazy and I said, "My God, something's happening to them." I ran right down and they were gone, but there were two cops in a car out there. They started to yell at me that they were going to take me to jail, because I shouldn't be on the street, because that was against the law, and I don't know . . . they scared me, but I kept saying "Where did my friends go?" They pointed to the park. I started to walk down there. I didn't think that they had gone there, but that's what the police said. They police started to follow me. All the way to the park, they just kept following me. It was pretty late and there weren't very many people on the street, and I got very scared of these cops, they just kept following me. . . .

While we were just rethreading the tape I was thinking why I was so uptight telling the story. The reason is because I still think that people aren't going to believe me. That's the effect it has had. Four or five years later I'm still afraid that you're going to say, "Oh, cops aren't like that." But anyway, after hanging out in the street for about two hours, my friends did not come back. It was probably two o'clock in the morning and it began to rain. I began to get very uptight because there were people on the street, and I knew the East Village was full of junkies and murderers and rapists, and I didn't know what to do. At that point I said, "Well, I'll go back up this guy's place because he's such a wishy-washy weakling, sort of, that I just doubt he would do anything." If I stayed on the street, I thought, "My God, I'm going to get raped, I can't stay out here all night." And I went upstairs and asked if I could sit in his kitchen. I sat down in his kitchen and I kept my coat on. Like around two minutes later he started to attack me. He pulled me over to the bed and we must have fought for a very long time. After a long time, my muscles sort of just gave out. I was very afraid of screaming because he seemed sort of scared anyway. I was very afraid that he would have a knife and that he would stab me. So he raped me. He didn't hurt me too much. The only thing he hurt was my arms which he was holding down and maybe my legs—to hold my legs down his knees kept pounding into my thighs. After he finished raping me I guess I got dressed, and I was sort of sitting there. I had left a note out on the door to my girl friends, saying, "Ring the buzzer when you get here." And sure enough, one had come back. The other one had taken the train home. They had gotten very scared of the cops; they thought the cops were going to bring them to jail like they threatened. So she came up, and I told her what had happened. She was like very shocked. I was just sort of sitting there. The guy got very scared, and he turned very white and he said, "Oh, I feel sick, I have to go out." And he left. We stayed there, and he never came back. I looked through all his stuff to try to get his address and his parents' name because I was scared I was going to get VD or get pregnant.

Anyway, when I got home I was very scared I was pregnant, and I was very scared I had VD. I knew I had to tell someone and so I told my uncle. My mother was very suspicious that I would talk to my uncle alone. She demanded to know what we were talking about. I guess one of us told her. My uncle sort of passed it off. He said, "Oh, so what." I said, "Oh, but . . .." And he said, "So this and that." And I said, "I'm afraid I have VD. I think I should go to the doctor." He said, "Do you burn when you go to the bathroom?" I said, "No." He said, "Forget it, nothing is wrong, nothing is wrong." I was still very scared. After my uncle left, I remember my mother even called me "Candy." This time I just burst out crying. It was just so awful that she didn't believe that I had gotten raped. She was sure I had asked for it. She even, I think, thought that I had gone to New York to fuck. It was so awful. They so totally brainwashed me that I wasn't raped that I actually began to doubt it. Or maybe I really wanted it. People said a woman can't get raped if she doesn't want to. I thought maybe I could have fought harder, maybe I should have kicked him in the balls, maybe . . . It was such a terrible thing that was happening between my mother and me as a result of it. It had long-lasting effects. Like when it came time to go to school, she would not let me go to New York. She wouldn't let me go to Berkeley or the University of Colorado. I ended up going to a school in Canada that I did not want to go to that was very strict. And I had to leave there. I didn't want to go there anyway. I finally put it out of my mind and realized that it had happened. But for about nine months I was sure I was going to die of syphilis. Finally, I had come to New York and I went to a doctor. He thought I was silly that I thought I had syphilis. To this day even I have a fear that I have syphilis.

Sandra: It's really strange that when it happens to you, it's something that you don't quite want to face, because I don't think any of us are prepared for the instance of rape. Women are raped psychologically and economically and every other way, and it's something that you kind of turn off your consciousness and take for granted. But we are still programmed in a way to believe that we do have sexual choice. This is a choice that we have, and when it is taken away, it is a very traumatic thing, it's very upsetting. Then when your friends and your doctors and your policemen and the district attorney act as if it's something you're not to be too upset about—it's a kind of deliberate indifference. That's even much more upsetting in a way than the rape itself. The thing that made me the most upset, I think, was the feeling I got from the others whom I had talked to that the one thing I didn't have the right to do was try to save myself by submitting to the rape, that really, you know, a virtuous woman fights back and screams. That was the time I really did get angry at the cops. I said, "God damn it, he threatened me with a weapon. I want you to do something about it." I did feel that I was not being treated fairly at that time, that it was like looking up a dead-end street. The whole experience of reporting the rape and of thinking about the rape made me realize that if I needed protection I was not going to get it anywhere, that I would have to put up my own walls.

Jane: When you were talking about reporting it, I just remembered that one of the reasons I was so afraid to scream was that I had been in this situation because of the cops. And I knew that the cops wouldn't do anything. I was afraid that if the cops came they would hurt me, take me to jail and threaten me that I couldn't be on the streets late at night and that it was against the law. So I was all alone. There was no one that was going to help me.

Sandra: I think that that's one of the things that keeps a lot of women from reporting rape. They do feel, and we all feel, that women are alone, they are isolated. When it happens to you, you feel like you're the only person it ever happens to. And you know, even though you know that logically speaking it isn't true, you have that feeling that you are totally alone. I think also there is the feeling in the society that if you don't get protection, if you don't play the game as well as possible and get money, and if you're a woman, a man to protect you from anything and everything, then there is something wrong with you. I hadn't been to the shrink that I finally ended up with at that time, but I had been to psychotherapists before. The first one was a really tragic old-fashioned type, who did not understand that a woman did not like repression. He felt that it was sick and abnormal not to want the traditional woman's role. And he felt that some of my protests were signs of neurosis.

Jane: What finally happened, I just sort of put it out of my mind. I thought, Well, that's something that happened. Then I had a lot of other bad experiences when I'd been traveling. I traveled for a couple of weeks with a boyfriend of mine—he wasn't my lover but we were traveling together. The thing that happened was that on the way back home we got separated. I was going to stay in New York because my mother was moving from _____ to New York that day. All of a sudden I decided that there wasn't a place for me to stay. I thought I was going to go to some friends' apartment, but they weren't there and I decided that I really wanted to go home and be there before my family moved. I only had two or two and a half hours to get there, so I decided to hitch. I took a ride from a truck driver. I always thought truck drivers were good people to get rides from. My father used to drive trucks when he was young, and my cousin was a truck driver—they must be good people to take rides from. I always thought it would be like a groovy thing to do, you know?

I got in the truck, and he said to me, "Aren't you kind of young to be hitchhiking?" And I got scared. Then he told me that he'd have to pull off the highway and go to, I think it was Greenwich, or some small town. I thought, My God, he's going to pull off the highway and drive into the woods and rape me or stab me—because there had been a case I had read about. I thought, My God, I have to jump out. And I think he realized that this was in my mind, because at that moment—we were on the highway, it was Bruckner Boulevard—he started to attack me while he was driving. He started to beat me down and he started to rip off my blouse. He unzipped his pants and started to beat my mouth and head down on his penis. It was so awful.

In the meantime the truck is swerving back and forth. I said, "Well, we're both going to die now." When I kept trying to get up to wave to the cars on the side, I was still hoping they would call the police right away and the police would come. But I didn't really think I would have that much time anyway if that had happened. I remember at one point I was thinking, Am I going to let this guy kill me? I was thinking. Why don't I just take the wheel and just swerve this fucking truck off the highway and end it? That was the only way I could end it, but I didn't want to die. I don't know if this is what I imagine now, but I think there was some type of understanding between us that if I gave him all he wanted he would let me go. I don't know if this was stated. The whole thing was such a shock anyway, it was hard to remember. But he just kept beating my head down, and finally had an orgasm. I don't know if he did this purposely, but he swerved to the side of the highway and almost hit the concrete bridge overhead, and I got out.

I stood on the highway crying, and no one would pick me up. Even the cops went by. When I saw the cops go by, I thought, Oh, no—I was scared—Oh, no, cops. And they didn't even stop. So I had my knapsack with me, and I put on my jacket, and tried to scrape off the semen from my hair, and went home. Of course I had to hide the whole thing because we were moving. "Hello, Mom," you know. I'm never going to hitchhike again. This is like a limitation which is really awful, that women cannot hitchhike. This is how I feel. I cannot hitchhike.

When I was hitchhiking with a man I was traveling with, these guys said that we could stay at their place. I was very suspicious of them, but Dan said, "Don't worry, don't worry, we'll stay in the basement." While we were sleeping next to each other, but he was sleeping in his sleeping bag and I was sleeping on a mattress, I heard them saying that they were going to rape me and hold a knife to him. I got very scared and I said, "Dan, they're talking about us." And he said, "Don't be silly." They started to move the furniture around, like building sort of a fort so we wouldn't get out. They both got on top of me, at which point I think I screamed, "Get off of me." The baby upstairs started to cry, and the father got up. They were petrified of the father because they had been talking about their drunken father, and they left. Then someone came down and screamed at us, and Dan and I left. But the rest of the night we were on the run from them. I was so petrified. We hung out in the bus station, but Dan was scared that the guys hanging out there were going to, you know, hurt us. We finally slept in a field for a couple of hours. I mean, the fact is, that until things change, we're limited. When people say, "Well, you asked for it by traveling," you know, well, that's like saying, "As a woman you're very limited. You cannot travel, you cannot be friendly with men, you can never go to a man's house, you can never go anyplace." We don't ask for it. We just want freedom to live. . . .

I thought about it and decided if men are so awful to rape us that was not reason enough for me to have to end my life. I'll try not to let it bother me as much. As a result, I have a mistrust of practically every man I see on the street. But I'm not going to let men take my life away.

Sandra: At the time I was raped, I was in the process of leaving my husband, and I had a regular boyfriend shortly after that, whom I trusted . . . I think that the main thing the rape did to me was to make me want to get a little more power, control, protection, whatever you want to call it. I felt a necessity for that because it wasn't going to come from any of the things that existed. I really felt because I was alone with a child and had to make my own living that I would really have to learn how to take care of myself. Some of the things I did worked and some didn't, obviously, but it was that kind of uptight situation.

Jane: Yes, I got into this thing where I realized, Well, it's dangerous to live alone and it's dangerous to travel alone. So I realized that I always had to have a boyfriend—right?—to be protected from being raped. Well, to always have a boyfriend, you have to sleep with him, right? So I realized that here I was sleeping with people sometimes when I didn't want to, to avoid getting raped by other people. And like now I'm trying to be very independent. I live alone and I get scared.

TWO WEEKS LATER

Sandra: This is the third time I've told about my own rape, but it's my first experience using a videotape camera. I have never operated one before. But Nellie and Jane both felt that the rapport that we would get by filming each other and relating to each other personally would be a great contributing factor to the warmth that you have seen in this tape. It was really an exciting experience for me. The first time I was on television talking about rape, someone called up and asked, "Is there a school for rapists?" And I said, "Yes. Life." Well, women are getting together now and starting something to combat the all-pervasive influence of rape in our society. It's called the Anti-Rape Squad, and it meets at the Women's Center.

Jane: When Nellie and I started talking about making this tape, I wasn't sure that I wanted to make the tape, because I wasn't sure I wanted to go back and deal with the experience that I had. The best way up to now that I had dealt with these experiences was to just leave them behind and forget about them. But after making this tape and after dealing with the experiences, I really feel very good about it. I can now take the energy from these experiences, from the anger and from the guilt, and channel it with other women into a direction where we can start dealing with the problem. I am very happy that I made this tape.

THREE

Feminist Analysis: The "Alleged" Victim and the Psycho-Sexual System

Introduction

What follows are papers delivered at the NYRF Rape Conference and papers that women wrote in response to that conference. Unlike other issues, such as prostitution or marriage, there is little debate on rape—its oppressive nature is obvious—but much real research and analysis had to be done because rape had never been an issue in a male-dominated society. Despite the violent and pervasive nature of the crime, sociologists have largely ignored it, while psychologists have been more interested in the rape fantasies of women, which, if they exist, remain fantasies, than the rape fantasies of men, which are acted upon. Nor has the treatment of rape victims by the police or the courts ever been an issue to civil libertarians and lawyers. Similarly, reviewers have gone on at length about the violence in novels and movies without including the multiple forms of sexual degradation that are celebrated not only in hard-core pornography but in modern novels and "art" films. In short, there was little to start with, other than the raw data of our lives and our feminist consciousness. Some of us documented our professional experiences and compared them to male-oriented studies. Others of us interviewed women or studied statistics to see the scope of the problem. And some of us, like Joan Mathews, found the very absence of research significant.

As we gathered more research and data for our papers and workshops we began to fully realize that we were not dealing with an isolated social problem, but instead our studies were leading us to an analysis of our major social institutions. Violence toward women is not only pervasive, it is perpetuated by the total psycho-sexual system. The papers that follow are indictments not only of the rapist but of those institutions and industries that continue to support the caste relationship between the sexes—the courts, law enforcement, social welfare agencies, psychiatry, films, novels, hospitals, publishing, and government, on every level. We became less interested in the individual and varied motives of the rapist as we compiled facts and figures on the extent to which society ignores, tolerates, and even encourages repeated acts of rape and sexual exploitation. The very process of writing, and in this case the process of planning a conference, became radicalizing. For NYRF the issue of rape became a theoretical tool with which to cut away at the romanticism that obscures the real relationship between men and women in this society.

We have entitled this section "The 'Alleged' Victim," a term found in legal journals and penal codes dealing with rape, because it symbolizes the attitude that is prevalent in all levels of our society from respected members of the academic and legal professions to the popular and pornographic press. It is an attitude that refuses to recognize that women are victims even when it comes to the violent act of rape. We discovered that one of the sources of mystification of rape in our society is its association with sexual passion, an association that reduces the crime to a problem of self-control ("He needed a woman") or a problem of latent intentions ("She really wanted it"), when in reality rape is an act of hostility and humiliation. This refusal to recognize the objective oppression of women, whether it is economic, psychological, or social, is one of the major mechanisms of social control. We are denied the right to protest.

There are still many more aspects of rape to be explored, and the following articles by no means exhaust the subject. A detailed historical and cross-cultural study of rape in different countries is needed if we are to fully understand our current laws and attitudes. Also, little reliable data is available on rapists other than the few that are convicted, and given our current class and racist society, they are inevitably from the lower class and racial minorities. Almost no data exists on Third World rape victims, and a thorough study of their oppression is still to be written. Rape in marriage also has not been studied yet, though we know that it is far more common than supposed. Slovenko suggests in his article on "Sexual Behavior and the Law" that men often fantasize about rape, and it would be of some interest to fully investigate and analyze what rape symbolizes to the male psyche. Similarly, the relationship between certain styles of pornography and ideology needs to be clarified, especially since sadomasochism has been associated with both the extreme Right and the anarchic Left. In many ways the issue of rape is the first serious attempt to analyze the interrelationship of sexuality and power from a political perspective, and as other issues develop, this analysis will continue to gain greater depth and scope.

The process of writing is unlike that of consciousness-raising because it goes beyond the formulation of a feminist point of view—our attitudes and ideas are tested and verified, not merely expressed. And it goes beyond speaking-out because it attempts to describe not only our oppression, but to analyze why and how women are oppressed. Long before there was even a women's movement there were feminist writers, such as

Mme. de Staël and Mary Wollstonecraft, who unmasked the true dynamic between men and women. And long after the suffrage movement had become a caricature, Virginia Woolf, Simone de Beauvoir, Ruth Herschberger, and Betty Friedan kept alive the possibility of a second wave of feminism. We know our history through their books, and for many of us they were the only support we had when faced with the pervading masculine myths. Their writings, however, are fundamentally different from those that appear on the following pages, in that they were the products of isolated intelligence, of individuals struggling to rectify wrongs that were not recognized, much less admitted. Sheila Rowbotham, in her book *Women, Resistance and Revolution,* describes the dilemma of feminist writers such as Wollstonecraft, "Though she felt most female 'follies' came from the tyranny of men, she cannot conceive of women becoming the agents of their own liberation. She can only hope to convince reasonable men to assist in the emancipation of their companions."[1]

A conception of women becoming a movement is no longer merely possible, it has materialized once again. Ruth Herschberger recounts her reaction to the women's meeting she attended twenty years after the publication of her book, "When I wrote *Adam's Rib*, I was writing for readers who wouldn't accept the first premise. Now there was a whole roomful of people and a whole new vocabulary. I could go a whole month on the ammunition I'd get at one meeting."[2] Feminist writing, which before was limited to intellectual argument and persuasion, has now become a form of political dialogue among women. It is a means of clarifying, analyzing, and expanding issues that have emerged from the process of consciousness-raising and speaking out.

It is not the object of any one conference or writers' collective to exhaust all the aspects of an issue, simply because we recognize that it cannot be done and need not be done. But it is important that all women enter into this type of dialogue. Consciousness-raising is limited to a small group, while feminist writing, either from a conference or through a newsletter, can be distributed nationally. While organizing a conference takes several months of hard thinking and hard work, it does not entail vast economic resources, a large number of women, or a great deal of experience. Several highly successful conferences have been planned by a handful of women with enthusiasm, determination, and absolutely no money. Often donations alone or one fund-raising event will supply enough money for the rent and for publicity flyers. The single most important task for any planning collective is intellectual, not organizational: it is to develop and expand an issue, whether it is marriage, employment, or child care, and the rest will follow. It will not be easy. While a speak-out is a means of discovering an issue that affects women's lives, a conference should begin to explain *how* and *why* the issue affects our lives. This is where the process of writing and research is invaluable. But it must also be related to concrete experiences of women, which is why a speak-out and workshops are equally as important as papers or panel discussions. A feminist conference by its very definition is structured for maximum participation, not passive listening—because it is both a theoretical exercise and a political act.

Since we live in psychological rather than physical ghettos, communication between women is an organizing tool of great importance. As Shulamith Firestone points out, "That women live with men, while on some levels our worst disadvantage—the isolation of women from each other has been responsible for the absence or weakness of women's liberation movements in the past—is, in another sense, an advantage; a revolutionary in every bedroom cannot fail to shake up the status quo."[3] Books, pamphlets, magazines, and newspapers can help to create a national network that will cut across the divisions among women and that will support—intellectually, emotionally, and politically—women who are not in contact with consciousness-raising groups or feminist organizations.

But feminist writing is more than an organizing tool, it is also a process of development. Women have begun to write for and about themselves, to struggle with new and sometimes painful images of what it is to be a woman in this society. While the movement has attracted many writers, it has also encouraged women to write by creating a forum of ideas and a supportive but critical audience. Editorial elitism is discouraged. This open-access to publication is a recognition of the validity of our life experiences, whether we are housewives, welfare recipients, secretaries, prison inmates, factory workers, nurses or caseworkers—and it is reflected not only in grassroots newsletters but also in commercial publications such as *Ms.* Indeed, much of the women's movement's spirit and scope has come from individual women who for the first time in their lives are given the opportunity and encouragement to put their thoughts and feelings down on paper. Most of the following articles were not written by professional writers, though some of these women have since gone on to publish articles and to write books, but by women who were involved in one way or another with the rape conference. They presented papers or conducted workshops because they wanted to explore the issue of rape, not because they were considered "experts" or "specialists." Their research and insights have created a body of knowledge where none existed. And politically they have helped raise the issue of rape to new levels of analysis.

NOTES

1. Pantheon Books, 1972, p. 44.
2. Susan Brownmiller, "Sisterhood Is Powerful," *Women's Liberation,* ed. Sookie Stambler, p. 147.
3. *The Dialectic of Sex,* Bantam Books, 1971, p. 38.

The Sexual Abuse of Children: A Feminist Point of View*

Florence Rush

When I was asked to talk on the sexual abuse of children, I was not certain where the subject would lead. I am a social worker, had worked for the Society for the Prevention of Cruelty to Children, and remembered that the sexual victims brought to my attention were always female children and that the offenders were always male adults. This triggered off other recollections. I had worked some years back in an institution for dependent and neglected girls. I dug up some old notes and discovered that all those in my caseload had been sexually victimized at one time or another, running the gamut from exposure to male exhibitionists, to touching and fondling, to rape, incest, and carnal abuse. There was not a single girl who did not have an experience to relate. With my memory set in motion, I went back to when I was twenty and worked in an orphanage one summer between school years. I lived in the institution and was in charge of a summer program for the girls between seven and fifteen years of age. Soon after I began on the job, I learned that the male director would regularly take some of the girls to his apartment and sexually molest them. One night, I returned to the institution late to find the director in the hall entrance where he began to fondle and kiss me. The next day I reported his behavior plus his other activities to the board of directors. I was questioned very carefully and gently asked if I hadn't encouraged him just a teeny bit. I held my ground, and the director was fired. Please do not get the wrong impression. I quickly learned that the director was stealing the institution blind but no one could prove this, and I accommodated the board by offering a perfect solution to their problem. A week later, I was dismissed on the pretext that the institution had run out of funds and could no longer pay my salary. As I walked out the door, the new director, a man, entered. Tearfully, the orphans and I said goodbye, and it appeared to me that these children and young women were helplessly prepared to

*Presented at the NYRF Rape Conference, April, 1971.

face the same abuse which might be heaped upon them by the new director.

I said to myself at the time that these were poor children, who were unprotected and exposed to the evils of poverty. They came from broken homes and were economically disadvantaged, and this could not happen to a child in a stable family situation. This line of thinking, however, did not sit right with me, and something kept prodding me to remember more. I did remember more, I remembered about myself. I came from a very stable family which was both culturally and economically advantaged. When I was six, my mother sent me alone to the friendly family dentist who did more feeling than drilling. When I told my mother of my experience, she did not believe me. At age ten, I was molested by the father of a boy I secretly loved, and I somehow connected my secret love with the father's treatment of me and felt ashamed and guilty. At thirteen, my uncle, my mother's brother, came to visit from Chicago and wouldn't keep his hands off me. Again I told my mother and she scolded me for making up stories. Repeated lack of success did teach me never to report such incidents again.

At about the same time, I became obsessed with movies. I loved them, went every time I could, but found I could never get through a double feature without finding the hand of some gentleman up my skirt. My girl friend Jane and I worked out a system. If a man would get "funny," that is, if in the middle of a great Fred Astaire and Ginger Rogers movie, one of us discovered a strange hand between our legs, it was time to get up and say in a loud voice, "I must go home now because my mother is expecting me." Jane and I would then change seats and hope we would be left alone long enough to see the end of the film. It never occurred to us to holler at the man, hit him, or even report him to the management. It never occurred to us to hold the man responsible for what he had done. This was our problem, not his, and we handled it as best we could. In subsequent years, Jane and I reported regularly to each other on the number of exposed men we had seen, how we handled attempts to be touched, and how we escaped from what might develop into something violent and dangerous. After a while, we became rather casual about our experiences, rarely outraged, but simply tried to develop greater skills in avoiding and extricating ourselves from the sexual aggression of men without embarrassing the offender. This was excellent training and prepared me in later years for the breast-grabbers, the bottom-pinchers, and the body-rubbers. The horror, the shame, and the humiliation never left me, but until recently I never knew I had the right to be outraged and fight back. I was, after all, trained to be a woman.

After these memories, my thesis for this presentation became clear. The sexual abuse of children is an early manifestation of male power and oppression of the female. For myself, I need no statistics or research to prove my point, but to make my presentation credible, I have searched for supportive evidence. There is, significantly, very little material on the subject of sexual abuse generally and particularly as it relates to children. I think I found enough, however, for my purposes today. I will refer to five studies. The first is the one I have chosen as my authority and is the one most sympathetic to child victims of sex crimes. It is entitled "Protecting the Child, Victim of Sex Crimes Committed by Adults," and it is put out by the American Humane Association. I found this report to be the least prejudiced and the most scholarly, most humane and most informative as compared to the other studies I referred to. The following statistics, statements, and conclusions are drawn from this study, which is based on the investigation of 263 child victims of sexual abuse.

1. National statistics on the incidence of sexual offences against children are wholly unavailable. The FBI's annual Information Crime Report is concerned with statistics on the offender and not the victim. It does not even carry a breakdown of the total incidence of all crimes against children. What makes an assessment even more difficult, except for rare cases of brutal attack or fatal situations, is that cases of sex offenses against children are not generally publicized by the press.[1]

2. The problem of sexual abuse to children is of unknown national dimensions, but findings strongly point to the probability of an enormous national incidence many times larger than the reported incidence of child abuse (physical abuse other than sexual).

3. By an overwhelming ratio—97 percent, offenders were male and ranged in age from seventeen to sixty-eight.

4. Victims were in a ratio of ten girls to one boy. The boys were victims of male homosexuals. The victims ranged in age from infants to children under sixteen, and the median age was eleven.

5. In 75 percent of the cases, the offender was known to the child or family, such as a father, stepfather, mother's lover, brother, uncle, or friend of the family—25 percent of the offenders were alleged to be strangers.

6. Sixty percent of the child victims were coerced by direct force or threat of bodily harm. In 25 percent the lure was based on the child's loyalty and affection for a friend or relative. Fifteen percent were based on tangible lures.

7. Children were subjected to sexual offenses of all types, varying from indecent exposure to full intercourse, rape, and incest. The majority of incest is between fathers and young daughters.

8. Two thirds of the child victims were found to be emotionally damaged by the occurrence, with 14 percent severely disturbed. Twenty-nine of the victims became pregnant as a result of the offense.

9. In 41 percent of the cases, the offenses were repeated and perpetuated over a period of time ranging from weeks to seven years.

10. All the cases in the study were reported to the police (263). They made 173 arrests, and 106 were released on bail; this resulted in bringing the offender back into the community, thus again exposing the child victim to danger.

11. More than 1,000 court appearances were required for the 173 cases prosecuted, and this resulted in extreme tension and stress for both child and family. Forty-four percent of the cases were dismissed for lack of proof.

12. In almost two thirds of the homes, the parents were found to be inadequate. They were deemed to be failing to provide care and protection necessary for their children's welfare. (I will come back to this last point later.)[2]

I will comment now on four other studies. The following quotations and my comments will focus on general and professional attitudes that relentlessly forgive the adult male offender and indicate little concern for the female child victim.* I will refer to the studies as Study Number 1, 2, 3, and 4. I will identify my source material later to anyone who wishes the information.

*In many of the quotations, words and phrases have been deleted only to clarify and emphasize. The deletions did not alter the essential meaning of the quotations.

Study Number 1

This was an investigation of 1,365 convicted male sex offenders—868 offenders committed offenses against children. The following are direct quotes taken from the study.

Not only do they [women] commit fewer illegal sexual acts . . . but society tends to ignore or tolerate their breaches. Persons hesitate to sign a complaint against a female, police loathe to arrest and juries loathe to convict.

The indifference is justifiable. The average female has a much lower "sex drive" than the average male, consequently she is least likely to behave in a sexually illegal manner.

If a woman, walking past an apartment, stops to watch a man undressing, the man is arrested as an exhibitionist.[3]

First I would like to establish the author's attitude toward women. The author feels that the biologically limited woman with her low sex drives is not driven to commit sex crimes. If she were, however, society would be loathe to punish her. On the other hand, men, biologically endowed with powerful sex drives, naturally commit sex crimes. Despite their natural propensity toward sex crimes, men are accused of sex crimes that they do not commit. It may be confused, but the author's feelings come through loud and clear. His opinion of women is not secret. Now let us hear what he has to say about children.

The horror with which society views the adult who has sexual relations with young children is lessened when one examines the behavior of other mammals. Sexual activity between adult and immature animals is common and appears to be biologically normal.[4]

Disregard for age, sex, and species need not be regarded as biologically pathological; it is precisely what we see in various animals, particularly in certain monkeys.[5]

I once saw my cat have kittens. After each kitten was born, the mother ate the afterbirth and cleaned her babies with her tongue. I've had three children and am delighted I did not have to follow the example of the mother cat. Maybe monkeys are more like us. I don't know, but it never occurred to me that the behavior of animals was the norm for human behavior. The author now explains one kind of sexual offender.

Exhibitionism is an expression of hostility and sadism; a way to frighten and shock. Very few of these people (exhibitionists) consciously feel hostility and on the whole are to be pitied rather than to be feared.[6]

I guess dirty old men need love too. Again the author's logic eludes me, but the contradiction and bias are obvious.

Study Number 2

Here we have an examination of forty-one children, and the study attempts to estimate the psychologically harmful effects of sexual assault on children. The author draws heavily on Freudian theories of infant sexuality.

> He [Freud] noted that the majority of children could escape from the sexual situation if they wished and he maintained that the silence shown by some children following seduction could be explained in terms of their own feeling of guilt in yielding to forbidden attraction . . .

> The girl will strive to counteract her fear of the bad or sadistic penis by introducing a good one in coitus . . .[7]

> Bender and Blau [experts in child study] noted that the most striking feature of sexually assaulted children was their unusually attractive personalities. This was so noticeable that the authors frequently considered the possibility that the child might have been the actual seducer rather than the one innocently seduced.[8]

> The myth of childhood innocence seems, in the main, to have been rejected and some degree of participation by the victim group is accepted by all studies.[9]

> The suggestion is therefore made that the sexual assault of children by adults does not have a particularly detrimental effect on the child's subsequent development. . . . The need for affection, which may have well predisposed the child to this form of sexual acting out, will be outgrown.[10]

Isn't it strange how victims are held responsible for offenses against them! Our sexuality as women and children is not used to understand us but to psychologically trap us so that, we are told, the woman seeks to be raped and the little girl wants sexual abuse. And while the woman invites rape and the child invites sexual abuse, men are permitted their sexual indulgences, American soldiers rape and kill Vietnamese women and children and the Hell's Angels roam free to raid and rape. The myth of consent, that is, the psychiatric and popular use of ill-defined sexual motivation and acting-out to explain and condone the victimization of women and children, is unforgivable and shameful.

Study Number 3

This study involved a general investigation into the sexual behavior of women. Over 4,000 women were studied and 24 percent of these reported pre-adolescent experiences with an adult male.

It is difficult to understand why a child, except for its cultural conditioning, should be disturbed by having its genitalia touched or disturbed by seeing the genitalia of another person . . . Some of the more experienced students of juvenile problems have come to believe that the emotional reactions of the parents, police and other adults . . . may disturb the child more seriously than the contacts themselves. The current hysteria over sex offenders may well have serious effects on the ability of many children to work out sexual adjustment some years later.[11]

With the usual male arrogance, the author cannot imagine that a sexual assault on a child constitutes a gross and devastating shock and insult, so he blames everyone but the offender. The fact is that sexual offenses are barely noticed except in the most violent and sensational instances. Most sex offenses are never revealed; when revealed, most are either ignored or not reported; if reported, a large percentage are dismissed for lack of proof, and when proof is established many are dropped because of the pressure and humiliation forced on the victim and family by the authorities.

Study Number 4

This study deals with twenty cases of incest and involves the fathers as offenders and daughters as victims. The preponderance of incest cases are between fathers and young daughters. The author, although sympathetic with the victim, still does not deal with the offender, but looks to the mother to control the problem.

There follows several examples of father behavior described by thirteen mothers and, in every instance, corroborated by the child victim; breaking a radio over the mother's head; burning the child with hot irons, chasing the mother out of the house with a gun; . . . locking mother or children in closets while he sexually abused the child victim . . . forcing sexual intercourse with the child in the mother's presence . . .[12]

After examining the character of the incest family . . . the unavoidable conclusion seems to be that the failure of the mother to protect the child against the contingency of incestuous victimization is a crucial and fruitful area of study . . .[13]

Considering the father offender as a possible source of control of

> incest behavior seems . . . like considering the fox . . . as guard in the henhouse . . .[14]

> The mother is the only possible agent of incest control within the family group.[15]

The father rapes and brutalizes and it turns out to be the mother's fault and responsibility. Has anyone thought of the fantastic notion of getting rid of the father? Let me read you a statement of a fourteen-year-old girl taken down by the police.

> I was about nine years old when my father first began to come to my bedroom, which I shared with my two sisters, at night and started to touch my breasts and private parts. This would usually happen in the evening when my mother went to the movies or when she was in the living room with my older sister, Anne, was looking at TV or taking a shower. It was within the same year that my father began to have intercourse with me, which is putting his penis into my private parts. This was very painful to me when it started. My father told me this was normal and all girls did this with their fathers. When I said I was going to tell my mother or someone about it, he said that what my mother does not know would not hurt her. Sometimes he would hit me when I would refuse him and at times he would take me in the car and, as we rode, touch my vagina.[16]

This completes my report on the studies. I would like to touch very briefly on the subject of female juvenile delinquency. Although female juveniles have a much lower crime rate than male juveniles, the female is reported to be involved in a larger percentage of sexual offenses such as sexual promiscuity, adolescent pregnancy, and prostitution. Although these offenses are all heterosexual and cannot be indulged without the male, the male is rarely regarded as the offender. When a girl rebels against her family or society, she is usually suspected by her family and the community of being sexually promiscuous and is thought of as either a slut or a whore. The young male offender, however, is associated with crimes against society, property, etc. Here is a statement from a psycho-analytic journal regarding male and female juvenile delinquency, which supports psychiatrically the popular attitudes toward male and female delinquency.

> The boy's typical delinquent activities contain elements of keen interest in reality; we . . . recognize his fascination with the struggle waged between himself and people, social institutions and the world

of nature. In contrast to this, the adolescent girl ... will ... take revenge on her mother, by whom she feels rejected, by seeking sexual relations. ...

In female delinquency, the infantile instinctual organization ... finds bodily outlet in genital activity. The pregenital instinctual aims ... relate her delinquency to perversion. An adolescent boy ... caught in an ambivalent conflict with his father, might defend himself ... by getting drunk, destroying property, or stealing a car ... His actions are ... an attempt at progressive development.[17]

If we get past the psychiatric mumbo-jumbo, we are told that delinquent boys are trying to grow and develop, while delinquent girls take revenge on their mothers and are trapped in perversion by their "pregenital instinctual aims."

Earlier, I referred to a statistic that noted that two thirds of the families of sexually abused children were inadequate. According to most anthropologists and sociologists, the purpose of the family is the protection of children. From what I have heard, read, and seen, it would seem to me that the protectors and the offenders are one and the same. The fact is that families generally are given the job of socializing children to fill prescribed roles and thus supply the needs of a power society. My mother's inability to protect me from sexual abuse did not occur because she was worse than any other mother, but because, like all women, she was guilty and repelled by her own sexuality and taught me to feel the same way. Seventy-five percent of the sexually abused children are victims of family members or friends. All children suffer at the hands of their family, whether the abuse be sexual, physical, or emotional, but children have nowhere to go outside the family. They have no options, no choices, and no power. Ingrained in our present family system is the nucleus of male power and domination, and no matter how often we witness the devastatingly harmful effects of this arrangement on women and children, the victims are asked to uphold the family and submit to abuse. Let me read to you from a publication called "Violence Against Children." The passage is part of a study on the physical abuse against children in the United States, completed at Brandeis University; Advanced Studies in Social Welfare.

Most societies, including America ... have not developed absolute cultural and legal sanctions against the use of physical force toward children by adults. Not only is such use of physical force not prohibited, but it is even encouraged by many societies. ...

Children were considered property of their parents in many societies and parents had, thus, absolute power over life and death.[18]

Children in America ... have always been subjected to a wide range of physical and non-physical abuse by parents and other caretakers ... and indirectly by society as a whole. Such abusive treatment of children seems to be inherent in the basic inequality of physical makeup and social status between adults and children, and ... permissive or even encouraging attitudes toward the use of physical force.[19]

It is assumed that because children are not fully grown, they have not the knowledge, the humanity, nor the feeling to know what they want. As women we are treated the same way, and children feel as we do, only more so, because they are even more helpless and dependent. It is interesting to note, however, how early and eagerly male children take on and integrate the attitudes and advantages of male supremacy. I talked one evening to a group of high-school students, young men and women about fourteen years of age. When I pointed to the similarities between the oppression of women and children, the male students objected vehemently, almost to the point of physical revulsion. Already contaminated, they could not bear to be identified with women. But for those male children who are not yet contaminated and for all the female children who are being abused, manipulated, and prepared for the role of subjugation and exploitation, we must offer help in light of our own oppression and new feminist understanding. We must begin to study and understand what is happening to children today.

From my personal experience as a woman, as a female child, as a social worker, and, after talking to countless women, after reading and researching, and with my deepened understanding and radicalization from my involvement in the women's movement, I have drawn some conclusions regarding the sexual abuse of children.

1. That the sexual abuse of children, who are overwhelmingly female, by sexual offenders, who are overwhelmingly male adults, is part and parcel of the male-dominated society which overtly and covertly subjugates women.

2. That the sexual molestation and abuse of female children is not regarded seriously by society, is winked at, rationalized, and allowed to continue through a complex of customs and mores that applaud the male's sexual aggression and denies the female's pain, humiliation, and outrage.

3. That sexual abuse of children is permitted because it is an unspoken but prominent factor in socializing and preparing the female to accept a

subordinate role; to feel guilty, ashamed, and to tolerate, through fear, the power exercised over her by men. That the female's early sexual experiences prepare her to submit in later life to the adult forms of sexual abuse heaped on her by her boyfriend, her lover, and her husband. In short, the sexual abuse of female children is a process of education that prepares them to become the wives and mothers of America.

4. That the family itself is an instrument of sexual and other forms of child abuse, and that in order to protect children, we must find new ways of rearing them so they may have optimum opportunity to achieve full human growth and potential.

5. That we must begin to think of children's liberation as being the same as women's liberation. The female child and woman are the same person, merely at a different stage of development. The growth from childhood to adulthood is a process, not a "gap" or separation. The female infant, child, woman, and old woman are subject to the same evils. The separations are false, provoke hostility, and are used to divide us.

In closing, let me read a passage from Shulamith Firestone's book, *The Dialectic of Sex*.

> Children, then, are not freer than adults. They are burdened by a wish fantasy in direct proportion to the restraints of their narrow lives; with an unpleasant sense of their own physical inadequacy and ridiculousness; with constant shame about their dependence, economic and otherwise; and humiliation concerning their natural ignorance of practical affairs. Children are repressed at every waking minute. Childhood is hell.

> Except for the ego rewards in having children of one's own, few men show any interest in children.... So it is up to the feminist revolutionaries to do so. We must include the oppression of children in any program for feminist revolution or we will be subject to the same failing of which we have often accused men; of not having gone deep enough in our analysis.

> There are no children yet able to write their own book or tell their own story. We will have to, one last time, do it for them. [20]

NOTES

1. Vincent De Francis, *Protecting the Child Victim of Sex Crimes,* The American Humane Association, Children's Division, Denver, 1965 (pamphlet).
2. Vincent De Francis, *Protecting the Child Victim of Sex Crimes Committed by Adults,* The American Humane Association, Children's Division, Denver, 1966, pp. 1-3, 215-33.

3. Paul Gebhart, et al., *Sex Offenders,* Harper and Row, 1965, pp. 9, 10.
4. *Ibid.,* p. 54.
5. *Ibid.,* p. 276.
6. *Ibid.,* p. 399.
7. Lindy Burton, *Vulnerable Children,* Schocken Books, 1968, p. 29.
8. *Ibid.,* p. 104.
9. *Ibid.,* p. 113.
10. *Ibid.,* p. 169.
11. Alfred Kinsey, et al., *Sexual Behavior in the Human Female,* Pocket Books, 1953, p. 121.
12. Yvonne Tormes, *Child Victims of Incest,* The American Humane Association, Children's Division, Denver, p. 27 (pamphlet).
13. *Ibid.,* p. 32.
14. *Ibid.,* p. 33.
15. *Ibid.,* p. 35.
16. De Francis, *op. cit.,* p. 112.
17. Peter Blos, "Preoedipal Factors in the Etiology of Female Delinquency," *The Psychoanalytic Study of the Child,* International Universities Press, 1957, Vol. XII, p. 232.
18. David Gil, *Violence Against Children,* Harvard University Press, 1970, p. 9.
19. *Ibid.,* p. 1.
20. Shulamith Firestone, *The Dialectic of Sex,* William Morrow and Company, 1970, pp. 117, 118.

BIBLIOGRAPHY

Blos, Peter, "Preoedipal Factors in the Etiology of Female Delinquency," *The Psychoanalytic Study of the Child,* International Universities Press, 1957, Vol. XII, pp. 229-49.

Burton, Lindy, *Vulnerable Children,* Schocken Books, pp. 87-169;

Cavan, Ruth, *Juvenile Delinquency,* J.B. Lippincott Co., 1962, pp. 102-109.

Chaneles, Sol, *Sexual Abuse of Children,* The American Humane Association, Children's Division, Denver, 1966 (pamphlet).

De Francis, Vincent, *Protecting the Child Victims of Sex Crimes Committed by Adults,* The American Humane Association, Children's Division, Denver, 1966.

Firestone, Shulamith, *The Dialectic of Sex,* William Morrow and Company, 1970, pp. 81-118.

Gebhard, Paul, et al., *Sex Offenders,* Harper and Row, 1965.

Gil, David, *Violence Against Children*, Harvard University Press, 1970.

Hirschberger, Ruth, "Is Rape a Myth," in *Masculine/Feminine,* ed. by Betty and Theodore Rozak, Harper and Row, 1969, pp. 122-30.

Inbau, Fred, and Reid, John, *Criminal Interrogation and Confession,* The Williams and Wilkins Company, 1967.

Kinsey, Alfred, et al., *Sexual Behavior in the Human Female,* Pocket Books, 1953, pp. 104-22.

Richette, Lisa, *The Throwaway Children*, Dell Publishing, 1970, pp. 212-33.

Rush, Florence, and Singer, Miriam, *Proposal for Young Mothers Educational Development Program,* Mt. Vernon, Community Action Group, 1966 (mimeograph).

Thompson, Hunter, *Hell's Angels,* Random House, 1966.

Tormes, Yvonne, *Child Victims of Incest,* The American Humane Association, Children's Division, Denver.

Verille, Elinor, *Behavior Problems of Children,* W.B. Saunders Company, 1967, pp. 266-378.

Rape and Psychotherapy*

Phyllis Chesler, Ph.D.

The kind of children that Florence Rush was talking about, whether they are orphans or whether they are victimized in the family, grow up. Like us, they have problems and they go to therapists, psychologists, or psychiatrists who could help them with these early traumatic experiences. Guess what? Psychiatrists do the same damn thing that the fathers did to begin with, which is what I am going to address myself to. But I'd like to make a few general comments first.

To continue Florence Rush's review of the psychiatric folklore, I've been looking at the analysis of incest in the psychological and psychiatric journals, maybe because I think that women in this society are encouraged to commit incest as a way of life. As opposed to marrying our fathers, we marry men like our fathers, or in short, men who are older than us, have more money than us, more power than us, are taller than us, are stronger than us ... our fathers. I wanted to see if this is what is being recommended. I wanted to see how it takes place or how it begins to take place. In general, in all the case histories of incest between fathers and daughters, not only is the mother blamed by psychiatrists for not having protected the daughter, but she is also accused of denying sex to the father. You see, the fathers were *forced* to turn to their daughters, according to these psychiatrists, because the wife allowed it to happen by refusing her husband's sexual demands or by secretly wanting her daughter to take her place. And they kept it in the family, you know, they were nice enough to keep it in the family! Also the daughters of "delinquent" females are seen as seductive and attractive and promiscuous—as sending off all the unconscious signals that allow the father to do this. Interestingly enough, some researchers find that such incest keeps a dysfunctional family together, which they find is sort of a good thing!

Now, the only case that I have uncovered in the last fifteen years

*Presented at the NYRF Rape Conference, April, 1971. Ms. Chesler is author of *Women and Madness*, published by Doubleday & Sons.

written about mother-son incest was entitled "The Psychodynamics of Consummated Maternal Incest." I could hear the tone of the writer . . . really hushed and sepulchral. Here, in this study, we have two really "schizophrenic" damaged men who were ruined beyond belief by their mothers, who slept with them. Now, it's interesting that both of these men—and there are only two—had recently come back from army combat duty. They had been making war. The researchers don't think that this fact could possibly have led to any kind of a breakdown. And the writer, who of course is male, begins to refer to these mothers in really mythologically misogynistic terms as Spider Women.

While many psychiatrists see men as irreparably damaged by these Spider Women mothers (because mother-son incest is thought to be a true violation of social relations), women's victimization by their fathers creates no such shock or horror from the male-oriented psychiatric literature. Women are encouraged to marry their fatherlike men, encouraged as children to be victimized by their real fathers or father-like surrogates (uncles, cousins, older brothers). When they grow up, they are encouraged to try to fall in love with and get some father figure to take care of them. And when none of this works out, if it all fails, they are told to go to psychiatrists and psychologists and psychotherapists, most of whom are male. And women are also conditioned to prefer males rather than females as therapists. And the therapists take this for granted. Father-daughter incest patterns are at the root of much psycho-therapeutic treatment—whether the treatment becomes overtly sexual or not.

When I originally started interviewing women who had been in analysis or in therapy, I said, "Gee, I wonder if they have sex with their therapist. Well, probably not." And then I started asking around. Every other person I talked with said, "Oh, I did (or my sister did or my friend did or my aunt did)." And it seemed to be a very pervasive phenomenon—although, as in all instances of victimization of women and other relatively powerless people, there are no hard statistics. And there are certainly many other sorts of psychiatric victimization of women. However, sexual relations between patient and therapist is a very serious phenomenon. The rationale usually given by the male psychiatrist or therapist is that if the female patient "falls in love" with and/or sleeps with him, it will help her with her frigidity and/or will help her to become a "normal," genitally functioning, heterosexual woman . . . and that's what transference is all about, or so the psychiatrists say.

I want to call this rape. But I'd like to place it in context, because several articles have already appeared in the professional literature that discuss sexual relations between female patients and their therapists as a exotic or very sensational occurrence. In a sense, I don't think it is.

I think that extreme forms of exploitation, injustice, and cruelty always signify the existence of the more invisible and therefore more pervasive forms of injustice in a society. Atrocities and scandals are every-day events—writ large. The My Lai massacre is only possible because of our involvement in Vietnam, which in turn signifies the daily existence of sexism, racism, and capitalism in America. The rape of Vietnamese women signifies the existence of prostitution, puritanism, and the wholesale rape of women in any father country in which women are economically dependent on men and do not control the means of reproduction. The brutality of our prison system crazy-mirrors the brutality of poverty. The sexual abuse of adolescent and other female mental patients and their so-called illegitimate in-hospital pregnancies (I don't know how a pregnancy can be illegitimate, but this is how it is referred to in the psychiatric and psychological journals) are an exaggerated form of the degradation of women in the society at large. Let me tell you, in a mental asylum not only are you given shock therapy, pills that you don't want—which can damage you over a long period of time; not only are you beaten up; not only are you either sexually abused or forced to remain celibate; but if you are a woman what you become is a domestic for the psychiatrists who live on the state asylum grounds. You do their cooking and their washing and their cleaning. This is slave labor and the state doesn't pay for it. (Men—and there are fewer men in asylums than women—participate in sex-typed slave labor also; they do the "heavy" and/or outdoor work.)

Now, take just a regular woman with a problem. She goes to a shrink. Physical and/or psychological violence can't happen to her, she thinks. She's not a nut. She has enough money to pay for help. But, in fact, physical and psychological brutality often occur in psychiatrists' offices too—sometimes in the form of rape, more euphemistically termed sexual relations with female patients—as a cure for female "mental illness" or unhappiness.

When I first started doing interviews with women in therapy and discovered the incidence of sexual relations between female patients and male therapists, I mentioned my findings to friends or colleagues, especially colleagues (other psychologists or psychiatrists). They said, "Oh, but Phyllis, really. Weren't those women really making it up? Or if they weren't making it up, wasn't it their fault—because they really wanted to, or because they fell in love with their therapists, as they're supposed to do, and they forced the poor man to do them a favor. Wasn't it really their fault?" This is from clinicians.

There are, surprisingly, some statistics about this phenomenon. Masters and Johnson, for instance, in their *Human Sexual Inadequacy*, say that if only one quarter of the reports of women having been seduced—raped—by their psychiatrists, that came to Masters and Johnson, are true, then it is a very, very prevalent phenomenon. The newspapers, over the years, have always had scandals breaking about prostitution rings or sexual abuse of female mental patients either by orderlies, attendants, or by members of the staff in mental asylums. There's been a paper published by Clay Dahlberg in one of the professional journals in which he cites nine cases—I was going to say of father-daughter incest because that's what it amounts to—of sexual relations between male psychiatrists and female patients.

Now there's one guy who actually published a paper in favor of it. His name is James L. McCartney and he is now dead. At the time of its publication he was thrown out of the American Psychiatric Association for doing it. His paper is titled "Overt Transference." He says that some women need to have this in order to become adjusted and "healthy," and he obliges. I calculated that he obliged about one hundred women over the last twenty years, and he began this when he was about forty-five or forty-six. What's very interesting about most of these self-proclaimed sexual pioneers is that they're against the incest taboos, they're revolutionaries, they're for sexual liberation. Now, this includes Sullivan, Wilhelm Reich, it includes Ferenczi, it includes Alexander, it includes most recently Martin Shepard, it includes a whole bunch of male names. But they're against bisexuality, they're against homosexuality. They're mainly in favor of the sexual aggression and emotional coldness of men, that's the sexual liberation that they're in favor of. They don't know anything about women. And, in fact, what McCartney says is that very often if the need for overt transference arises in male patients and they are with male therapists, they don't have to be transfered to a female therapist who will sleep with them because they can go out in society and practice on women. He says women allow themselves to be practiced upon for the sexual growth of men, for the psycho-sexual development of men. And he's perfectly right, we do allow ourselves to be practiced on. Whereas, he says, women have a harder time of it, because men will not be "practiced on" in the larger society, so therefore, he, McCartney, is setting himself up as a kind of a temple prostitute, a religious do-gooder, who will oblige all of his young, attractive female patients who want to practice on men but the men won't allow it. He also, by the way, like the other sexually courageous pioneers in psychiatry, views the mental health of his female patients whom he has screwed in terms of whether the women got married and had children. That was a sign of good adjustment—that it didn't *hurt*, the father-daughter incest didn't hurt, it only helped—because, as Florence Rush pointed out, it turns them into the wives and mothers of today.

Now let's view the composite picture of female patient-male therapist sexual relationships as drawn by other people in the psychiatric literature and by me in talking to women. There is usually a fifteen-to twenty-year age difference between them. Basically the female patient, like all women, is naïve, is lonely, and is highly socialized as a "feminine" female. The male rapist-psychiatrist is very gradiose, is middle-aged, is very heterosexually biased. They're also lousy lovers, but then, rapists are. It's very interesting that only in a few cases did the women really enjoy themselves sexually. For the most part, the analysts just climb right on top and they kind of jerk off into somebody's vagina and they say, "Okay, you're cured." James L. McCartney is in favor of the analyst remaining unemotional and detached, which is no different from what we find in men in general. (Why do we have to pay for the damn thing!) They're consummate con artists. They also believe in "sexual magic"—sex will make you free, sex is "revolutionary," or, in my terms, male sexual aggression is the revolution.

Male psychiatrists are also involved in a very aggressive form of competition with their male patients. I really wonder what's going on. One of the things that I've thought about, and I haven't been too particularly concerned with, is what happens to men with their therapists: namely, the Oedipal situation is played out again. The male therapist gets involved in a form of male bonding. You and me, baby, against the women out there. Every time you can go out and lay a broad, screw a broad, that's one up for us men and you're on your way to mental health as a man. I think this is what some male therapists covertly or overtly encourage their male patients to do. They encourage them to beat up their wives, to leave their wives, to take mistresses, or to sleep with a different woman every night as a sign of growing male psycho-sexual maturity. I think also what the male therapist is saying is that in this office (just as their male patients' fathers said to them), I am the boss. That woman (your mother) is my property, you can't have her, you can't identify with her, and if you want power to go out and fuck other women elsewhere in the world you've got to obey me right here. Do as I do, watch me. I think this is what some male therapists do with male patients in this composite picture that I am drawing.

You know, women are always said to send out the unconscious signals men can't resist and that's why rape is the woman's fault. All right, these are the unconscious signals that any rapist in the psychiatric setting sends out: power, money, the promise of romantic love, the promise of instant identity, the promise of protection. Now, what woman can possibly resist this in a patriarchal society? Well, I almost begin to think: why don't all women sleep with all their male therapists, because the signals that male therapists send out are everything that a woman has been conditioned to respond to in men. This composite picture is not a sensationalistic one.

This is a portrait of any man in our society, any middle-aged businessman who tries to screw the secretary is doing the same thing.

All right. What I would like to get to now is the kind of action that I have in mind that could be taken. Just because I've said that rape is very prevalent in therapy and therefore Lieutenant Calley is not any more guilty of Vietnam than anyone else in the army or any of the men in government running the war, this is not to say that I don't think each and every one of them should be penalized for that act at any level on which they can be gotten. I think that psychologists and psychiatrists can be gotten on at least two levels. One, legally—they should be sued. It is against the Hippocratic Oath, against the American Psychiatric Association's Code of Ethics, to have sexual relations with patients. Now, I'm not sure whether they should be sued for producing such damage in a woman that she is a total mental wreck, because male lawyers especially would love nothing better. I've been involved with male lawyers who are handling a case in New York City in which a woman is suing her therapist for having seduced her. She is suing him for $1,500,000. The lawyers portray this woman as terribly distraught and broken up, which would have to be proven legally in order to collect damages in such a case. Anyway, lawsuits can be brought against these rapist-psychiatrists.

Information about these lawsuits should be made public. Which gets to the other level of penalizing them. Which means women should be told to avoid them. We have to get up a shit list, at least in New York City, of male therapists who engage in this particular practice. We have to boycott them. They're screwing us, they're abusing us, and we're paying them for it. Now this is women's business. We have to take care of that. I think that when such a shit list is gotten up (I've collected a goodly number of names and I'm sure there are many more to be collected), we should get together a little handbill. After consulting a lawyer as to possible libel suits, this handbill should be written. It should say that such and such a therapist sleeps with his female patients, refuses to sleep with his male patients, encourages his male patients to sleep with as many women as possible, and, in short, that he is a sexist. And women ought to stand outside the office of the offending therapist, preferably with the victims at their side, to give these handbills to women as they enter. So that at least the women are aware this is going on and that they are not very uniquely chosen for the privilege of being doubly fucked over and that they should also be disabused of the belief that the man's in love with them. They never are.

The Psychology of the Rapist and His Victim

Lilia Melani and Linda Fodaski

The attempt of the rape conference was to examine the nature of sexual assault. Although the direction of the study was only vaguely suggested by the criminological and psychiatric literature, the conviction grew among feminists that women are victimized and abused not only by street violence and deviant sexuality but, indeed, by the total sexual system of the present culture, a culture that deprives them of sexual autonomy and exploits them as inferior sexual objects. By *rape* we mean any assaultive or humiliating act perpetrated on a woman through her demeaned sexual status. It is understood that rape is fundamentally an aggressive rather than a sexual act, that its motivation and dynamics arise out of hostility rather than sexual need, and that this hostility is only the final expression in a series of indignities and prejudices continually heaped on women in this culture.

One problem that arises in analyzing the motivation and behavior of the rapist is that of identification—just who is to be classified as a rapist? The legal classifications of rape, statutory and assaultive, are inadequate for many reasons. The charge of statutory rape, designed to protect virgins by setting an arbitrary age of consent (varying from sixteen to twenty-one in various states), is a fundamental denial of female sexual autonomy. A young woman is discouraged from experimenting sexually with male companions of her own age level. [1] Boys who satisfy their sexual desire with similarly motivated girls are legally declared rapists and fall into the same category as assaultive offenders. The only real connection between statutory rape and assaultive rape is that both deny the female the right to *choose* the sexual experience; on the one hand, the law restricts the female minor from having sex, on the other, the rapist forces her to submit to it. Even discussions of assaultive rape, however, have limited application since they represent only the barest minimum of actual rapes. Few of the forcible rapes by strangers—let alone acquaintances, friends, or family—are reported to the police; government agencies conclude that rape is one of the most under-reported crimes—the crime that victims are most reluctant to talk about. Of the small number of men arrested for the few forcible rapes reported in 1967, only 62 percent nationwide were prosecuted for the charge of rape; 34 percent were found guilty of rape, 17 percent were convicted of lesser charges.[2] Furthermore, records often show only the charge for which a person was *convicted*, and this is frequently a lesser offence than that for which he was arrested. What this means is that few of the men who commit rape are ever arrested, much less convicted. Yet most studies of rapists survey men in prison, although it is clear from other sources—Attica, for example—that the prison population, with its high concentration of oppressed groups, does not reflect our society as a whole. In other words, the phenomenon of rape is a great deal more pervasive than we think and is conspicuous, for the most part, only where it is considered socially repugnant (as in the South, when a black man rapes a white woman) or excessively brutal (as in the cases of rape-murder).

Bearing in mind that current reports of rapists may apply only, or primarily, to men in prison, we can still profitably examine the psychological and sociological opinion in the literature on sexual offense. The studies persist in grouping rape with what are, legally, classified as sex crimes, i.e., homosexuality, voyeurism, indecent exposure. This classification, however, disregards the true nature of sexuality and the real rationale of the dynamics of sexual laws. Sexuality includes actions that give an individual pleasure through erotic contact and stimulation. It is valid as long as it involves responsible and mutual consent and is not injurious to the persons involved or to anyone else. Our sex laws, however, originate from a belief in the necessity for population increase and consequent sexual conformity. Every form of sexual activity that neither produces children (e.g., homosexuality) nor produces them in a socially acceptable way (rape and fornication) is made illegal. Our sexual laws, in other words, deny the individual the right to free and full sexual experience. The association of the rapist, who violates another person, with the homosexual, who exercises a natural sexual option, reflects the degree of control that society exercises over individual preference. This basis of our sexual laws is shown by its extension into and justification by psychiatry. Benjamin Karpman, a pioneer in the psychodynamics of sexual offence, comments, "It is entirely true that many modern humans' sex acts are often engaged in without the thought of procreation; but most humans are bent on raising a family, which is the foundation of our society and assures the continuation of the race. Where the individual lacks this trend and only recognizes the need for sexual intercourse as a need *per se*, we are, I am sure, dealing with a neurotic situation."[3]

It is, to a great extent, sexual nonconformity that strikes the most intensive blow at our collective morality. Homosexuality and rape can evoke equivalent distaste because they both transcend the limits of "proper behavior." That the latter brutally violates another person becomes, in the legal and moral scheme, essentially obscured. Indeed, rape, in its great variety of forms, may be more acceptable, because the elements that produce it (viz., aggression-submission) function in all human relationships, most of which are structured, to a very great degree, around the exertion of power.

How different is predatory criminal rape from "normal" sexual behavior? We suggest that the difference is essentially one of degree, that we live in a culture that, at best, condones and, at worst, encourages women to be perennial victims, men to be continual predators, and sexual relations to be fundamentally aggressive. First, psychiatric and popular opinion maintain that woman is by nature masochistic, and that this trait achieves its fullest expression during the sex act. For example, "it should be borne in mind that a masochistic component is present in the female at the height of sexual passion."[4] We find Freud remarking that everything active and powerful is masculine, everything passive and weak is feminine. "To the end of his life he maintained his assumption that the libido (the energy of the sexual instinct) is always masculine. Consequently, he could not account for any positive manifestations of sexual feeling or any voluntary sexual activity in the female except by making another assumption, that all such feelings and activities arise from a masculine component of their nature."[5] In other words, men assert themselves sexually and women do not. Men are again and again encouraged to show force and dominance, to disregard the weak refusals of the female, and when persuasion fails, simply to overpower the passive partner with aggression and control. The pressure to be masculine, in fact, is implicitly an underlying factor in much sexual assault. Some studies have discovered an unconscious passivity in violent sex offenders which was concealed by excessive aggression. Disregarding the dignity of women, many of the assaulters (studied by Glueck) "showed no concern for their partners' sexual response or gratification, and many . . . had no idea of how a woman responded, that she could have an orgasm, or that she might be an important component of sexual intercourse."[6] Many men, in fact, achieve greater potency when confronted with female resistance; overcoming the resistance is one mechanism of rape: it degrades the woman and satisfies the rapist's need for sexual control. Through the sense of dominance he belittles the sexual object and satisfies hostile impulses directed toward women.[7]

Two patterns are significant in sexual domination: (1) it fulfills the cultural image of male supremacy; and (2) it symbolizes the inferiority of the offender and expresses what is actually an overcompensation for his sexual inadequacy. In the first case we find, in the early lives of many convicted rapists, an indication of great parental friction, with a violent father abusing an ineffectual mother. The culturally established images of male aggressiveness and female weakness, learned from the parents and approved by society in general, are thus duplicated symbolically and physically in the explosive act of rape. In the second case, concerning male inadequacy, we find many suggestions of insecurity and submissiveness in the offenders' childhoods. The submissiveness, used to conceal the hostility toward parental authority, later becomes a source of fear and insecurity for the adult male. For aggressiveness and destructiveness constitute acceptable male behavior, while femininity is identified with passivity. Passivity, therefore, represents the greatest threat to the "sense" of masculinity, and it is not surprising that studies have revealed "a substratum of unconscious passivity" in perpetrators of violent crimes, the offenders having concealed this with an exaggerated or pretended masculinity.[8] It is the unconscious fear of femininity that drives this type of rapist, again and again, to attack the submissive female; he destroys what he fears most in himself. An interesting and tragic illustration of this power of the *feminine* can be found in a report on the Philadelphia prison system filed on September 2, 1968. Male homosexual assaults were epidemic although the vast majority of aggressors and victims had no previous homosexual history. "Virtually every slightly built young man committed by the courts was sexually approached within a day or two after his admission. Many of these men were overwhelmed and repeatedly raped by gangs of inmate aggressors. Others were compelled by the terrible threat of gang rape to seek protection by entering into a housekeeping arrangement with an individual tormentor."[9] The report stated that none of the aggressors considered himself homosexual. Rather, he saw his behavior as an "impression of masculinity." What do we have in this prison picture, in this microcosm of society's power plays, but the enforcement of our own sexual codes with force operating on the weaker from the more aggressive? The kept prisoner, like the married woman, protected at home by the husband, is cautioned to avoid the "world" with its physical and sexual dangers. The female or the surrogate female becomes the property of the male, the most obvious illustration of this occurring in the marriage ceremony where the father "gives the woman away," or transfers ownership.

The woman whose connection to, or ownership by, a man is not immediately clear, is vulnerable to attack by any man, fair game for all men. That is why a woman's place is in the home where her husband (as in the territorial imperative) has total reign. The real motive behind imprisoning the woman in the home is to force her to perform society's tasks (e.g., bearing and raising children), and one way to keep her there is to make the outside environment threatening to females. A woman who is raped while alone at night or in a deserted place is blamed for "asking for it." The implication is that her behavior disregards safety precautions; the extension of this is that she is responsible for any harm done to her, and she is, in fact, frequently accused of desiring her own rape. A man in the same situation, who might be robbed or mugged, is not judged this harshly. The actuality is that both men and women are attacked in such circumstances because of their vulnerability. And the crux of rape is woman's vulnerability. Women are conditioned to be helpless property requiring the protection of a male owner. We find John Kercher implying that the home is the right place for woman, and that she may be raped because she leaves it, when he says:

> Before the First World War women were satisfied to be housewives. After the war, they enjoyed independence, they lived and worked as men did. Men lost their jobs owing to women's competition and found it hard to build up a family because of women's independence. Millions of men without jobs, without money, without home and mates, without ability to work off surplus energy, with enforced idleness and sexual urge ungratified, and with animosity towards women in general, committed an unusual number of sex crimes or rape.[10]

Kercher, apparently, sees no connection between the war itself as a brutalizing force and the violent expression of hostility. An interesting illustration of this traditional idea that "a woman's place is in the home" occurred on February 24, 1968, after two women were murdered in the street. *The New York Times* reported that a task force of plainclothesmen was set up to protect women who *have to use* the streets at night (emphasis added). Such a phrase would seem strange indeed used with reference to men. The formation of this squad and its implicit suggestion that women should remain at home are especially remarkable since they ignore completely a third rape-murder which occurred at the same time, that of a twenty-one-year-old mother who was killed in her own apartment. The fact that a considerable percentage of reported rapes occur in the victim's home is generally ignored when we think or talk about rape.

The focus on the kind of rapist who attacks strangers on deserted streets obscures the fact that nearly everything in our sexual system implies the rape relationship and encourages the male to go out and "take" the female. A common male belief, arising, naturally enough, from our sexual miseducation, is that when a male feels the sexual urge, "he's got to have it." This misconception leads, in fact, to a whole set of misguided notions about rape—primarily, that it arises out of excessive potency and great sexual need. But it is true that rapists have no source of sexual outlet? A surprising proportion of the rapists studied are or have been married. John Mohr found in his study that fourteen out of the thirty-eight rapists were married and three separated; only one of the rapists over twenty had not been married.[11] Bernard Oliver presents 59 percent as married or living in common-law relationships.[12] In addition, the idea of the rapist as unusually potent was rejected by most experts, as well as by the fact that many rapists are unable to maintain an erection or to ejaculate. Glueck rejects sexual desire as a motive for rape; indeed the rapist emerges, from Glueck's studies, as a man who experienced difficulties from his earliest sexual encounters. Only 10 percent of all rapists enjoyed their first ejaculation, 43 percent experienced mild anxiety or disgust, 37 percent severe anxiety or disgust. Seventy-three percent still suffered moderate to severe anxiety after intercourse, a lack of pleasure Glueck believed to be a significant factor in rape. Sixty-three percent regarded women in a derogatory manner, dissociating sexuality from love. This distaste for women is reflected by the fact that approximately half of the rapists avoided sex with women menstruating, many feeling extreme disgust like nausea or hostility. Very few had the "concept of an equal, sharing, mutually satisfying relationship with women."[13]

As distasteful and inferior as the female may be, she remains an object of desire, to be had, as the concubines of American slavery; and the *having* remains an enhancement to the sense of masculinity. In addition, the male has been told that women like strong, commanding men, that women do not know what they want, that they say "no" though they mean "yes," that he must insist. If the woman is a "tease," the man may feel he has the right to punish her with rape. Gebhard comments on the "curiously self-righteous" attitude of this type of rapist, whose moral hypocrisy extends to the female who has had or is believed to have had sexual encounters (i.e., the "school whore" who is actually a virgin). By having had previous sexual experience, without belonging to one man, she has forfeited the right to refuse any man. Menachim Amir found a significant association between rape and victims with "bad" reputations in victim-precipitated rape: that is, rapes which ensued because the man interpreted the woman's behavior as an invitation or a sign of availability.[14] In any case, overpowering even the not-too-willing female is implicitly condoned, encouraged, or accepted as biologically inevitable. We find one of the experts saying:

Any reasonably experienced male has learned to disregard [the] minor protestations of the female ... a male is supposed to be physically forceful in his sexual behavior. ... Actually there is some sound biology behind this supposition. In many mammals coitus is ordinarily preceded by a physical struggle. ... The physiological by-products of excitement and exertion—the increased heart rate, increased breathing, muscle tension, the greater supply of blood to the body surfaces, etc.—all of these are also a part of sexual response and it is easy to see how these physiological conditions could facilitate a subsequent sexual response.[15]

Once we accept the relationship of aggression and submission; once we recognize force or struggle as an integral component of the sexual courtship (as in the battle of the sexes), it follows that the sex act itself is only a less emphatic expression of all those elements that make up criminal rape. The connection between rape and "normal" sex is concealed and made generally ambiguous in our society. On the one hand, men react to rape with the same horror that they experience in seeing their property damaged (which is no small emotion considering our great "love" of property). On the other hand, sexual abuse is minimized and covertly accepted in all but a few cases (those which concern total strangers). Although murder and aggravated assault are clearly related to forcible rape in being aggressive acts against the person, rape is, in effect, dissociated from the others. the FBI Uniform Crime Report comments that most murders and aggravated assaults are committed by relatives or friends of the victim.[16] In the case of sexual assault, however, the more closely acquainted the victim is with her attacker, the less likely are the police and courts to believe the charge of rape. The implication is that the woman who agrees to the company of a man is, automatically, making herself sexually accessible. This illogicality is carried to its ultimate conclusion in the legal fact that there can be no rape in marriage, the wife having given her permanent sexual consent to her husband.

The frequently stated belief that there are few crimes in which false charges are more easily and confidently made than in rape, leads, in the courtroom, to the victim herself being on trial; suspected of lying, she must prove her innocence. Furthermore, she must be prepared to defend her entire sexual mode; any deviation from conventional morality weakens her credibility, a fact that causes many rapists to charge, in their defense, that the woman was a prostitute seeking revenge for nonpayment. One defense based on these assumptions occurs in gang rapes: " ... but I was fifth."

Another assumption, this one from medical jurisprudence, also operates against a woman's credibility in courts: that is, that no healthy adult female resisting vigorously can be raped by one unarmed man. This belief is asserted universally, though it has never actually been proved; in addition, it conveniently ignores many psychological factors in the woman. A comparable statement would be that no healthy adult can be robbed or mugged if he resists a single, unarmed assailant. Opinions and judgments unfavorable to women radiate from this premise, like tentacles from an octopus. It is at the heart of the reasoning for the stringent corroborative evidence required by many states. Morris Ploscowe objects to defining as rape any assault in which the penis merely touches the vulva or vagina; he believes the penis must penetrate fully, as this is more susceptible of proof.[17] Again, apply this criterion to other assaultive crimes: how deep must a stab wound be, how deep a bullet, to penetrate?

The myth of woman's physical un-rapability ignores the fact that the woman is, all her life, discouraged from asserting herself physically, emotionally, socially, or financially; she is encouraged generally to submit to men's demands. Women, constantly propositioned by men and even manhandled (the phrase is no accident), are trained to feel that they must be gentle and inoffensive in their rejections. This conditioning, which makes many women afraid or incapable of opposing men (the woman's marriage vow runs, significantly, "love, honor, and obey"), also reduces the verbal and physical forcefulness of their resistance, and it is thus easy for men to ignore or mistake their meaning, with disastrous consequences to the woman. Furthermore, women are advised by expert and layman alike to submit to rape rather than be killed. Yet a glance at statistics about murder reveals that there are, relative to the number of murders, few rape murders. Edwin H. Sutherland, after tabulating the murders reported by *The New York Times* in 1930, 1935, and 1940, found that of the 324 women murdered, only 17 had been raped or seem to have been raped. He concluded that:

> The danger of murder by relative or other intimate associate is very much greater than the danger of murder by an unknown sex fiend. In fact, in one of the three years as many females were reported to have been murdered by policemen—two cases, both involving drunkenness of the policemen—as by the so-called sex fiends.[18]

This myth of the murderous sex fiends serves the valuable function of keeping women frightened and submissive. Gebhard reports that few of the rapists interviewed had been even bitten or scratched, so intimidated were the women; he adds that few women are willing to commit the necessary brutalities to defend themselves, as in most rapes the attacker's eyes or genitals are vulnerable at some moment.

The victim's encounters with police only duplicate and intensify the defenselessness she has already suffered through sexual attack; many policemen, believing that women invite rape, show a prurient interest in the crime and persist in asking questions about its details (i.e., "Did you climax?"). Even if the policeman is sympathetic, it seems unreasonable to expect a woman, just violated by a man, to turn to other men for comfort, guidance, and redress. But this illogicality makes sense if we remember the appropriate female role: that is, to turn to the male for protection and security, the male who has humiliated her, degraded her, and traditionally, rendered her powerless. The source of her weakness is not only concealed but presented as the source of her strength and salvation.

Why this distrust on the part of police, of courts, of men in general? The male is aware, apparently, at some level of consciousness, of the hostility that exists in relationships between the sexes, a hostility that arises inevitably when men have power and women do not. Knowing how he had used his power against women, sexually and nonsexually, the male also feels vulnerable to a charge of rape; he has probably forced or manipulated some woman to submit to him, a woman not in a position to deny his sexual demands, because she needs the job, because she needs his approval, or his money, because she needs his help as an alalyst, a lawyer, or a teacher. So, of course, men in self-protection, and in common cause with other men, have been reluctant to believe a woman's claim that a male friend, relative, or acquaintance has raped her.

Women's outrage and injury are perpetually minimized by the courts, by police, and by men in general. Women are accused of enticing men into sexual uncontrollability or of seeking revenge after a quarrel (hell hath no fury like a woman scorned). This view of women as seductive or acquiescent to male desire figures significantly in the fact that convicted rapists denied their guilt more frequently than nonsexual prisoners. Gebhard found that only 52 percent admitted their aggression to authorities, 57 percent to his staff.[19] That many of these rapists charged that women encouraged them or became aroused during the course of the rape made them sound sincere; they were perhaps mistaken through distorted beliefs rather than lying. It is this ring of sincerity that contributes to the difficulty of prosecution. Glueck received the impression that "most of the men were partially or completely seduced by their so-called victims. Gebhard's staff held a similar belief until they checked official reports, which indicated that a supposedly willing woman required five stitches in her lip. For this and other reasons Gebhard recommends that "in the absence of witnesses or evidence, the woman's word weighs more than that of the man."[20]

Psychologists and other experts have little sympathy with the female victim. They are acquainted with theories of female masochism and hidden sexual motivation and hence of her consequent responsibility for victimization. Bernard Oliver discusses an article written by a rape victim; she states that the rape she experienced at age thirteen has made her neither bitter nor ashamed, though one wonders why she wrote anonymously. She compares the rape to the breaking of a leg or an arm with accompanying discomfort, awkwardness, and a mild unhappiness which soon disappeared. Oliver approves of her submission and concludes: "Victims can usually escape prolonged effects of the experience of rape if they are able to develop a sound emotional attitude toward it."[21] What this means is, a great number of women who might understand the horror of rape dissociate themselves, ultimately, from the victim, through their identification with male power and their fear of association with someone who is suspect. "Did she ask for it?" the other woman wonders, and thinks, smugly or fearfully, that she is impervious to rape. If the victim is held responsible other women can comfort themselves with the belief that "proper behavior" will protect them.

For the man who is connected with the rape victim, his masculinity is affected in two ways: (1) his possession of the woman is no longer complete (the importance of exclusivity or possession is clearly indicated by our cultural emphasis on fidelity, particularly for the woman); (2) he has failed in his obligation or role as protector and may experience her rape as his failure, with resulting resentment and hostility.

Clearly it is necessary for society that rape be seen as an aberration, that the rapist be seen as a man different, fundamentally, from other men in his sexual nature and emotional structure. In reality, his behavior and attitudes are shared in varying degrees by everyone in our culture. Indeed, the rapist has been shown to have more in common with the general population than all other types of sexual offenders. Studies that use control groups of nonsexual offenders (chosen from the general prison population) consistently indicate that rapists are more closely related to the control than to other sexual offenders. Glueck found that, "in terms of their general personality organization these men [rapists] were closest to the offender-controls in every area investigated. They showed a more aggressive, outgoing, impulsive type of personality . . . and were somewhat better integrated into community activities because of this."[22]

In the final analysis it seems clear that we have all been raised on sexual images of male conquest and female acquiescence. From the earliest ages we are exposed to male fantasies about females; thus, women, struggling with and guilty for their own active urges, came, tragically, to identify with the male sensibility, so pervasive is it. *Female sexuality remains painfully undefined and unfulfilled.* When a woman attempts to become a sexual being instead of an object, she is regarded with suspicion or condemned outright. For the female adolescent who engages in sex is "incorrigible," the female adult who has premarital or extramarital sex is promiscuous, and the woman who tries to affirm her own sexuality, to be active and directive, is called castrating or nymphomaniacal.

There is little in womanhood that we can identify with power or sexual dynamism. Women are called sexy, to be sure, but more for their physical qualities than for their sexual sensitivity. And after all the cultural encouragement of male sexuality and the repression of female sexuality, we are told that men, biologically, have greater need and desire, that it is more painful for men to go sexually unsatisfied, that men have a harder time doing without; and the proof of this barrage of nonsense is the sex maniac whose uncontrollable urges compel him to attack. Interestingly, the few women who are believed to have uncontrollable urges (i.e., nymphomaniacs) attack no one, not being trained for aggression and violence.

In actuality, it is not only female sexuality that is thwarted in women but also the sense of herself as a "being." It is indeed more comfortable to see her in her relation to men, to see her, in de Beauvoir's terms, as the "other." Morris Ploscowe introduces his discussion of rape with this idea:

> His [the rapist's] activities strike a sphere where *man* is most sensitive: the sexual honor of the female, whether the female be wife, mother, daughter, or sister.[23]

The implication here is that, for men, rape is reprehensible because it threatens their honor or power. Women, that is, have no power or honor within themselves; they are defined in terms of their relationship to men. This sort of depreciation is part of the general depersonalization of women, a phenomenon that makes it easier to commit aggressive acts against them; indeed women's bodies when not sold directly in prostitution or marriage, are used to sell other objects like cars or cigarettes or plane rides. The depersonalization that allows men to attack women enables them also to dismiss women's attempts at justice for the indignities that burden them. And, as we have seen, women are indeed blamed for the many ways in which they "ask for it." A woman alone is "asking for it." A woman who is enticing "asks for it." It seems, then, that woman is trapped by a contradictory and paradoxical set of demands and expectations. She is programmed from the beginning to groom herself, to adorn herself, to display herself. Yet she remains vulnerable to attack when and because she performs these functions. Men continually regard women as sexual objects, their primary function being to fulfill sexual needs and fantasies. Despite recent acknowledgements of the fact that women, too, have sexual needs, they are not yet regarded as important as men's, or as necessary of fulfillment. The reason is simple: women are selling. They have been taught to sell, to be conscious of their bodies, to be eyed, but to barter well for financial support, security, or status. One of the single most curious facts in the study of sexual assaults is that the mothers and/or wives of many convicted rapists have been characterized as "seductive and rejecting." Is this not, however, what most women are taught to be? Are we not entreated again and again to make ourselves attractive but cautioned at every turn, always, always, to remain "good girls"?

NOTES

1. The problem of the solicitation of children or teen-agers by older men is another issue discussed in Florence Bush's paper on the "Sexual Abuse of Children."
2. FBI Uniform Crime Report of the U.S., 1969.
3. Benjamin Karpman, *The Sexual Offender and His Offenses*, New York, 1954, pp. 502-503.
4. Walker Bromberg, *Crime and the Mind,* New York, 1965, p. 335.
5. Hervey Cleckley,*The Caricature of Love*, New York, 1957, p. 80.
6. Bernard Glueck, *Final Report Research Project for the Study and Treatment of Crimes Involving Sexual Aberrations,* Minnesota, 1952-55, p. 32.
7. Karpman, *op. cit.,* p. 121.
8. Bromberg, *op. cit.,* p. 98
9. *The New York Times,* September 12, 1968.
10. Karpman, *op. cit.,* p. 80.
11. J.W. Mohr, "Rape and Attempted Rape," in *Sexual Behavior and the Criminal Law Preliminary Report*, Toronto, 1965, p. 2.
12. Bernard J. Oliver, *Sexual Deviation in American Society: A Social Psychological Study of Non-Conformity*, New Haven, 1967, p. 58.
13. Glueck, *op. cit.*, p. 33.
14. Manachim Amir, "Forcible Rape," *The Journal of Criminal Law, Criminology and Police Science*, 1967, pp. 497-99.
15. Paul H. Gebbard, John H. Gagnon, Wardell B. Pomeroy and Cornelia V. Christenson, *Sex Offenders: An Analysis of Types*, New York, 1965, pp. 177-78.
16. FBI Uniform Crime Report of the U.S., 1967.
17. Morris Ploscowe, *Sex and the Law,* New York, 1951, p. 180.
18. Paul Tappan, *The Habitual Sex Offender, Report and Recommendations of the Commission on the Habitual Sex Offender as Formulated by Paul W. Tappan,* New Jersey, 1950, pp. 21-22.
19. Gebbard, *op. cit.*, p. 197.
20. *Ibid.*, p. 177.
21. Oliver, *op. cit.*, p. 66.
22. Glueck, *op. cit.*, p. 85
23. Ploscowe, *op.cit.*, p. 155.

That's All She Wrote:
Popular Rape Fiction by Women

Lynne Farrow

Everyone remembers the scene in *The Fountainhead* where the wealthy, antiseptic Dominique Francon scratches the marble in her bedroom fireplace so that it may be replaced by Howard Roark, the quarry worker with the uncompromising stare. We learn shortly that the novel's hero is soon to be a rapist and that the act is thoroughly compatible not only with Ayn Rand's sexual politics but with her larger social vision as well. What is the political-social context of rape within the conservative design?

The Fountainhead strings together a series of Howard Roark's struggles against outside forces, in contests to control or dominate. He struggles against nature in the quarry, against the woman Dominique, and against society's evil impulse to collectivize. To Howard Roark, the author's mouthpiece, the world is a place where all human activity bears some essential antagonism. Camps must always form. The logical extension of the social-political paranoia that is conservatism is Roark's persistent "Us against Them" attitude. Similarly, the emphasis is always placed on what makes the individual distinct and *different* from the rest of society. Man against society boils as an issue of constant irresolvable conflict. All characters are drawn either as weak or strong, good or bad, in a world where every action taken is deliberate. Nothing happens without purpose or outside of a strict cause-and-effect relationship. Society is a culture divided between perpetually hostile camps.

The first quarry scene shows how the hero's struggle with nature is interwoven with strong sexual metaphors, foreshadowing the soon-to-come rape.

> To hold his fists closed tight, as if the skin of his plalms had grown fast to the steel he clasped—to keep his feet steady, pressed down hard, the flat rock an upward thrust against his soles—not to feel the existence of his body, but only a few clots of tension: his knees, his wrists, his shoulders and the drill he held—to feel the drill trembling in a long convulsive shudder—to feel his stomach trembling, his lungs

trembling, the straight lines of the stone ledges before him dissolving into jagged streaks of trembling—to feel the drill and his body gathering into the single will of pressure, that a shaft of steel might sink slowly into granite—this was all of life for Howard Roark, as it had been in the days of the two months behind him. . . .

He liked the work. He felt at times as if it were a match of wrestling between his muscles and the granite. . . .

Each evening he walked the two miles from the quarry to the little town where the workers lived. The earth of the woods he crossed was soft and warm under his feet; it was strange, after a day spent on the granite ridges; he smiled as at a new pleasure, each evening, and looked down to watch his feet crushing a surface that responded, gave way and conceded faint prints to be left behind.[1]

Later when Roark is lying on the ground, he even finds the earth an opponent.

He pressed his hips, his back into the earth under him; the earth resisted, but it gave way; it was a silent victory; he felt a dim, sensuous pleasure in the muscles of his legs.[2]

Similarly, the author's physical description of the hero reveals a contestant who glories in commanding the environment to his will.

It was a body of long straight lines and angles, each curve broken into planes. . . . His face was like a law of nature—a thing one could not question, alter or implore. It had high cheek bones over gaunt, hollow cheeks; gray eyes, cold and steady; a contemptuous mouth, shut tight, the mouth of an executioner or a saint.

He looked at the granite. To be cut, he thought, and made into walls. He looked at a tree. To be split and made into rafters. He looked at a streak of rust on the stone and thought of iron ore under the ground. To be melted and to emerge as girders against the sky.

These rocks, he thought, are here for me; waiting for the drill, the dynamite and my voice; waiting to be split, ripped, pounded, reborn; waiting for the shape my hands will give them.[3]

Where Howard Roark functions as an abstract of male authority, Dominique Francon embodies the tall, pale-skinned aristocratic female whose sole occupation amounts to cultural masochism. Rand's every sentence describing Dominique boasts her satisfaction capitulating to a will not her own, a pain or discomfort inflicted by someone else. Dominique is a female totally enraptured by the theater of her own passivity; her thoughts are filled with the terms of her own defilement and submission, almost as if she were seeking new occasions to be acted upon, bigger contests to lose.

> Dominique walked to the quarry. The thought of seeing it on that blazing day was revolting; she enjoyed the prospect.[4]
>
> She thought of the many distinguished men whom she had refused. She thought of the quarry worker. She thought of being broken—not by a man she admired, but by a man she loathed. She let her head fall down on her arm; the thought left her weak with pleasure.[5]
>
> She found a dark satisfaction in pain—because that pain came from him.[6]

The rape of Dominique, the impudent virgin, by Howard Roark creates the quintessential sado-masochistic resolution. It follows that the author creates the rape scene as the epitome of sexual encounters, a mock contest where if it wasn't clear before where dominance and submission are cast, it is now made specific with the brutalization of the female. There appears no passing suggestion that the violent forced experience be viewed as a crime. To the contrary, it graphically endorses the relationship between man and women as it should be: defilement. Both sexual identities are reinforced by every detail the author gives us about the rape. Dominique is meticulously groomed, clean and perfumed in the elegance of her family's summer home, whereas Roark comes straight form the quarry with a dirty work shirt and pants still smeared with granite dust.

> It was an act that could be performed in tenderness, as a seal of love, or in contempt, as a symbol of humiliation and conquest. It could be the act of a lover of the act of a soldier violating an enemy woman. He did it as an act of scorn. Not as love, but as defilement. And this made her lie still and submit. One gesture of tenderness from him—and she would have remained cold, untouched by the thing done to her body. But the act of a master taking shameful, contemptuous possession of her was the kind of rapture she had wanted.[7]

The author sees Roark's relationship to women as similar to his relationship to his work, building. They both exist as objects to be conquered, then left for new challenges. Predictably, the day after the rape Roark leaves town to resume his career as an architect, saying in so many words, "A man's gotta do what a man's gotta do," or now that the woman has been put in her proper place, it's time to get back to work. This cliché is the seduced and abandoned motif found in many stories where the man passes through town, sexually takes the lady of his choice, then moves on to larger and more important exploits. It is the man who controls the relationship, who is moving places, creating a bigger and better world.

Rape, therefore, fits into the social-political design of conservatism as yet another measure of man's response to challenge and threat. It is another essential struggle that clarifies his identity and social definition as that of the controller. On a class level it divides the world into the potential rapists and the potential victims. Rape functions either by actual assault or persistent fear as sexual lynching to keep women aware of their place in the rigid social design: a man rapes women, he breaks stone, he creates buildings. It is these, according to Rand, that make a man conscious of his existence.

> In some unstated way, last night had been what building was to him; in some quality of reaction within him, in what it gave to his consciousness of existence.[8]

Jacqueline Susann's most recent novel, *Once Is Not Enough*, does not pretend to be the novel of ideas *The Fountainhead* does, but it certainly puts forth some ideas as to how men and women function given the options of a sexist society. Where Ayn Rand's novel stands as an abstract of conservatism, endorsing rape as part of a social vision where men dominate and women submit, Jacqueline Susann's convictions about rape and the ideal relationship between the sexes are ambivalent. Her female characters are complex, strong, provocative figures, all victimized somewhat differently by a sexist society. The male characters are interchangeable, only occasionally sympathetic and obsessed with their power over their work world and women.

The Susann characters show what the female experience can be. January Wayne, the principal, is the lovely, motherless (she committed suicide because of her husband's infidelities) daughter of an ambitious, wheeling-dealing Hollywood producer. She sustains a severe automobile accident in her late teens at the hands of a reckless male escort, then remains paralyzed or somewhat handicapped for almost three years in a hospital in Switzerland recovering.

January's physical paralysis and attempt to integrate back into the culture may symbolize the social-political handicap of sex. This theme weaves in and out of the story in a series of traumatic vignettes. Because January has been cut off from the mainstream of society while hospitalized in Switzerland, she returns to New York an observer of social values and customs and has less vested interest than those around her do. Wide-eyed and disillusioned, she tries to explore what possibilities exist for herself as a woman in the world of work and in relationships between men and women.

January first meets Dee Granger, powerful and fantastically wealthy heiress who marries men for their "use value" and eventually discards them. The role reversal here appears in that it is January's father, the handsome, charming Mike Wayne, who marries Dee for financial security. Dee is calculating, knows what she wants, and just happens to be in love with Karla, the Polish actress.

The next female character the author exposes January to is Linda Riggs, ambitious woman's magazine editor, efficient, talented, totally dedicated to her career and frustrated by a series of ineffectual men in her life. January eventually goes to work for her at *Gloss* magazine. As they become friends, Linda recites to the bewildered January survival politics for the sexually "liberated" female. In the course of these sisterly lessons Linda is portrayed as bitter at her fate as a female in search of bigger and better orgasms, and finding continually men who are intimidated by her ambition and agressiveness.

Karla appears on the New York Scene as an elusive feminist specter. No one really knows anything about her apart from legend. Slowly we learn she has come from Poland where she was raped by Russian soldiers at the beginning of her ballet career. At one time Karla was in love with Sister Therese, her teacher, and since has had a series of lesbian affairs in her long career as an actress. As the sought-after social misfit, Karla intrigues January and serves as the likely rape victim.

The male characters the author has thinly drawn appear cardboard and for the most part interchangeable, like January's father, Mike Wayne. He is portrayed as the hero to January, but otherwise as a watered-down Norman Mailer type, concerned with his own exploits and image, whereas the more intricate female characters are struggling for an identity apart from second-guessing the men in their lives, and they appear to be succeeding.

January's search for a social context unravels in the setting of these essentially independent men-less women. But from there the author creates a rape, in flashback terms, that reveals some basic ambivalence in her feeling about sexual politics. The rape scene takes place in Russian-occupied Poland during World War Two. Russian soldiers break into a convent to rape the nuns living there. One of them is Sister Therese, Karla's teacher and first love. Karla, hiding in the dark, observes the scene.

And then Karla saw Sister Therese. Blood was smeared between her thighs as one Russian got off her. Another picked her up by the neck and kissed her violently. Then his mouth began to ravage her body, beginning at the breasts as he chewed away on each of them, his dirty fingers groping between her legs. While he was enjoying himself, slobbering down her body, another soldier approached her from the back, spread her buttocks apart and rammed into her. At the same moment, the soldier in front opened his pants and also rammed into her. Karla couldn't believe it—two men tearing at her insides . . . one from the front . . . one inside her back! Mercifully, Sister Therese passed out.[9]

A week later Karla is raped.

A week later the same soldiers returned. They were more raucous than before. And this time Karla did not escape. They pulled off her glasses and her clothes. She was thrown on the floor and her head struck against a chair. She prayed for unconsciousness but was jolted into awareness with the knifelike pain as her legs were forced apart and the soldier ripped into her. Rhythmically, roughly, they rode her, one after another—five, six, seven, eight . . . her blood mixed with their orgasms . . . their wet mouths biting at her lips, her breasts.[10]

These rapes are created to horrify and shock us. Not only are the victims nuns protecting starving Polish children but they are assaulted multiply and sodomized in grotesque fashion. As powerful an impact as the scenes may stir, they serve as a bizarre fantasy. Susann's rapists are soldiers infused with the savagery of war in a strange country. This brutal scene could only successfully fit into the novel as a flashback, as an event dreamlike and unreal, a complete social aberration. Susann's rapists are drawn as near-psychopathic animals. Rape, she is telling us, is horrible, but it is a freak of war or an event essentially outside our culture, a social obscurity. Susann is sensitive to how rape brutalizes women but is totally naïve as to the regularity with which rape pushes in to the lives of women, and by men consistently considered harmless and normal.

The author clearly perceives a culture that exploits women in subtle and obvious ways, yet she does not see rape as a symptom or part of that exploitation. Rape erupts only as a hateful isolated crime with no social underpinnings.

Susann's ambivalent social perspective focuses again with her curiously sympathetic characterization of the Russian captain. When Karla becomes pregnant from the multiple rapes and wants to rid herself of the fetus, the handsome young Russian captain who rescues her from further abuse offers a suggestion of dubious value.

"Oh God—if there is a God—how can I rid myself of this thing growing in me?"

He colored slightly. "I know of a way that might work. I . . . I saw it happen one night last week. Some soldiers were searching homes . . . looking for some escaped prisoners from work camps. Suddenly I heard a scream . . . I rushed upstairs . . . one of the soliders had raped a woman—" He sighed. "You must understand, some of these men are peasants . . . they are lonely . . . they have never been away from the farm . . . they have never had much to drink . . . suddenly they have Polish vodka . . . there are pretty women. And—" He shrugged. "They rape. This man . . . he raped a girl in your condition. Only it was a baby she wanted . . . from her husband. She had pleaded with him . . . told him she was three months' pregnant . . . that she might lose it." She shuddered. "I heard her begging . . . but when I got to the room it was too late . . . and she lost the baby . . . or what was the beginning of the baby. I shot him."[1 1]

First, Karla's knight-in-shining armor captain presents an alternative to childbearing that can only be construed as suspiciously lecherous. Secondly, considering he shot one of his fellow soldiers for doing exactly what he proposes doing to Karla, it might be suggested that he invoked righteous indignation only when it suited his purposes. The rapist he shot had victimized a respectable, heterosexual married woman. Thus, the soldier was defending the sanctity of marriage and the defilement of some man's property. Karla participated in none of these socially sanctioned institutions, so the protection they insure did not apply to her and the soldier felt no compunction about aborting Karla by having violent sex with her. The only reservation he mentions is that the child might be a boy with gray eyes. Finally, although Susannn has violently condemned the rapes previously, now using the captain as a mouthpiece, she sees the rapes as somewhat excusable because the soldiers are part of a drunk, confused peasant class in a foreign land.

With these obvious questions going unanswered, the captain moves into the sex-for-therapeutic-abortion scene with the complete endorsement of the author. If the reader entertained any doubts about Karla's knight being there for her own good, they are quickly confirmed.

He lay beside her on the bed and stroked her body. She was rigid. When his lips went to her breast she pushed him away. "Please . . . do your business and be done with it."

"No . . . first I make love to you." And against her will he gently caressed her . . . kissed her lips . . . her neck . . . her breasts . . . And soon she found herself relaxing. And when he lay on top of her and took her smoothly, rhythmically and fiercely, she suddenly felt an odd sensation. She held him close, and when the unbelievable explosion shot through her, she cried out in agonized delight. . . . [12]

Elements of a classic rape fantasy surface in this scene. Big, strong, handsome soldier meets celibate lesbian woman who sees sex only as an instrument of brutality. But the man changes all that and makes her enjoy the experience against her will. He proceeds to make her, the sexually and socially aberrant female, normal. "All she needs is a good fuck" seems to be only one of the clichés operating here.

The question arises whether Susann, in this context, sees rape as a punishment or an instrument of socialization. The chapter ends with Karla thinking, "She was grateful for all he had done," as if the entire experience had come from the captain's paternalistic heart. Whatever consciousness the author reveals through her female characters about the complexity and extent of women's dilemma, she suspends when it comes to rape as if it had practically nothing to do with men and women, no roots in cultural climate that treats women as objects to be acted upon.

Where the sexual politics of *The Fountainhead* may be seen as reactionary, i.e., rape is seen as the ultimate sexual encounter, and the sexual politics of *Once Is Not Enough* seen as ambivalent, i.e., where rape is an abhorrent social anomaly, Grace Metalious's *Peyton Place* presents a perspective that falls more on the left, feminist side of the scale. Rape appears not an isolated crime of a disturbed personality but as much a common occurrence and accepted value of our culture as paying taxes and bills.

Peyton Place attacks the values of a small New England town by presenting an array of otherwise likeable, believable characters involved in malicious situations. Constance MacKenzie and her daughter, moderately prosperous, attractive, and Waspy, quickly surface as the town's favorites. When Constance is raped by the town's new principal and Greek embodiment of machismo, Thomas Makris, her major concern is that the lights are out and the door is locked. After looking at Jacqueline Susann's novel, one might be perplexed at the anticlimactic rape because the two people involved know each other and the victim is ashamed that her neighbors might find out and think of her as the enticer. But as investigations have shown, this is a most accurate picture of rape as it occurs on a day-to-day basis in small towns and large cities. The book does not dwell on this rape but shows it only as an embarrassment for Constance, which, although understated, is an accurate profile about how women learn to regard their own sexual abuse.

The way the town reacts to its misfits brings the author's sexual politics into clear focus. Nellie Cross, for example, one of the novel's most sympathetic characters, echos a quivering feminist voice as the casualty of an impoverished patriarchal household. We meet her in her late forties, slatternly, overworked, cleaning other people's houses, then returning to the shack where she lives to endure the violent abuse of her drunken husband, Lucas. While Nellie is cleaning the MacKenzie house one day, Allison insensitively siezes the opportunity to ask her, in effect, why she is such a misfit.

> Two years earlier she had been content to let books answer her questions, but now she tried to learn from people. She asked questions of everyone whom she dared to approach, and the most sympathetic of these was Nellie Cross.
>
> "How did you ever come to marry Lucas, anyway?" she asked Nellie one day.... Allison had learned to be patient with Nellie's inarticulateness ...[13]

Predictably, Nellie married for the same reasons most of us do. It seemed like a good idea at the time.

> "I dunno that I ever did come to it, like you say," said Nellie finally. "Marrin' Lucas wa'nt nothin' I ever come to. It was just one of those things that happened."[14]

Allison, typically and predictably socialized to think opression is the direct responsibility of the oppressed, responds, "Nothing ever just happens. There is a law of cause and effect that applies to everything and everybody." After a while Nellie recalls that if there was any reason she married, it was by necessity. She really hadn't any options.

> "Now that I think of it," said Nellie, "there most likely was a reason why I married Lucas. I had Selena. Tiny, she was then. Just barely six weeks old.... It seemed like a good idea, at the time, my marryin' Lucas, I mean. He was alone with Paul, and I was alone with Selena. Don't do for a woman to be alone, or a man either. Besides, what could I do? I wa'nt in no shape to work right then, bein' as how I just had a baby, and Lucas was after me...."
>
> "But how could you stay with him?" asked Allison. "How come you didn't run away when he beat you, and beat your children?"
>
> "Why, honey, beatins don't mean nothin'." Nellie cackled again, and this time her eyes did turn vague. "It's everythin' else. The booze and the wimmin. Even the booze ain't so bad, if he'd just leave the wimmin alone...."

"Oh, he'll get his someday," whispered Nellie, matching her voice to Allison's. "He'll get his, the sonofabitch. They all get it, in the end, the sonsofbitches. All of 'em."[15]

Nellie's muttering refrain indicting men, "sonsofbitches. All of 'em. Booze 'n' wimmin. Wimmin 'n' booze," weaves hauntingly throughout the story. This plaintiff chant causes the town to disregard everything she says as part of her "bitterness." They are able to bear her slatterliness and hard life in their presence, but when she responds logically to her oppressive situation with righteous indignation, many of the town's people become outraged that Nellie doesn't accept her victimization more complacently. Nellie's bitterness implies consciousness and consciousness implies resistance. The town recoils from it defensively.

> Allison sighed and stood up. When Nellie began to croon and curse, it was futile to try to talk sense to her. She would go on for the rest of the day, swearing under her breath, unaware of all questions put to her. It was this trait in Nellie that caused Constance MacKenzie to remark frequently that something would have to be done about her. But somehow Constance never got around to doing anything, for Nellie, eccentric or not, was still the best house worker in Peyton Place.[16]

Nellie's fifteen-year-old daughter by a previous marriage, Selena, is beaten and raped several times in the course of her adolescence by her stepfather, Lucas. Eventually she becomes pregnant and goes to the town's doctor, Matthew Swain, who performs an abortion in secret. Dr. Swain becomes the novel's feminist inquisitor when he goes to Lucas and threatens him until he confesses. He begins by asking how many times he raped Selena.

> "A couple," said Lucas in a low whisper. "I was drunk, Doc. I didn't know what I was doin'."
>
> Automatically the doctor's mind registered the first of Lucas's excuses. I was drunk. I didn't know what I was doing. It was a standard with men like Lucas, for everything from fighting and stealing, to apparently, the raping of children.
>
> "She was a virgin when you started, wasn't she, Lucas?" asked the doctor in the same sly voice. "You busted your daughter's cherry for her, didn't you, Lucas, you big, brave virile woodchopper?"
>
> "I was drunk," repeated Lucas. "Honest, Doc. I was drunk. I didn't

know what I was doin'. Besides, it ain't like she was my own. She wa'nt mine. She's Nellie's kid." ...

Lucas gasped as the doctor's fingers twisted in his hair. "Yes," he said. "I knew. I seen her one day, and I seen she was almost grown. I don't know what got into me."

The second standard excuse had now been presented. I don't know what got into me. It was as if men like Lucas expected men like Matthew Swain to believe in the existence of strange devils who lurked, ready and eager to invade the minds and bodies of men like Lucas. The second excuse for misbehavior was always tendered in a wistful, half-apologetic tone, as if the speaker expected the listener to join with him in wonder at this thing which had got into him. I don't know what got into me, but whatever it was, it was none of my doing. Something just got into me, and there was nothing I could do. . . . .

"I dunno how many times it was," said Lucas thickly. "A couple— maybe three—when I was half drunk and didn't give a shit." His eyes went blank with remembered lust. "She's a wildcat, Selena is. Always was. I used to hit her till she didn't fight no more."[17]

This is the first occasion in any of the three books in question where anything resembling a social analysis of the rapist occurs. The doctor does not hide behind system-blaming generalities to give the rapist excuses. Instead he attempts to demystify the system to show how certain people are continuously advantaged by this system and that it is they who must be held responsible in order to change the way things are. Grace Metalious creates a culture in which Selena's rape and her mother's subsequent suicides are events we cannot dismiss philosophically as inevitable because of cultural values. We see that someone who participates in sex or class privileges directly maintains those values and capitalizes on them whenever possible. It is he who must be defined and held responsible for the rape, the suicide, and the system that supports them.

Very often in literature and films the rape victim has to suffer some further punishment for being raped because of the general belief that she must have asked for it. She is either forced to have the baby, becomes a lesbian or prostitute, or commits suicide. Although these things almost never happen in real life to rape victims, where a writer can control the course of events, the cultural belief that the rape victim should be punished finds its way into the story. To the contrary, *Peyton Place* gives us an unusual literary event where Selena not only has a successful abortion but a positive future provided for her. Grace Metalious's purpose is to focus on the sexual politics of the rapist and the rape culture, not to hammer the nails into the coffin of the victim. The suffering of Nellie Cross hangs heavily over the whole sexual-political scheme of Peyton Place as she becomes increasingly despondent and driven incoherent by fleeting images of her husband raping Selena. Even though Jacqueline Susann does not comprehend the pervasiveness of rape, she points consistently to the elaborate social webs that paralyze every woman character in some way. Popular fiction of this kind that deals with the issues and fears of women's everyday life runs the risk of being dismissed as frivolous tear-jerking trash. This is especially true when the author happens to be a woman. We have been consistently pressured to dismiss our anxieties and invalidate our experiences as women—to see them as unimportant, isolated sob stories with no political significance. Like Nellie Cross, when we complain and locate the responsibility for our social condition with men, we are approaching a consciousness that is on the brink of active resistance. Just as Nellie's experience was dismissed as eccentric, bitter, female carrying-on, so has the literature of women's experience, including rape, been subjected to mockery and dismissal. We must reevaluate what all women authors, not just those accepted by the male-dominated literary establishment, have chosen to write about. If a woman writes a book and thousands of copies are bought by women readers, something important is going on in those pages.

NOTES

1. Rand, Ayn, *The Fountainhead*, New American Library, 1964, pp. 194f.
2. *Ibid.*, p. 195.
3. *Ibid.*, p. 7f.
4. *Ibid.*, p. 197.
5. *Ibid.*, p. 199.
6. *Ibid.*, p. 202.
7. *Ibid.*, p. 210.
8. *Ibid.*, p. 211.
9. Susann, Jacqueline, *Once Is Not Enough*, William Morrow, 1973, p. 213.
10. *Ibid.*, p. 214f.
11. *Ibid.*, p. 217.
12. *Ibid.*, p. 217f.
13. Metalious, Grace, *Peyton Place*, Julian Messner, 1956, p. 129.
14. *Ibid.*, p. 129.
15. *Ibid.*, p, 130f.
16. *Ibid.*, p. 131.
17. *Ibid.*, p. 159.

The Independent Woman
and the Cinema of Rape

Lynne Farrow

The act of rape has grown so common in recent films that when it's going to happen on the screen you can feel it coming, as if it were the logical conclusion to certain antecedent events. I discovered one prevalent rule in the Cinema of Rape: men never arbitrarily rape women, they are set up. That is, men are "victims" of of uncontrollable situations that independent wicked women supposedly create.

Town Without Pity, made in 1961, is a case in point. The story takes place in a German town in which there are American troops stationed. A sixteen-year-old, very pretty German girl has a fight with her boyfriend while they are swimming. She tartly leaves him at the lake (still wearing her bikini) and is raped by American GIs.

Clearly the girl, Karin, displays what might be considered aggressive and "whore" behavior by her attackers and even the audience. She was, after all, wearing a bikini, and what's a sixteen-year-old girl doing alone at a secluded lake trying to seduce her boyfriend, especially in 1961? Not only that, but she's uppity. She did leave him and walk through the woods alone, right? With these events in the background you just know she's about to be raped. "She's just aksing for it," like the man says.

Justice does not stop there. The rest of the movie covers the military trial and justification of this gang rape. Kirk Douglas, as the GIs' defender, comes from the States to defend the men. He comes on super-male (the prominent chin), super-military (a major), and super-American (Steve Garrett). You cannot say "Major Steve Garrett" without sensing the growling macho embodiment Kirk Douglas gives this leading character. Similarly, in the course of the movie, Garrett defends three things: male privilege, military privilege, and American privilege. His job as the defense lawyer actually is to enforce the authority of all three of these privileges. And he does.

First he snoops around town and finds a peeping tom shopkeeper who swears that there were times before the rape when Karin had forgotten to pull down her windowshade. That does it. She's a proven whore. He drags that fact into the trial of the four soldiers and it is considered admissible evidence. In the course of his snooping he also reveals how ignorant and eccentric "those foreigners," the Germans, are and how intimidated they are when he marches his shiny, uniform-bedecked torso into their living rooms. He speaks slowly, effectively, and precisely. They tell their stories quickly in broken English and become confused.

As a man, a soldier, and an American, the major sets everything straight in the course of the trial. By this time the townspeople have become so confused and awkward in the presence of this articulate authority that they will say almost anything he wants so that the ordeal will be over and they can resume their self-respecting lives. The audience is manipulated into thinking that it is not the major but the town that has no pity on the girl and that indeed it is the town at whom we should point the finger. The townspeople ostracize Karin (for pretending to be an innocent schoolgirl when all the time she was a whore!) as the major has encouraged to save the guilty necks of his defendants.

When the town has been manipulated and tormented and Karin finally commits suicide, the major goes into the bathroom and throws up. But Male, Military, and American authority carry on. This is the cultural climate of rape. The events in *Town Without Pity* corroborate the testimonies at the rape conference in that rape is rarely an act of purely sexual passion but rather an act of aggression against women, a reassertion of male dominance.

In *Town Without Pity* we are assured repeatedly in the course of the film that Karin is a whore, asked for it, etc. In *Last Summer* the raped teen-ager, Rhoda, is a plump, freckled prude. She is characterized as offensively brainy and throws around psychological jargon with arrogant facility. In this way she can be seen as another stereotyped rape victim, another kind of independent woman. Her behavior is construed as baiting potential attackers because of her indifference to men. Both Karin and Rhoda share one characteristic, they cannot conform to the code of behavior men have set up for women that dictates that females should act in a manner that most accommodates men. That is, they must never lapse into either prudish braininess or whoredom because there they trespass on male prerogative. Any act of independence like Rhoda's disregard for appearance or Karin's sexual casualness are interpreted as acts of sexual aggression and are considered willful attempts at undermining male authority.

The two stories are similar to detective stories; however, the rapist is never the criminal sought after and punished. The raped woman is. *Town Without Pity* focused on gradually revealing the wanton character of the criminal, Karin. *Last Summer* focuses on the crime of Rhoda's consistent arrogance and the interaction of the other three characters. Whereas the rape (the punishment of the criminal) takes place in the beginning in *Town Without Pity* and the remainder of the film justifies it, the rape in *Last Summer* takes place at the end, and the first part of the film explores the crime of Rhoda's righteousness and why punishment is deserved.

Last Summer uses a fascinating and incredible device to incriminate Rhoda. The rape is executed by two teen-age boys with a female accomplice, Sandy, the male-identified heroine. The logic created through this device is that, if another woman collaborates in rape, it must be justified. Women are usually the compassionate sex and if one turns on the other, this, in a sense, sanctions the aggression. But the phenomenon of the male-identified woman goes deeper than the film takes it. Sandy is not just an anonymous female who happens to side with the male aggression on the single issue of manipulating and assaulting Rhoda. She consistently draws a sense of strength from doing lip service to the male viewpoint. As sort of a male groupie, she gets approval for putting down her mother for taking all her father's money in alimony. By aligning herself with the faction calling the shots, the male-identified woman taps a measure of that power. She flatly refuses to see herself as the victim in sexual situations. To do this would be to say, "I have been exploited" or "I am weak." Sandy has found her own way, however ignoble, to survive with a measure of self-respect in our male-defined, male-ruled culture. Identifying with the stronger, the establishment, or the oppressor is a way always to be on the winning team—a sort of misguided guerrilla warfare survival tactic.

Other details contribute to her magnificent but frightening male-identified characterization. "Sandy" is a name that does not betray her sex. In the middle of the film she even kills a lame seagull, a definitely unfemale thing to do. Tormenting animals is always considered the mainstay of the cruel-little-boy sports. By her cruel whims she tries to out-male the males, beating them at their own game. Peter and Dan are horrified by the killing, but it's not clear whether they consider it unfemale or just plain cruel.

In the course of the film the two boys and Sandy manipulate Rhoda into seeking their (male) approval. Sandy even takes her shopping so she can replace her saggy one-piece bathing suit with a bikini. Previously Rhoda had said, "But I like my old one." Slowly her tastes change, as the three withdraw approval and affection when Rhoda says something that displeases them. Sex is the one area they see as Rhoda's sensitive point— she is terribly shy and inhibited. Sandy's aggressiveness embarrasses Rhoda and she openly disapproves of her swimming bottomless with the boys in the ocean. As the film proceeds, the three manipulate Rhoda into dropping most of her prudishness and even her precocious vocabulary. She gradually seeks to be included in their summertime activities. When she behaves as they do, they reward her with affection, and when she occasionally lapses into her former intellectual self, they snap at her.

They seemed to have changed her dress, her speech, and her righteousness, and they are satisfied. But the one thing Rhoda refuses to change her attitude on is their sexual exploration. They intimidate her about it, but she won't be changed. In the final scene when they go off into the woods, Rhoda reprimands Sandy for beginning to take off her bathing suit. The three are infuriated with her for going along with their values this far and then turning independent on them at the last minute. So, held by Sandy and Peter, she is raped by Dan.

Where *Town Without Pity* examines the independent woman as criminal and *Last Summer* explores the nature of her crime, a more recent film, *A Clockwork Orange,* achieves something entirely different. The rape act is glorified and made into high art. The events and characters leading up to it or following it fall inconsequentially into the background. The brief rape scenes in *Town Without Pity* and *Last Summer* appear primitive and awkwardly carried off in comparison with Kubrick's creation. They needed a logical plot to justify rape. Not so in *A Clockwork Orange.* Rape exists for its own sake, concertized as a thing of beauty.

The story is about Alexander, a young man who beats up old men and rapes and murders women. Finally, when he is imprisoned, he volunteers for some antiviolence treatments so that he may be discharged early. The treatments consist of forcing him to watch movies of violence and rape while injected with a nauseant so that in the future he will associate violence with sickness and feelings of dread. Heavy-handedly, we are supposed to believe the bad guys are the police, the doctors, the prison officials, the establishment, and it is they that created the poor, brutal waif. But before so simpleminded an antistate statement can be made, we are forced to watch what seems hours of Alexander's rapes, beatings, and sordid slashings. He has a boundless imagination when it comes to brutalizing and degrading people (mostly women) and we must be shown all the possibilities until finally we tire of looking for a redeeming social message.

It becomes obvious after the first half hour that whatever the plot, moral, or theme of this story, it is all an excuse to display some arty antifemale violence for an eager audience. But the film is not without the company of other recent films that pretend to the philosophical conclusion that "man is basically evil" and thus dramatize some kinky kind of brutality that hasn't been tried before. Trying to outdo each other at this game, the filmmakers stage their yearly rip-offs to "artfully" exploit woman-hating violence. Just as *A Clockwork Orange* was last year's and

Straw Dogs this year's, there will certainly be a whopper again next year pretentiously putting forth the authoritarian notion that we are all utterly depraved and must not be allowed to go unchecked.

Take the first rape. Not only is it a gang rape, but the woman is extraordinarily shapely and beautiful, and it is, of all places, on the stage of an enormous abandoned theater. One street gang barges in on the other gang doing the raping and there ensues a very bloody fight. We know right away which gang we will see the most of because they are wearing all-white jumpsuits with hard, protective shells over their genitals. Somehow in the shuffle the woman gets away but the tone is set for the way females are to be treated in the following scenes.

Cut to the Corona Milk Bar, a posh nightclub of the future. Here we have one of the other explicit ways women can be violated by cinema. To receive the drugged milk the establishment serves one must deposit a coin between the spread legs of a kneeling white figure of a naked woman. The spiked milk then comes out of the nipple into the glasses. All the female figures have different-colored wigs (purple, pink, blue) and matching pubic hair. The same white figures in a backbend position are used as cocktail tables. This utilitarian, purely exploitive fantasy use of women is just the beginning.

The next rape is choreographed to music. After gaining entrance to the house of an elderly and famous writer, Alexander and his white hoods, dressed in dancers' costumes, kick the old man and proceed to stage the rape of his young wife in his presence. Our hero Alexander cuts holes in the woman's jumpsuit with elaborate flourishes, so that her breasts protrude through. Next he cuts away piece by piece until there is nothing left but the huge tape across her mouth, then he rapes the terrified woman. This rape establishes women as depthless, incidental, and interchangeable characters in the story, leaving the way Alexander moves his graceful leotarded body to the music ("Singing in the Rain") to capture our full attention.

If we are not convinced by now of our hero's imagination for raping women we are soon to be convinced of his super-male prowess in the next male fantasy par excellence. In a music store of the future Alexander comes across two pretty sweet young things, licking some penis-shaped lollypops. He promptly picks them up and brings them home to his room. There he proceeds to have sex with both of them at the same time and singly, in every conceivable position, to the accompaniment of the "William Tell Overture." The film is speeded up rapidly (à la Keystone Kops) to give the illusion Alexander has the amazing super-sexual energy that could only be the product of a wish-fulfillment male fantasy. Although this sequence has nothing to do with the rest of the film, it might have been thrown in to assure us that not only is the hero good at imaginatively raping women and nastily beating old men, but he has sufficient all-American boy sex appeal to attract two horny young things back to his room to make it nonstop double-time speed with both of them.

A Clockwork Orange does have a climax about half way through the film. You can tell because that's when they made the music the loudest. The scene begins when Alexander, his friends waiting outside, breaks into the house of a well-known yoga and health foods woman who is home alone. When he surprises her, she tells him to get out, she's not afraid of him, he's a creep and more. This independent woman is characterized as arrogant and unfeminine, that is, straightbodied, aggressive, and sharp-tongued. She lives alone with her yoga and health foods and, to complete the fantasy that a woman cannot live without the penis, she has a huge sculpture of a phallus (white again) enshrined as a work of art in her living room. After chasing her around the house he picks up the super white incarnation of male aggression and murders her with it. We are supposed to imagine the exact details of the brutal murder, for all we see is Alexander raising the phallus to Beethoven, then blood coming from the woman's mouth. This climaxes the Cinema of Rape.

A Clockwork Orange should be labeled and filed away somewhere in feminist archives because it makes such a complex study in female humiliation. What's more, it's such an ambitious film. Rape is staged in a theater, choreographed to music, and finally incarnated in the giant white phallus as it becomes the instrument of a symbolic sexual murder. The many clever details like Alexander's pet snake slithering up the crotch of a giant female pinup also contributes thickly when cataloguing the film's persistent misogyny.

Kubrick has even constructed a protest move, protesting the nasty way rapists are locked up by the establishment. But justice reigns in the end when Alexander is literally spoon-fed (visual pun) by the government big-wigs who apologize for his mistreatment and vow to be sympathetic to his kind in the future. The theme, as I see it, is "Viva la rape," or "How dare the civilized establishment try its high-handed, mind-controlling tricks on perpetrators of the all-American sport."

We expect a film to crystallize through plot and characterization what a culture emanates. But *A Clockwork Orange* pulls off more than that. For example, in *Town Without Pity* the audience is cast pretty much as audience by the camera angles and film editing. We are shown fleeting glimpses of the rape and things gradually unfold that we cannot know because we are not there. *Last Summer* follows the same pattern with one exception, in the rape scene when the camera becomes the rapist and records each body thrust by zooming up and down on Rhoda's face.

A Clockwork Orange goes beyond showing us a wedge of our woman-hating culture. We are made partners in rape by Kubrick's easy skill. He accomplishes this by creating so little dialogue that a spectator has little to react to, to stand away from and evaluate. You hear the hero's breathing, you see what he sees, you walk along with him. Finally you listen to Beethoven so loud you forget who you are and become inextricably enmeshed in the character of Alexander. In the safe fantasy world of the future you travel unrecognized by your old world. Liberated from the puritanical hang-ups of the 1970's, you plunge into a new age where you can participate in a festival of rape, murder, and machismo undetected.

The timing of the three films is also interesting to consider. In 1961 when *Town Without Pity* was made, veiled threats of rape to "loose" women like Karin were cinematically viable. An average female might have even tempered her behavior after seeing the plot unfold to Karin's eventual suicide. In 1969, when *Last Summer* was released, the sexual revolution was in full swing. Of course it has been said before that this is not our revolution and the film corroborates this by showing sex as acceptable when it conforms to male demands. Rhoda is a prude, out of time with the sexual revolution, hence, she is punished. Even Eleanor Perry, who wrote the screenplay, said, "She [Rhoda] almost asked to be victimized."* Obviously, a woman had better not be out of step with the sexual mores of the times.

Now in 1971 Kubrick creates the rape and brutality festival. From the use of female figures as tables and dart boards to the artful elimination of one victim by a crushing blow of a twenty-pound penis, the misogynist message is clear, unadulterated by any extended justification of rape. One wonders if *A Clockwork Orange* might not be part of a Women's Liberation backlash, a statement that whether women are "good girls" or "independent," they are merely objects, esthetic or otherwise, in the male fantasy of sex and violence.

---

*Quote from an interview by Kay Loveland and Estelle Changas, "Eleanor Perry: One Woman in Film," *Film Comment*, Spring, 1971, p. 68.

Rape Bibliography*

Joan Mathews

Having chosen the subject of rape for my term paper,* I spent an afternoon at the main branch of the Brooklyn Public Library looking for material. The card catalogue contained such books as *The Rape of Lucretia, The Rape of Africa, The Rape of Art, The Rape of the Lock*, but *not one single book on the rape of women*. It occurred to me that the library might not classify crimes as such, and to check out this point, I looked up murder. There were *ninety* books on murder, not including fiction.

I decided that rape might be treated as part of puberty or initiation rites and found several books by anthropologists dealing with these subjects, but none dealt with rape or even mentioned it. One book, Bruno Bettelheim's *Symbolic Wounds* (on initiation rites), which is kept in a special spot in the closed stacks in a locked cage, had been stolen. I found it later in a paperback bookstore, but although it contained some interesting material, again it did not deal with rape.

Next I tried the Marboro Bookstore on Eighth Street in Manhattan and went through their sociology/anthropology section. I found one book, *Primitive Peoples Today* by Edward Weyer, which contained a couple of sentences on the Camayuras of Central Brazil who use rape as a form of punishment for women if they touch the ritual pipe of the males of the group (somewhat like the Hell's Angels). That was the extent of what I found on rape there.

My next stop was the reference room of the main library on Forty-second Street in Manhattan. Their catalogue showed twenty books on the rape of women, several of them falling into the category of curiosa; that is, they are accounts of trials of rapists that took place as early as the eighteenth century. I mention this because, of the twenty books on the subject, eight deal with crimes committed one hundred years ago or more.

*"Rape Bibliography" was written as a term paper for an anthropology course at New York University in the summer of 1971 with the encouragement of Professor Ethel Alpenfels.

Nine are in other languages—German, French, Italian, Spanish—and they have apparently not been translated into English. (Anyway, translations are not available at the public library.) Most of these latter books were written in this century. I found only *one* book in English out of the twenty that could be considered a serious study of the general problem of rape, *Girls on City Streets: A Study of 1400 Cases of Rape* by Rosamond W. and Jacob A. Goldberg, published in 1935.

After this, I visited the Marboro Bookstore opposite the library. They have a reader's guide, *Paperbound Books in Print*, that lists thousands of books, but not a single one on rape. It may be included under other headings, but it is obviously not thought important enough to rate a classification of its own. (I think I should mention here that I was too reticent to ask the man behind the counter if he knew of any books on the subject of rape. I have found that men respond to any mention of that word in various ways: sometimes with a grin, or raised eyebrows, or hostility. They are seldom "supportive." I know I shouldn't let this stop me, but it does. It's still hard, even for a feminist like myself, to bring this subject out into the open.)

New York University's library contains three books under the category "Rape," one a Danish book dealing with the treatment of sexual offenders in that country (this has been translated into English), another in Italian dealing with the rape of Christian virgins during the Roman Empire, and a third dealing with religious myth and symbol, which peripherally includes rape.

The next place I visited was Brentano's at University Place and Eighth Street. Their paperback department's reader's guide showed five titles under rape, *all* of which turned out to be works of fiction! Upstairs I found two books that included rape. One is *Crime in Urban Society* edited by Barbara McLennan. The amount of space allotted rape is not very significant, but the findings are: although the overall rate of this crime is one woman in every 10,000 in the United States—a high percentage, in some cities (Chicago is one), the chances of a woman's being raped are one in *100*. The second book, *An Outline of Sexual Criminology* by Nigel Morland, an English book, puts most of the blame for rape on the victim.

Having received a tip that there was a new book out entitled *Rape*, I visited Scribner's and two Doubleday bookstores on upper Fifth Avenue and checked Brentano's again. Nobody at any of these bookstores had heard of it nor was it listed in their indexes of new and soon-to-be-published books.

At this point I decided to go back to the main library and check the Union Card Catalogue, which lists every book in every branch library in the city of New York. The subject "Rape" does not appear in this catalogue. I was advised to consult *Books in Print*, an exhaustive listing of books available anywhere, not just those in the library system. There is no such category as "Rape." Under "Sex Crimes" there are are ten books, none of whose titles mentions rape or sexual assaults on women. I checked out these books at the Mid-Manhattan Library and found they had only five of them, three of which were not available, being neither on the reference nor on the circulating shelves. Another book, which dealt primarily with the personal backgrounds of sex offenders, seemed a bit remote for my purposes. The only remaining book, *Crime and the Sexual Psychopath* by Paul De River, dealt seriously with the subject but only devoted a few pages to it.

The Cumulative Index in Room 315, the reference room of the main library, shows nothing under "Rape." the Periodicals *Reader's Guide*, in the same room, shows the category "Rape" and lists *one* article which appeared in the January 25, 1971, issue of *U.S. News and World Report*, entitled "Violence Is a Part of the Times," by M.A. Lipton. (*New York Magazine*, which carried an article on the NYRF Rape Speak-out in January, 1971, is not included in either of the two periodicals indexes in the main reference room.) *The Reader's Adviser* that lists books does so by title only and had nothing on the rape of women, at least under that heading.

I decided to see if *Girls on City Streets: A Study of 1400 Cases of Rape* was a worthwhile book and ordered it up from the stacks. It is a serious work, sympathetic to the victims. It does not go into any of the psychological mumbo-jumbo that invariably puts part, if not all, of the blame for rape on the victim (enticement, wishful thinking, etc.). It also views rape as a major crime and treats it as such.

A number of books on rape and crime in general are published by Charles C Thomas, but are available at only a few bookstores, and are directed toward law enforcement and its agencies. I think it's safe to say that one won't find anything in these books that isn't already a part of the official police attitude, which is, to put it kindly, skeptical of all rape victims.

It appears that rape is considered a crime, a deviation, a perversion, etc., *but not as a special sort of weapon used against women almost exclusively*. One seldom hears of a woman committing rape, if ever. Do the writers of books on "sex crimes" consider these facts when they wedge rape in between their chapters on indecent exposure and foot fetishism? Do they consider the fact that it frequently ends in murder?

In concluding, I would like to quote some lines from Ruth Herschberger's excellent *Adam's Rib*, which has a very profound chapter on rape.

> Rape is a form of violence involving the personal humiliation of the victim . . .

> Murder is a form of violence forced upon an unwilling victim; but murder does not humiliate its victim unless sexual elements are added. Not so with the raped woman. She is rendered passive, shamed, dejected . . . Her honor has been taken from her by force, and no recourse is possible . . .

> . . . As women began to discover their own instincts and inclinations [in sexual matters], husbands found their wives less and less amiable. The demands that were made in sensory matters alone contradicted everything a husband had been accustomed to expect from a wife . . .

> Just as in the situation of rape, the man finds on his hands, secure within the bonds of marriage, an unwilling woman . . . He finally tells himself that sexual aggression toward women is the natural state of things, and he is only carrying out nature's plan.

> The rape rumor . . . not only agrees entirely that sexual aggression is the natural state, but it rather suspects that the natural woman is unwilling. It promises even more. For the rape myth conjures up an image of an unwilling stranger who, *unlike the unwilling wife*, instantly recognizes her assailant's right of sexual aggression—and loves him for it.

> When the man turns to the sensational image of rape, he learns of a sex act which, if effected with any unwilling woman, can force her to enter into a sexual relationship with him. She can be forced into a psychological intimacy with him, as his wife stubbornly is not. Thus in the dream world of gross aggression, the husband finds the same unwilling woman of his marriage situation. But in the rape victim the unwilling woman magically becomes willing . . .

One final word. Every man, every husband may not be a rapist, but all of them *benefit* from the existence of rape in their daily struggle to subjugate women, physically and psychologically. This may be the reason why the libraries and bookstores are singularly unequipped on the subject. By minimizing its importance, blaming women for it, or even denying that there is such a thing, men permit rape to continue, and *all* of them continue to benefit from the fear it casts over *all* women, a fear that inhibits the growth of our independence.

Books on Rape in Room 315, Main Library, Manhattan

What follows is a potentially radicalizing list of books on rape available at some of the major libraries in New York City. On the surface, their irrelevance is humorous, but Joan has included them because they are indicative of academia's total disinterest in a crime that affects mostly women.

—EDITOR'S NOTE

Class Mark

Dost, Oskar Paul   E-11
Psychologie der Notzucht; Untersuchung, Verfelgung,   9264
Vorbeaugung, Hamburg, Kriminalistik (1963) 464 p.

Nisot, Pierre   SLE p.v. 86,
L'age et le consentment de la victime en matière d'infrac-   no. 3
tions contre des moeurs perpetrées envers des filles mineures;
étude de droit comparé par Pierre Nisot ... Renaix: J. Le-
herte-Courten et fils, 1926, 155 p.

Schulz, Gunter   D-12
Die Notzucht; Tater, Opfer, Situationen. Hamburg, Kriminal-   1774
istik, 1958. 178 p.

Ullgren (E.)   Illegible
De Raptu Feminarum in lvecia ... Upsaliae (1791). 9 p.

Jurisprudence—Crete   Illegible
_____rnet, Louis [first part of name illegible] Observations
sur la loi de Gortyne (Revue des Etudes Grecques) Paris,
1916.

Rape—Jurisprudence—Cuba   SNR
Estefano Pisani, Miguel A.
... El rapto (su doctrina y evolucion en el derecho positivo
Cubano) por el Dr. Miguel A. d'Estefano Pisani ... La
Habano, J. Montero, 1945.

Rape—Jurisprudence—Cuba: Mantanzas   SLE p.v. 63,
Tejera Garcia, Diego Vicento   no. 2
.... El rapto. Memoria le ida por el fiscal de la audiencia de
Matanzas en la solemne apertura de los tribunales el 1 de
Septiembre de 1921. Matanzas: Soles y hnos, 1921.

Rape—Trials—Great Britain   6-SLN
Baltimore, Frederick Calbert, 7th Baron, 1731-1771, Defen-   *
dant. The trial of Frederick Calbert, Esq., baron of Balti-

more, in the kingdom of Ireland, for a rape on the body of
Sarah Woodcock; and of Eliz. Griffinburg and Ann Harvey,
otherwise Darby, as accessories before the fact, for pro-
curing, aiding and abetting him in committing the said rape.
At the Assizes held at Kingston, for the county of Surry ...
the 26th of March, 1768. Taken in shorthand by Joseph
Gurney. London, W. Owen (etc.) 1768, 74 p.

Rape—Trials—Great Britain   SLN p.v. 31
The trial of John Motherill, for a rape on the body of
Catherine Wade, daughter of John Wade, Esq., master of the
ceremonies at Bright-Helmstone. Tried before Mr. Justice
Ashurst, at the Lent assizes for the county of Sussex, held at
East Grinstead, on Tues., the 21st of March, 1786. London:
printed for E. Macklew, 1786. 34 p.

Rape—Trials—Italy   NANA
Bentini, Genuzio
Il ratto della bella americanina. Contro Rocco Barbaro.
(L'Eloquenza; antologia, critica, cronaca. Roma, 1939. 1939,
set.-ott., p. 373-397).

Rape—Trials—U.S.—New York   8-*KD
New York (state). Courts: Court of Oyer & Terminer. Report   1800
of the trial of Richard D. Croucher, on an indictment for a
rape on Margaret Miller; on Tues., the 8th day of July, 1800.
Taken in shorthand. N.Y. Printed by G. Forman, pref. 1800,
28 p.

Rape—Trials—U.S.—New York   SLN p.v.
Wakely, Charles   (rest
Trial of Charles Wakely, for a rape on Mrs. Rebecca Fay, wife   illegible)
to Dr. Cyrus Fay, physician; before the Court of General
Sessions of the Peace for the City and County of N.Y. ...
1810. New York: M'Carty & White, 1810. 80 p.

Rape—France   BTZE p.v. 106
La loi du male, a propos de l'enfant du barbare ... Vigot   (part of card
frères, 1915. 64 p.   missing)

Rape—Germany—Bonn   SLA
Wessel, Gerhard
Das Delikt der Kindershandung im Landgerichtsbezirk, Bonn,
von Dr. jur. Gerhard Wessel. Jena: Frommann, 1939, viii,
85 p. incl. tables.

Rape—Great Britain—England—Totnes   NCE

A blazing starre seene in the West at Totnes in Devonshire on
the 14th of Nov., 1642. Wherein is manifested how Master
Ralph Ashley, a deboyst cavalier, attempted to ravish a
young virgin, the daughter of Mr. Adam Fisher ... Also how
at that instant, a fearefull comet appeared ... likewise declaring how he persisting in his damnable attemt, was struck
with a flaming sword, which issued from the comet, so that
he dyed a fearefull example to al his fellow cavaliers. London, printed for Jonas Wright and I.H. 1642. (Ingram, Pa.,
1939)

Rape—Hawaii   SLO p.v.
Goodhue, E.S.   (rest of mark
Letters of Julius Commedius Brutus and the reply.   illegible)
Francisco: Blair-Murdock Co., 1913 (55) (1) p.

Rape—U.S.   6-SNY
Goldberg, Jacob Alter, 1890–
Girls on City Streets; a Study of 1400 Cases of Rape by
Jacob A. Goldberg and Rosamond W. Goldberg. Foreword
by Wm. F. Snow. N.Y.: Foundation Books (1940) 358 p.

Rape—U.S.—Alabama   XAH p.v. 372
Conrad, Earl
Equal Justice under law, by Earl Conrad & Eugene Gordon;
foreword by Henrietta Buckmaster, cover by Bert Adams,
N.Y., Committee for equal justice for Mrs. Recy Taylor
(1945), 15 p. illus.

Rape—U.S.—Connecticut   Illegible
Rogers, Ammi, 1770-1852.
Memoirs of the Rev. Ammi Rogers, A.M., a clergyman of the
Episcopal Church, educated at Yale College in Connecticut,
ordained in Trinity Church in the City of New York—perse-
cuted in the State of Conn., on account of religion and
politics, for almost 20 years and finally, falsely accused and
imprisoned in Norwick jail, for two years, on the charge of
crimes said to have been committed in the town of Griswold,
in the county of New-London, when he was not within about
100 mi. of the place, and of which he was absolutely as
innocent as the judge who pronounced the sentence, or as
any other person in the world. Composed, compiled and
written by the said Ammi Rogers ... Schenectady, G.
Ritchie, June, 1826, 272 p.

Rape—U.S.—Connecticut—Danbury   *KD 1798
Langdon, Timothy, 1758-1801
A sermon preached at Danbury, Nov. 8th, A.D. 1798, being
the day of the execution of Anthony, a free Negro, pursuant
to sentence of death passed upon him by the hon. superior
court, for the crime of a rape. By Timothy Langdon ...
Danbury, Conn.; printed and sold by Douglas & Nichols.
1798.

Books on Rape in New York University Main Library

Rape—Denmark   Social Work
Sturup, George K., 1905—   HV
Treatment of Sexual Offenders in Herstedvester, Denmark;   4989
the rapists. Copenhagen, Munksgaard, 1968. 62 p. (Isaac Ray   .S7
Award Lecture, No. 3)

Rape—Rome   BV
Crescenti, Giovanni   4647
La condanna allo stupro delle vergini cristiane durante le   .C5
persecuzioni dell 'Ampero Romano. Palermo, Flaccavio.   .C7
(1966) 155 p. (Collana di saggi e monografie. Nuova serie,
21)

Rape (in religion, folklore, etc.)   BL87
Eliade, Mircea, 1907—   .E413
Mephistopheles & the Androgyne; studies in religious myth   1965
and symbol. Translated by J.M. Cohen, New York, Sheed &
Ward (1965), 223 p.

Selected Bibliography

This is a list of books and articles that are sympathetic to the victim. Most
of them were written by women. Women write about this subject best
because they have had to live with the threat of rape and have had a lot of
time to think about it. Much of this material has appeared since the
emergence of the women's movement and particularly since the Rape
Speak-out and the NYRF Rape Conference.

—Joan Mathews

Briffault, Robert, *The Mothers: The Matriarchal Theory of Social Origins,*
    Grosset & Dunlap, 1927.
De Beauvoir, Simone, *The Second Sex*, Bantam, 1949.
De Gramont, Nancy and Sanche, "Rape, True and False," *Vogue,* June
    1971.

DeRiver, J. Paul, *Crime and the Sexual Psychopath* Charles C Thomas, 1958.

Goldberg, Jacob A. and Rosamund W., *Girls on City Streets: A Study of 1400 Cases of Rape*, Foundation Books, 1935.

Herschberger, Ruth, *Adam's Rib*, Har/Row Books, 1970. (Orig. pub. 1948).

Lacks, Roslyn, "The Politics of Rape—A Selective History," *Village Voice*, February 4, 1971.

Lichtenstein, Grace, "Feminists Hold Rape-Defense Workshop," *The New York Times*, April 18, 1971.

Reiss, Albert J., Jr., "Assessing the Current Crime Wave," *Crime in Urban Society*, ed. Barbara N. McLennan, Dunellen, 1970.

St. John, Mary, "Requiem et Caveat," *Everywoman*, Los Angeles, California newspaper, January 1, 1971.

Sheehy, Gail, "Nice Girls Don't Get into Trouble," *New York Magazine*, February 15, 1971.

Taylor, Angela, "The Rape Victim: Is She Also the Unintended Victim of the Law?", *New York Times*, June 15, 1971.

Unsigned article, "Women Speak Out on Rape," *Woman's World*, New York City newspaper, April 15, 1971.

Unsigned article, "Jack the Raper," in *It Ain't Me, Babe*, Berkeley, California newspaper, September 17, 1970.

Unsigned article on rape in *Ain't I a Woman*, Iowa City, Iowa newspaper, December 11, 1970.

Other Books

These books are included as a concession to "objectivity." Most of them were written by men and reflect "official" attitudes, which place some or all of the responsibility for rape on the victim. The fact is, women are raped because they exist, not because of anything they do. Some of the books in this list do more harm than good. The distortions of the past will impede the formation of a new attitude toward rape. The less we are impeded by the conventional male definition, the easier it will be to come up with a new female definition.

—Joan Mathews

Amir, Menachim, "Forcible Rape," *The Journal of Criminal Law, Criminology and Police Science* 1967.

Bromberg, Walter, *Crime and the Mind*, New York, 1965.

Cohen, M., and Seghorn, T., *Profile of the Rapist*.

Drzazga, John, *Sex Crimes*, Charles C Thomas, 1960.

Duffy, C., and Hirshberg, A., *Sex and Crime*, Pocket Books, 1967.

Ellis, A., and Brancale, R., *The Psychology of Sex Offenders*.

FBI Uniform Crime Reports of the U.S., 1969.

Gebbard, P.H., Gagnon, J.H., Pomeroy, W.B., and Christenson, C.V., *Sex Offenders: An Analysis of Types*, New York, 1965.

Geis, Gilbert, "Group Sexual Assaults," *Human Sexuality Magazine*, May, 1971.

Glueck, Bernard, *Final Report: Research Project for the Study and Treatment of Crimes Involving Sexual Aberrations*, Minnesota, 1952-55.

Hervey, Cleckley, *The Caricature of Love*, New York, 1957.

Karpman, Benjamin, *The Sexual Offender and His Offenses*, New York, 1954.

Kling, Samuel G., *Sexual Behavior and the Law*, Pocket Books, 1965.

Lipton, M.A., "Violence Is a Part of the Times," *U.S. News & World Report*, January 25, 1971.

Mohr, J.W., "Rape and Attempted Rape," *Sexual Behavior and the Criminal Law Preliminary Report*, Toronto, 1965.

Morland, Nigel, *Outline of Sexual Criminology*, Hart, 1966.

Oliver, Bernard J., *Sexual Deviation in American Society: A Social Psychological Study of Sexual Non-Conformity*, New Haven, 1967.

Ploscowe, Morris, *Sex and the Law*, New York, 1951.

Schultz, Gladys D., *How Many More Victims: Society and the Sex Criminal*, J.B. Lippincott, 1965.

Tallman, Frank, *California Sexual Deviation Research*, 1963.

Tappan, Paul, *The Habitual Sex Offender; Report and Recommendations of the Commission on the Habitual Sex Offender as Formulated by Paul W. Tappan*, New Jersey, 1950.

Thompson, Hunter, *Hell's Angels*, Random House, 1966.

Van Emde, Boas, "Some Reflections on Sexual Relations between Physicians and Patients," *Journal of Sex Research*, 1966.

Weyer, Edward, Jr., *Primitive People Today*, Dolphin, 1961.

FOUR

Legal Aspects: Rape by Statute

Introduction

Of all violent crimes the conviction rate for rape is the lowest, but the fault does not lie exclusively with the police and their reluctance to investigate. We have chosen to devote a separate section on the legal aspects of rape because it is our institutions of law which reflect society's *intent* to pursue justice. The issues are complex and many-sided, but the simple fact remains that in every courtroom in this nation the rape victim, and not the rapist, is put on trial, judged, and found guilty or innocent. She is subjected to stringent requirements of evidence and her general conduct is subjected to close examination without regard to her right to privacy. If witnesses exist, if she has been severely beaten, and if her demeanor and past conduct cannot be criticized, then she will be found "innocent" and the rapist will be convicted, though possibly on a lesser charge. But the victim's case may not even reach the trial stage if no witnesses exist, if she submitted because the rapist threatened her with a weapon, or if some past impropriety is discovered.

It must be made clear that rape is not a law-and-order issue. Women are not demanding castration nor are women demanding capital punishment— our demand is to abolish those laws and legal procedures which support male supremacy. As Rita stated in the consciousness-raising session in Section One, "The authoritarian society is our enemy. It's what oppresses us, and I think it's the authoritarian society that's distorted sexuality to this extent, making it an instrument of power. If we begin to adopt the same flaw in treating rape in punitive terms, then we can only deal with it symptomatically as it turns up, bit by bit; there will still be new rapists, because rape is the psychology of sex in our society." We do not want to make rape laws more punitive, but we do want the courts to recognize the rights of women to a fair and equitable trial as a first step in eliminating sexism in our legal system. The laws as they stand now reflect only suspicion and mistrust of the victim.

Corroboration and the Adversary Presentation of Evidence

In all other criminal proceedings the adversary presentation of evidence is held to be a sufficient aid to the accurate determination of the facts. But in rape cases the testimony of the victim must be corroborated, and that is the central issue in the articles that follow. *The Concise Oxford Dictionary* defines the word as "confirmation by further evidence." At common law, that is, law not enacted by legislative act but law made by judges following the example of previous court cases, corroboration is needed for three specific parts of the rape victim's testimony: (1) *identification*, that the man accused is the rapist, (2) *penetration*, that intercourse or its attempt occurred, and (3) *lack of consent*, that the intercourse was not a voluntary act on the part of the woman.[1] Corroboration is not supporting evidence that can be used to strengthen the prosecutor's case, it is evidence that is *required* to prove that rape occurred. A woman's testimony alone is insufficient grounds for conviction even if it is probable and consistent. Thus, the requirement of corroboration makes the victim's testimony the central object of inquiry and not the rape incident itself. While the defendant is innocent until proven guilty, the prosecutrix in rape cases is guilty of making a false accusation until proven innocent.

One of the consequences of the corroboration requirement is that women who submitted to rape because they were threatened by knives or at gunpoint cannot corroborate lack of consent because they do not have physical bruises that can serve as evidence. The District of Columbia Task Force on Rape concludes, "The underlying assumption seems to be that any woman worthy of the protection of the law would defend her virtue by at least undergoing a significant degree of physical harm before 'giving in,' . . . No person should be required by law to make a choice between being injured and being able to prove a charge of rape."[2] And one could further add that no person in our society because of her sex should be required to provide extraordinary proof that her allegations are true.

That the rape victim is put on trial rather than the accused rapist is not an unintended consequence of corroboration. It has been suggested that corroboration is necessary in rape cases because of the gravity of the crime. If so, why hasn't corroboration been made a requirement in murder cases? The statements of the following legal authorities on the subject of rape suggest that it is the nature of the victim and not the nature of the crime that necessitates corroboration. Numerous legal articles on rape begin with the observation made three hundred years ago by Lord Hale to the effect that rape "is an accusation easily to be made and hard to be proved, and harder to be defended by the party accused, though never so innocent."[3] The assumption is that women, given their nature, will make numerous false accusations of rape—and so corroboration is a means of preventing women from doing so. When women are on the stand the courts seem to feel that additional measures are needed. Professor Wigmore states in his authoritative *Rules of Evidence,* "No judge should ever let a sex-offense charge go to the jury unless the female complainant's social history and mental makeup have been examined and testified to by a qualified physician."[4] Similarly the American Bar Association Committee on the Improvement of the Law of Evidence reported, "Today it is *unanimously* held (and we say 'unanimously' advisedly) by experienced psychiatrists that the complainant woman in a sex offense should *always* be examined by competent experts to ascertain whether she suffers from some mental or moral delusion or tendency, frequently found especially in young girls, causing distortion of the imagination in sex cases."[5] Such statements, made by legal authorities, are not that far removed in spirit from statements made more than a century ago as to the unreliability of witnesses that were black, American Indian, or Chinese. While these racial distinctions have been abolished, at least on paper, sexual distinctions as to the credibility of a witness's testimony have remained intact in rape cases.

In Iowa the requirement of corroboration is written into the penal codes on rape, but in fourteen other states the laws in one form or another require corroboration to secure court conviction.[6] In some states, and sometimes within a single court jurisdiction, corroboration is required by the court, even though it is not part of the law. In his article "The Trial of a Rape Case: An Advocate's Analysis of Corroboration, Consent, and Character," Richard Hibey, after listing twenty-one states where corroboration has been held unnecessary, concludes, "The majority of jurisdictions do not require corroboration of the victim's complaint in order to establish a *prima facie* case for rape. Yet cases in those jurisdictions never fail to recite the litany of facts which support the victim's testimony and, thus in reality, to evidence corroboration of identification and/or penetration. One must conclude that while the articulation of the rule speaks in terms of the sufficiency of uncorroborated proof, the fact remains that proof of rape in most cases is sufficient only when the evidence is corroborated."[7] It would seem, then, that corroboration is a universal requirement whether it is written into the laws, a decision on the part of the presiding court, or ruled unnecessary. However, where corroboration is required by the state penal code and when corroborating evidence is unavailable, as it often is, then the district attorney will probably decide not to prosecute at all. Where corroboration is the requirement of the court alone, the judge may instruct the jury that the case be dismissed because the victim's testimony, no matter how convincing, is not sufficient grounds for conviction. And, indeed, the conviction rate for rape is significantly lower in those states where corroboration is required by law, possibly because it discourages criminal prosecutions. For example, in New York City in 1971, when the state law required corroboration of penetration, identification, and lack of consent, the conviction rate for rape was three tenths of one percent. In 1972 the New York State Legislature passed a new rape law which required corroboration only for lack of consent, and by 1973 the conviction rate was 3 percent.[8] Now that all corroboration requirements have been repealed by the state legislature, New York District Attorneys will no longer be as hesitant to bring rape cases to the trial stage, so there should be an increase in the conviction rate for rape. However, it is also possible that even though corroboration will no longer be necessary for the district attorneys to prosecute, corroborating evidence may still be a critical factor in whether they can secure convictions. In that case the conviction rate for rape may remain low.

Rape as "Unjustified" Sexual Assault

The elimination of corroboration must go hand in hand with efforts to change other blatant injustices in our rape laws and their interpretation by the courts. At common law rape as a crime is defined as sexual assault by any man who is not the victim's husband. While a wife may bring charges against her husband for assault, she may not accuse him of rape. The rationale for this is that rape in such a situation would be difficult to establish in court. Yet even when a couple is legally separated, sexual assault is not viewed as rape. The District of Columbia Rape Task Force* points out, "The rule of spousal exclusion grew up at a time when a married woman had no legal rights, or even legal existence independent of her husband; at a time when a wife was considered the property of her husband, to be treated as he saw fit . . . she is still viewed as the sexual property of her husband. This attitude, sanctified in the law of rape, is outmoded."[9] But the issue is much broader than the legal rights of women in marriage. In a paper presented to the Michigan Sociological Association, Janice Reynolds pointed out that spousal exclusion is just one more instance of a general pattern of narrowly defining only certain sexual assaults as rape, the others as "justifiable." She writes, "Although it is *not* specified in rape laws, a husband can't be charged with raping his wife. Similarly, in practice, a man is never charged with raping or sexually assaulting a prostitute, and if a woman has had a sexual relationship in the past with a man who later attacks and rapes her, no matter what the level

*See Appendix III.

of brutality, her rape allegation is viewed by the court as highly doubtful. Again it appears that the raped woman must prove not only that she was raped but that the rape was 'unjustly' meted out."[10] The unstated assumption of the courts is that if a woman has ever voluntarily had intercourse with the rapist, then by definition she could not have been raped. The lack of a distinction between voluntary and involuntary sex in these cases only reveals a male supremacist attitude that all women should be sexually available to men, whether the men are husbands or boyfriends. The courts view rape as a crime only if it is committed by a male who does not "own" the woman.

Sexual Conduct as an Indication of a Witness's Credibility

A closely related bias of the court system is that the honesty of a woman can be judged by her past sexual conduct. Frequently the strategy of the defense attorney in rape cases is to concede that the accused had sexual intercourse with the victim, because then the central issue becomes whether or not the victim consented to intercourse, and her reputation for "prior unchastity" is admissible evidence.[11] In fact, Richard Hibey goes so far as to suggest that even if consent is not an issue, "The jury should be allowed to hear *general* reputation evidence of the complainant's unchastity in order to weigh and credit her testimony in the context of the character of person she is reputed to be."[12] He then cites Wigmore's suggestion that such evidence is admissible "because a certain type of feminine character predisposes to imaginary or false charges of this sort and is psychologically inseparable from a tendency to make advances, and its admissibility to discredit credibility . . . cannot in practice be distinguished from its present bearing."[13] If, indeed, the woman has a history of falsely accusing men of rape, evidence of that nature would seem to be appropriate, but Hibey and Wigmore state clearly that "a general reputation for unchastity" has a direct bearing on a woman's credibility. The assumption that if the rape victim is unchaste she could not possibly be telling the truth is founded on the medieval logic that anyone who cannot walk across a bed of coals must indeed be a heretic. No such confusion is shown toward the defendant. Since rape is a crime of violence, past conduct that does not have bearing on his reputation for peace and order is deemed inadmissible. That the accused may have been previously convicted of a nonviolent crime, such as larceny, is immaterial because it is not evidence that he is capable of committing a violent crime. While such rules of admissibility of evidence are the tradition in criminal proceedings, only in rape cases is the defense allowed almost free rein to discredit the reputation of the prosecutrix. Given society's strict standards of acceptable behavior for females, the revelation of any impropriety damages the chances of convicting the rapist, not because such a revelation shows the woman to be a liar but because such impropriety may suggest that "she had it coming to her."

Changing the Legal System

The essential question for feminists is how to make rape trials equitable so that when women are sexually assaulted they know that they have some recourse to the law. In New York State feminist groups launched a highly successful lobbying campaign to repeal all corroboration requirements in the rape laws. Within a period of three years legislators who had been strong advocates of corroboration became advocates of its repeal. Since the new rape law has just been enacted, it is impossible to report on what impact its passage has had on the trial procedure. The legislative repeal of corroboration does not automatically mean that women will get a fair trial; it only means that they will at last get a trial. It may be, as Richard Hibey suggested, that the standard of proof for conviction remains that of corroborating evidence even though it is not articulated in law. For a short time within the feminist community in New York State there was some debate as to whether women should fight to repeal the corroboration requirement or whether the rape law should be reformulated altogether so that rape is categorized as assault. A model law drawn up by the New York University Law School Clinical Program in Women's Legal Rights is included in the following section. The advantages of making rape into a crime of assault are three-fold: first, there would be no corroboration requirement; second, the sexual nature of the crime would tend to be diminished and more attention would be paid to the amount of physical and psychological injury inflicted on the victim; and third, the sexual conduct of the victim would be immaterial. Yet it was decided that feminists should lobby for repeal rather than a reclassification of the crime. Women have learned through bitter experience that reforms that they have fought for can be used to further their oppression. It is not inconceivable that our male-dominated legal institutions would greatly lessen the penalties for rape if it were viewed as assault, especially since many lawyers and judges seem unable to distinguish between voluntary and involuntary sexual intercourse. In fact, one unnamed lawyer quoted in *The New York Times* stated that since sexual mores have been relaxed, rape no longer seems such a serious crime.[14] However, if there is no change in the conduct of rape trials, then it is possible that feminists will again begin to think of reformulating rape so that it is made a crime of assault.

If the laws are not reformulated altogether, the question remains of how feminists can stop the courts from subjecting women to a detailed review of their conduct and motives. Even in states where there is no requirement of corroboration, an accused rapist can be found innocent if the rape victim is found unworthy of protection. Through legislative pressure, can women force the courts to change the rules of evidence in rape trials? Can laws be drafted and enacted that stipulate that "prior acts of unchastity" are not relevant to the credibility of the rape victim's testimony? It must be remembered that despite federal prohibitions against laws forbidding labor organizing, the courts continued to support punitive measures against labor organizations for more than forty years.[15] If the vast majority of judges and lawyers continue to be men, then it is conceivable that the rape victim would still be viewed with suspicion despite legislative reform. On the other hand, these questions may not be important ones in the long run, for as women begin to educate the public in their attempt to change rape laws, the attitudes of judges, lawyers, and juries may also change.

Another important consideration is that the criminal trial, unlike the civil trial, is structured to safeguard the rights of the defendant, and corroboration and the admissibility of evidence as to "prior acts of unchastity" are viewed as safeguards, even though they do not reflect any civil humanitarian respect for the accused but only a deep-seated distrust of all women. Feminists in effect are arguing for the rights of the prosecutrix. Though the American Civil Liberties Union changed its policy on corroboration just recently, most liberal legal groups have shown little interest in expanding the rights of the rape victim because of their traditional concern for the rights of the defendant. We are all reminded that at one time in our history black men were lynched on trumped-up charges of rape, yet the fact that the rape of black women was tolerated and condoned by the legal system is ignored. When Billie Holiday was raped at the age of ten, her rapist was sentenced to five years in prison, but *she* was also sentenced to a youth institution. Surely, had she been a white child, he would have been executed. Even now, black women are not encouraged to report rape, because they know that their accusations will be met with suspicion and sometimes hostility. "A fair trial" has always been associated with the treatment of the defendant, not the prosecutrix, and so essentially feminists will have to reeducate the so-called liberal establishment to defend the right of women to testify about crimes committed against them without harassment and intimidation.

But even if the legal definition of rape were to be broadened to include all sexual assaults, if a woman's reputation for "unchastity" were to be considered immaterial, and if corroboration were eliminated, the conviction rate for rape would not change dramatically as long as the myths about rape remain in the larger society. As Pamela Lakes Wood points out in the article that follows, jurors may be more biased against the rape victim than the judges. Richard Hibey states that jurors often believe that women who hitchhike or who sleep in the nude are inviting sexual assault.[16] Thus, even if no references were made in court to the private life of the prosecutrix, if the jury were to find out that she was a cocktail waitress, or a hitchhiker, or was wearing a short dress when she was attacked, then again she would be viewed with suspicion and distrust. In short, women must continue to speak out about rape and to raise the issue so that societal attitudes toward the rape victim—and all women—change. However equitable rape laws become, if the sexual conduct of a woman remains the basis upon which her character and her credibility are determined, then essentially no change in the status of women either in court or in the larger society will have occurred. If laws against sexual assault are still enforced only for women who are "chaste," then our institutions will continue to support male supremacy. We must not settle for the symbolic justice of laws; rather, we must seek to change the subtle mechanisms by which we are oppressed as human beings. Under ancient Jewish law and under ancient Roman law the crime of rape was punished by death, yet it was viewed as a crime committed against either the father or the husband of the woman.[17] Now that we are no longer legally considered property or chattel and now that we seek justice on our own behalf, rape is one of the most difficult crimes to prosecute because our laws and courts have demanded elaborate "tests" of our honesty and character. We do not want rape to be once again a capital crime, but we do want the institutions of law to view rape for what it is and always has been, an act of violence against women.

In the following section we have included Edith Barnett's and Jan Goodman's discussion of the 1967 and 1972 New York rape laws so that the reader can understand the effects of the corroboration requirement and how they were modified. While to some extent the history of these changes is relevant only to those states which have corroboration requirements written into the state penal codes, these articles discuss some of the legal issues involved in all rape laws.

—N. C.

NOTES

1. Richard A. Hibey, "The Trial of a Rape Case: An Advocate's Analysis of Corroboration, Consent and Character," *The American Criminal Law Review*, Vol. 11, Winter, 1973, No. 2, p. 310.

2. "Report of the Public Safety Committee Task Force on Rape," July, 1973, District of Columbia, p. 32. See Appendix III.
3. Sir Matthew Hale, *Pleas of the Crown*, 635. Cited in Hibey.
4. J. Wigmore, *Evidence* §924(a) (3d ed., 1940). Cited in Hibey.
5. 1937-38 Report by the American Bar Association Committee on the Improvement of the Law of Evidence. Cited in Hibey.
6. Judith Miller, "Ally of the Rapist," *Village Voice*, August 23, 1973, p. 27.
7. Pp. 313-4.
8. Nancy Lewis, "The Behind-the-Scenes Story of the Unanimous Repeal Bill Victory," *Majority Report*, Vol. 3, No. 11, p. 6.
9. P. 50.
10. "Rape as Social Control," paper presented at the Michigan Sociological Association, November 12, 1971, at Wayne State University, p. 3.
11. Hibey, *op. cit.*, p. 325.
12. *Ibid.*, p. 328.
13. J. Wigmore, *Evidence* §62 at 467 (3d ed., 1940). Cited in Hibey.
14. Paul L. Montgomery, "New Drive on to Make Rape Convictions Easier," *The New York Times*, November 13, 1973, p. 47.
15. Derek Bok and Archibald Cox, *Cases on Labor Law*, The Foundation Press, Inc., 1965.
16. P. 310.
17. William Blackstone. *Commentaries on the Laws of England: Of Public Wrongs*, Beacon Press, 1962, pp. 235-6.

Legal Aspects of Rape
in New York State*
Edith Barnett

While the number of forcible rapes reported in New York State has continued to show a steady and dramatic increase, the percentages of those complaints resulting in grand jury indictments and convictions have decreased just as steadily and dramatically. According to a 1969 report of the New York State legislature, arrests for rape in New York State increased from 1,500 to 1,800 between 1960 and 1967. Since rape is one of those crimes that is grossly under-reported (see FBI Annual Uniform Crime Reports), we can assume that actual numbers of rapes showed even more of an increase. Indictments decreased from 600 in 1960 to 400 in 1967. Convictions decreased from 120 in 1960 to 50 in 1967, or from 8 percent of those arrested in 1960 to 2½ percent of those arrested in 1967.[1]

Rape is a felony. In 1967, 30 percent of all New York State felony indictments resulted in convictions. Only 13 percent of rape indictments resulted in convictions. Even acknowledging that our court system is tremendously overburdened and there is a great deal of plea bargaining which results in convictions for lesser crimes than those charged in indictments, it is clear that a rapist has a much better chance of escaping conviction in New York than do other criminals. We can attribute this phenomenon to the peculiarly stringent evidentiary requirements for proof of rape, as enacted by the state legislature and as interpreted by the New York State courts. These requirements are the stiffest in the United States.

In 1967, the New York legislature enacted into law the requirements of corroboration formerly laid down by the New York courts. Penal Code §130.15 says that no person shall be convicted of a sexual offense, including rape, sodomy, and sexual misconduct, on the uncorroborated testimony of the alleged victim alone. Corroboration means some indepen-

*The following remarks were prepared for presentation at the conference on rape sponsored by New York Radical Feminists, April 17, 1971. In 1972, modifications were made on the law Ms. Barnett discusses (see p. 000), but it was not until 1974 that the corroboration requirement was totally repealed.

dent evidence tending to prove the guilt of the defendant by connecting him with the crime and extends to every material element of the crime.[2] Thus, in the case of a charge of first-degree rape, there must be some kind of independent evidence as to force, penetration, and the identity of the assailant. No other felony in New York needs to be proved in such detail; depending on the credibility of a complaining witness, a conviction may be had on his or her testimony alone in crimes such as larceny, burglary, etc.

These requirements are obviously extraordinarily difficult to meet. If a victim is threatened with a knife or physical abuse, and simply, and perhaps wisely, submits without resistance, she may have no bruises to show. A married woman or nonvirgin may have no evidence of penetration, especially if the assailant has ejaculatory impotence. Corroborating his identify is also difficult, since crimes of rape do not tend to occur in the presence of eyewitnesses.

The New York State court has put an all-or-nothing construction on the corroboration requirement. If the victim testifies to a completed rape, but can only corroborate an attempt, for example, because she lacks evidence of penetration, the alleged victim cannot be convicted merely of an attempt. Thus, where there is alleged to be a completed rape, the defendant is convicted of rape or nothing.[3]

Nor can an assailant who is alleged to have completed or attempted a rape be convicted of assault in the third or second degree,[4] the less aggravated assaults, because in 1967, when the legislature "reformed" the penal code, it excluded from the category of assaults committed "in furtherance of the commission of attempted or attempted commission of a felony" assaults committed during the commission of sexual offenses. In other words, if a man tries to beat you up, pure and simple, you may have him convicted of assault on your word alone. But, if he tries to beat you up because he wants to have intercourse with you, you cannot have him convicted of assault but only of attempted rape—and only if you meet all the stringent requirements. From these rules it appears that a woman who has been sexually attacked might profit from denying that her attacker has attempted or completed a rape in the course of his attack, since if she does not mention the rape, her proof burden will be considerably lightened. Of course, she might then face a conviction for perjury.

Since 1967, the New York courts have extended the corroboration requirement to crimes inherently unrelated to sexual offenses. Thus, if a man rapes you while holding a knife at your throat, he cannot be convicted of felonious assault with a knife and possession of a dangerous weapon with intent to use unlawfully against another without corroboration that you have been raped.[5]

If the 14th Amendment of the U.S. Constitution protected women (and the U.S. Supreme Court has never held that it does), we might argue that women in New York are denied the equal protection of the New York laws because their burden of proof is much heavier than that of men who are victims of the identical felonies, the only difference being the sexual intent of the assailant. The trend seems to be toward making it harder and harder for women to prove crimes committed against them where a sexual attack is involved.

In most felonies, criminal defendants are considered to be sufficiently protected by the traditional presumption of innocence and the necessity for the state to prove, by a preponderance of the evidence, guilt beyond a reasonable doubt.[6] Tough cross-examination of witnesses is also a considerable protection, and women have never been considered too tender to be exempt from it.

The original corroboration requirement seems to have been instituted by judges fearful of the possibility of sick women making up charges against men whom they wish to punish or control.[7] Such women may exist, as may those men who will also falsely accuse others of felonies. This does not excuse the New York courts and legislatures effectively removing protection from women who are indeed the victims of sexual attack.

A bill to substantially relax evidentiary requirements for rape and remove some of the other inequities of the rape laws has been introduced to the New York State legislature by the Association of District Attorneys who became educated to the problem by the ever-decreasing rates of rape indictments and convictions. The conference should support the bill and lobby for it. The bill would do a great deal to tip the scales of justice back in favor of the woman victim, instead of the rapist.

NOTES

1. Table 2, p. 11; table 11, p. 20; table 5, p. 14, 1969 Report of the New York State Joint Legislative Committee on Crime, its Causes, Control and Effect on Society, legislative document No. 16 (1969).
2. People v. Page, 162 N.T. 272, 56 N.E. 750 (1900) for example.
3. People v. Moore. 23 N.Y. 2d 565, 245 N.E. 2d 710, 297 N.Y.S. 2d 944, cert. den. 394 U.S. 1006 (1969).
4. Penal Code § 120.00 & 120.05.
5. People v. Sigismondi, 21 NY 2d 186 (1967).
6. People v. Radunovic, 21 NY 2d 186 (1967). Scileppi, dissenting.
7. People v. Friedman, 139 A.D., 795, 124 NYS 521 (1910) for example.

Interview with a Feminist Lawyer*

Wilson: Has there been any fundamental change in the rape law since the New York Radical Feminist Rape Conference in April, 1971?

Goodman: There has been a new law passed which will be effective July 1, 1972, I believe. It revises the old law specifically as to the corroboration requirements to prove rape. What they have done is essentially change the corroboration requirement to make it applicable to only one element of the crime. Let me go over the old law. It said that every element of the crime must be corroborated, which meant that you had to have corroborating evidence as to penetration, as to identification, and as to coercion or lack of consent. The new law does away with the corroboration of identification and of penetration, but retains a form of corroboration as to consent. And it uses very, very vague language which I think might even be constitutionally improper language. What the statute now provides is that, "A person shall not be convicted of any offense defined in this article or of an attempt to commit the same solely on the testimony of the alleged victim unsupported by other evidence tending to: (a) establish that an attempt was made to engage the alleged victim in sexual intercourse, deviate sexual intercourse, or sexual contact, as the case may be, at the time of the alleged occurrence; and (b) establish lack of consent of the alleged victim, where such is an element of the offense." So really there are still two requirements for a form of corroboration—that's the fact of consent and the fact that the crime itself has actually been committed. I find it very hard to understand what "evidence tending to establish lack of consent" means. It leaves a very broad level of discretion with the courts, and I think the courts are going to be unclear as to how much evidence is needed. Indeed, any defendant could challenge the law on

*The following is an interview with Jan Goodman, a partner in the New York law firm of Bellamy, Blank, Goodman, Kelly, Ross, and Stanley, a feminist law firm formed in 1973. The interview was conducted by Cassandra Wilson just after the New York State legislature had passed a new rape law in June, 1972.

its being an unconstitutionally vague statute. In other words, you can't convict a person of a crime unless the statute is specific and tells a person exactly and precisely what the crime is.

Wilson: You mean they haven't established what consent actually means?

Goodman: No. There is nothing here. The new law reads, "evidence tending to establish lack of consent." Well, as an example, that could be rumpled clothing that could tend to show forced sex has occurred. Under the old law, where you needed the same corroboration for consent, some judges would say there was sufficient corroboration if a woman would appear disheveled and her clothes were askew. Another judge, though, in a similar type of circumstance made the remark, "Well, that's not corroboration. That's just the nature of the sex act itself." So that's what happens when you have very vague language. We can rest assured that Legal Aid, which is in the main part charged with the responsibility of defending persons accused of this crime, and paid attorneys as well are going to challenge the constitutionality of such vague language. And the courts are going to have a lot of trouble determining what it means.

Wilson: What does this mean for the victim?

Goodman: Oh well, now they've added this wonderful language about the "alleged victim"—I mean they just keep turning the screw there. I think the rape victim is in precisely the same situation she always was. By reading the legislative history in the Memorandum of the bill which states its purpose, you get to what they're really all saying. They state that this law is a great change. They're trying to defend their law. The Memorandum reads, "The present requirement of corroborating identity in forcible sex cases has no basis in the policy underlying the corroboration requirement—fear not that the complainant will accuse the wrong person of a crime . . . ," which is a real fear. I mean, misidentification can often happen. That's not what they're worried about. What they fear is that the complainant will "invent the crime." We're back to the same concept in this law—the Assemblymen who are writing these bills do not trust women. They are making the assumption that women lie. The lawmakers put rape victims under stricter scrutiny than victims of any other crime.

Wilson: Are you saying that it's actually a better law for the rapist than it is for the victim? In other words, could the defense find ways to avoid conviction of rapists because of the vagueness of the law?

Goodman: I think there will be challenges because of the vagueness of the law. We don't know yet what the effect of this rape law will be, though I don't think there's going to be a substantial difference. I don't personally feel that this law is going to effectively insure women of a fair prosecution. I think that they are still mistrusted and their word is mistrusted. If a guy gets up on the stand and says, "Well, sure I had intercourse with her. She invited me. I met her at this bar," a woman needs corroboration to prove she did not invite him, but was assaulted by him. That's the kind of problem we've always been in.

But there has been one area of substantial change in the law and that is as to the corroboration needed for the other crimes committed at the time of the rape. In the past, if a case for alleged rape came to trial and if the victim alleged any other crime such as assault or breaking and entering or carrying a dangerous weapon, the courts had decided that because rape was involved all other crimes committed simultaneously with the rape fall within the corroboration rule. No longer. This law changes that substantially. So what you probably will be having is more people copping a plea to carrying a dangerous weapon. That's one possibility. Although that's conjecture on my part, that is one possibility. I think as long as a law in any way indicates that women rape victims shall be trusted less than victims of any other crime, then it's offensive. And it is clearly a statement that the woman witness is not a reliable witness. Such a law reflects how the prosecution will go, it reflects how the police will treat her, it reflects how the DA will treat her, and I think it reflects how juries will treat her.

We've got to remember that corroboration is not required in any other crime situation. There is only one other situation, and it's of relatively recent vintage, where corroboration is now required. It is required when accomplices testify against each other. But that's clear. See, if you and I were involved together in a crime, it would be easy for the cops to buy either one of us off to accuse the other, whether we did the crime or not. There really is a tangible benefit that an accomplice would gain by testifying against an accomplice because he is turning state's evidence. So to protect against that kind of abuse—and it's really police absue because they put pressure on one court victim to squeal— they have put in a corroboration requirement as to accomplices. But rape in essence is unique in terms of traditional crime. You don't need corroboration for murder, which is a much more serious offense.

Wilson: What would you consider to be a good rape law?

Goodman: A group of students at New York University developed a law which I think is the only way to handle the whole issue fairly. Rape would be put into a category of assault. What you have now are degrees of rape, but they are not really degrees of rape because there is no difference and no distinction between rape in the first degree and rape in the second degree, except age in the case of statutory rape. What we should have are degrees where first-degree rape is a completed rape with a deadly weapon and second-degree rape is without a weapon and so forth. You should put rape right in the assault category because rape is clearly a form of assault. This is a neutral rule and my own feeling more and more is that women should seek neutral laws, not special laws which give us special protection. Every time they've attempted to give us special protection like rape laws we wind up getting screwed and getting no protection at all. So what we want are neutral laws, and I think by putting rape in the assault laws we get treated like any other assault victim. You would no longer have as high a penalty if rape were integrated directly with the assault laws. Rape in the first degree is now from eight to twenty-five years and I think assault is now a maximum of fifteen years, so you might be lessening the penalty, but I don't think the length of prison sentence is what we're concerned about, but in getting protection for women and getting people to take the crime of rape seriously.

Wilson: By putting rape in an assault category there would be no corroboration?

Goodman: Right now if two men get into a brawl, one of them could go to the police and say, "He beat me up, unprovoked, and he was using a knife." On that man's testimony alone he could take the witness stand. Now that doesn't mean the jury has to believe him. They might not believe him. But he can take the stand and testify as to what happened, and he doesn't need corroboration. The jury is then just directed and instructed that there are only two people who are witnesses, the person who is the victim and the person who is the defendant. The jury is then given two instructions: one, they must find the defendant guilty beyond a reasonable doubt—that means that no set of circumstances could point to innocence; and two, they must make their determination on the basis of the credibility of the witnesses.

Wilson: That leads to the question of how one can prevent a prosecutor from questioning the rape victim about her sexual conduct before the actual rape occurred.

Goodman: That's not written into the law but they've been allowing it. I think it is legitimate if a woman takes the stand and says John Q raped me—I think it's legitimate to ask if she had prior sexual relations with that person. I think that it does add credibility to her as a witness if it can be determined whether it was a rape or a consensual sexual act. I don't think we should assume women are more or less apt to lie than men. But it is totally irrelevant whether she has had prior sexual relations with anybody else. And I think every lawyer should agree that she could be the most promiscuous person in the world but if she says No to that one person and that one person decides to rape her, the rape is an offense. I think we should have to make that distinction. It does not come up in the law. It is really a decision made by a judge at some point during the trial. I would say, strictly speaking, that in terms of evidence it is not relevant, and I think that if you ever had a chance to test it in the courts it would not be found to be a relevant question.

Wilson: It may not be relevant from a strictly legalistic point, but from my "Perry Mason" watching you can influence the jury with something like that.

Goodman: It's a fantastically important factor, no doubt about it.

Wilson: Does this leave too much to the judge and too little to the lawmakers?

Goodman: Well, it's dangerous—it's harmful sometimes to be too specific in the law. Furthermore, if we try to push that point they might say all prior sexual behavior is relevant. In New York there are "rules of evidence" that say that prior bad acts may be introduced to challenge the credibility of a witness. In other words, when somebody takes the stand, the defense attorney or the prosecuting attorney has every right to cross-examine that person to find out whether he is generally a truthful person or not. So the attorney tries to trap him as you see on "The Perry Mason Show." It doesn't make any difference what the witness has lied about, but he tries to show that he lied, and the attorney is allowed to challenge the credibility in terms of prior bad acts. Now the question is whether having other sexual relations is a prior bad act. I think clearly today it would not be, twenty years ago it probably would have been.

Wilson: Has the new law made a visible change in the courts in the treatment of rape victims or in the general consciousness of the crime of rape?

Goodman: I think I should make it clear that the new law has been in effect too short a time to evaluate whether there is any visible change. And I'm not in the criminal courts often enough to have observed it myself.

Wilson: I recently read in the paper some statistics which show that the incidence in reporting rape has increased. That is, the incidence of rape has not increased as much as people willing to report it. Do you think this law could possibly encourage women to. . . .

Goodman: I don't think this law is what is going to encourage women to report rape, but I think what has encouraged them—and in fact, has encouraged this new law—is that the women's movement has been discussing it. Rape is really starting to come out in the open and I think the New York Radical Feminist Rape Conference has played a vital role in raising the issue and its political significance—the methods used to intimidate women. I think the movement has made women less fearful because it has shown them how to fight back when they are attacked and they are more ready to stand up to the police when they are given a lot of gaff.

Wilson: Do you think that the attempt of the women's movement to bring this issue into a public forum really brought about the attempt to make a new rape law?

Goodman: No doubt. Probably the district attorney wanted a new law for a long time. But I don't think the DA alone would have succeeded without the pressure from and the consciousness of women. There have been a lot of articles written about rape, and the women's movement has worked on this issue. As a matter of fact, I was on a committee at the New York Civil Liberties Union, which is a defense-oriented group, and they couldn't bear taking any position against the defendant. They feel, and it's a legitimate position, that corroboration should be required in every crime, and I wouldn't have any objection to that. I don't think corroboration would be bad if every crime required it. But even in the last year, the NYCLU hasn't taken a position. They cannot go all out for the elimination of corroboration. However, they have since retracted their position in support of the corroboration requirement. Then you have organizations like New Democratic Coalition that is actively supporting change in rape laws. But I think all these movements and actions stem from the original interest of feminist groups.

The Victim in a Forcible Rape Case:
A Feminist View*
Pamela Lakes Wood

> Force and consent are the significant issues in rape trials. Many times a female will submit after a lot of talk, liquor, and lunges, and later, for a wide range of reasons, decide that she was really raped. Some girls rape awful easy. So many chicks say no no when there's yes yes in their eyes, and their thighs seem to spread at a mere flick of the finger. The rape law is often used by a woman to "get" a former boyfriend or a hoped-for boyfriend who never materialized.[1]

The most curious thing about forcible rape[2] cases, despite common misconceptions, is the amount of sympathy which is afforded the offender, and the callousness, or even hostility in some cases, which is felt for the victim. Because of the assumption that jurors are likely to feel sympathy for the victim and convict the assailant without adequate evidence, many states have more stringent proof requirements than would be necessary for other crimes.[3] Nevertheless, many commentators still are obsessed by the fear that innocent men are often convicted of rape due to the malice of "sick" women, who either fabricate stories of forcible rape or "trap" men in situations from which they can reasonably infer consent. These fears are largely groundless. It is more likely that guilty assailants escape due to the reluctance of victims to report the crime, police and district attorneys to prosecute, and jurors to convict. Due to the traumatic experience which a victim must go through in order to secure the attacker's successful prosecution, it is amazing that any rape cases ever come to trial.

Requirements of Proof: Traditional Justification

The law of rape is such that it is highly unlikely to produce an inordinate

*Reprinted with permission of the American Criminal Law Review and the American Bar Association, 1973. *The American Criminal Law Review,* Vol. 11, No. 2, Winter, 1973.

number of false convictions. Although most jurisdictions still pay lip
service to the common-law rule which permits a conviction based upon the
uncorroborated testimony of the complainant, corroboration is usually
required whenever the testimony is incredible, contradictory, or improbable.[4] Moreover, several states have, by statute, required corroboration in all rape cases; a number of others have required it in special
circumstances; and still others do not require it, but prefer it.[5]

Feminine Malice

One argument raised by commentators to justify more stringent proof
requirements for rape accusations is the greater possibility of convicting an
innocent man. It is assumed by some writers that men are often unjustly
imprisoned because of accusations brought by malicious women who all
too often are afflicted with sexual and emotional problems.[6] These alleged
victims, it is argued, are able to take advantage of the irrational sympathy
which jurors inevitably feel for a woman who alleges that she has been
"wronged."[7] These assumptions are at best questionable. Although Wigmore, for instance, strongly implies that men are often falsely convicted of
rape,[8] he fails to cite even one illustration of this having occurred. What he
does rely on are five case histories of mentally ill girls who made false
sexual accusations against men.[9] In none of these cases was a man
convicted of a sexual crime.[10] One author does cite a 1931 case in which
nine black men were falsely convicted of raping two white women,[11] but
such interracial rape cases are hardly typical as the vast majority of rapes
are intraracial.[12] In addition, there is reason to suppose that due to racial
conditions in the South at the time of the alleged assault blacks may have
been unjustly convicted of other crimes as well.[13]

It would, of course, be foolish to assert that fabricated stories of rape
never occur. However, there is no reason to conclude that juries are less
able to deal with fabrications in rape than they are in any other types of
cases. The "beyond reasonable doubt" standard should be adequate to
guard against unjust convictions. A study by Kalven and Zeisel, to be
discussed in more detail later, shows that juries, in fact, are more likely to
sympathize with the offender than with the victim, whenever there is an
indication that her character is less than flawless.[14]

Feminine Masochism

Another justification raised in support of stringent proof requirements is
the notion that the woman may have really wanted to be raped.[15] In cases

in which the victim and assailant are acquainted, some authors assert that it is often difficult to tell whether or not the victim did, in fact, consent since it is "customary" for a woman to say "no" when she means "yes."[16] Further, others submit that a woman may have an ambivalent attitude toward intercourse due to fear that her date will have a low opinion of her whether she consents or not. He may consider her a "prude," a "tease," or an "easy lay," depending upon her degree of resistance.[17]

But can one assume that the assailant could reasonably infer consent due to such "social phenomena"? Statistics indicating the amount of violence used upon rape victims tend to negate such a conclusion. A Philadelphia study[18] showed that in 85.1 percent of the reported rapes some sort of violence—either roughness, beating, or choking—was perpetrated upon the victim.[19] The study further showed that violence was used in 93 percent of the cases in which the rape was victim precipitated[20] (when the victim placed herself in a "dangerous" position or did not react adversely enough when the assailant's intention to have intercourse was first made clear), but violence was employed only in 83 percent of the non-victim precipitated cases.[21] It is difficult to conclude that assailants were misled in this preponderant number of attacks.

Victim Precipitated Forcible Rape. Some authors go further and suggest that in many cases the victim actually sets up the rape either consciously or unconsciously. It is asserted that women are so inherently masochistic that rape may actually be a "pleasurable event" or a "liberating experience."[22] Supposedly this attitude leads women into unconsciously taking unnecessary risks. It has also been suggested that because of a "riddance mechanism" a woman may unconsciously expose herself to dangerous situations. The victim is thought to fear rape so much that she wants to "get it over with."[23] Moreover, in cases in which the prosecutrix attempted to arouse the offender, without the intention to have intercourse, the "assumption of risk" is asserted, even though it would not constitute a valid legal defense. In such cases the defense may allege a "rape trap."[24] The concept of "assumption of risk" is also applied to situations in which the victim agreed to have a drink or go for a ride with a stranger (showing a reckless attitude) or in which she failed to react strongly enough to the advances of the assailant.[25]

All of these situations constitute what Professor Amir calls "victim precipitated forcible rape."[26] What the victim does is less significant than how the assailant interprets her actions.[27] The effect of this theory is to make the victim partly responsible for the crime having occurred, thereby mitigating the guilt of the assailant.[28] Such a conclusion is likely to focus the blame on women for having innocently participated in "dangerous" situations. If a woman goes drinking with a man her accusation of rape is weakened "since by drinking she took a chance, made herself vulnerable, and also introduced an element of stimulation for the male."[29] If she allows a man to come to her house, or if she goes to his, she is either indicating a willingness to have sexual intercourse or showing her readiness to assume the risk of attack.[30] If she allows any sexual intimacies, she is playing "the dangerous game of posing as a possible 'bad' girl who in the end turns out to be a 'good' girl."[31] It is dangerous for her to trust her friends or relatives since in 29 percent of primary relationship cases "gentlemen forfeited their positions of trust and committed the crime of forcible rape."[32] A woman could not remain blameless under such an analysis unless she lived in a constant state of fear that every man she encountered was a potential rapist. This hardly would constitute a healthy attitude, yet it would fail to counter suggestions that unconscious behavior precipitated the rape.

The real danger of this victim precipitation—assumption of risk doctrine, however, is its frequent extension to the point where the offender is freed from guilt.[33] Jurors, in particular, tend to think in terms of assumption of risk and victim precipitation.[34] The extent to which the doctrine is applied can be seen in the results of a study by Kalven and Zeisel. The entire study, which analyzed many crimes in addition to rape, relied upon 3,576 trials which were included in two surveys.[35] For each trial, a questionnaire was sent to the judge which asked him questions concerning the fact pattern, what outcome was reached by the jury, and how he would have decided the case if he were sitting without a jury.[36]

In two cases from the study, the judges thought that the jury had weighed the conduct of the prosecutrix in reaching their result:

Case 1: A seventeen-year-old girl was raped during a beer drinking party. The jury probably acquitted, according to the judge, because they thought the girl asked for what she got.[37]

Case 2: The prosecutrix and the defendant were divorced but were considering getting back together. The defendant alleged that they had continued sexual relations, but the prosecutrix denied this. According to the judge, the jury decided that she couldn't complain about the results of her own conduct.[38]

In a series of other cases, the judge noted circumstances which Kalven and Zeisel interpret as suggesting assumption of risk:

Case 3: The complainant was raped after she got into a car with the defendant and three of his companions. Prior to the attack she had had several beers. The jury acquitted.

Case 4: The victim, a thirty-three-year-old woman who had been married twice and divorced, met the assailant at a dance, went to a nightclub with him, and was raped on the way home. The jury acquitted.

Case 5: The complainant met the defendant at a dance and both had been drinking. She was raped in a deserted wooded area on the way home. The jury acquitted.[39]

In order to test their hypothesis that juries take factors such as contributory behavior on the part of the complainant into account, Kalven and Zeisel broke up the rapes in the study into two groups: (1) aggravated rape—when there was extrinsic violence, more than one assailant, or no prior acquaintance of the defendant and the victim, and (2) simple rape—all other cases. This division was based upon the lesser chance of contributory behavior present in the aggravated rape cases.[40] As expected, it was found that the judge and jury agreed much more frequently as to what the result should be in the aggravated rape cases than in the simple rape cases.[41] In 12 percent of the aggravated rape cases the jury acquitted when the judge convicted, but the comparable figure for simple rape was 60 percent.[42] In 9 out of 10 cases of simple rape in which the jury was given the opportunity to convict of a lesser charge, they did so.[43] These figures seem to indicate that in the simple rape cases the jury feels that the assailant is guilty of some crime, but they think rape is too severe a charge.[44] Since the jury lacks the discipline of the judge, it retains a certain amount of discretion and autonomy regardless of what the judge's instructions are.[45] As a result, the jury may take such factors as assumption of risk, victim precipitation, or reputation of the victim into consideration.

The Victim's Character and Mental State

The concentration upon the reputation of the prosecutrix, almost as if she were the one whose guilt or innocence were to be determined, is an indication of the bias against the rape victim in the current system. Police may dismiss a case merely because the victim is suspected of being promiscuous, particularly if she is black.[46] At trial, evidence of bad reputation or unchastity is generally admissible as substantive evidence bearing on the consent of the prosecutrix.[47] In a few jurisdictions, the moral character of the complainant may actually be a defense to the crime under the theory that an unchaste female or one with a bad reputation is likely to have consented.[48] Even when unchastity is not considered a defense, evidence of the parties having engaged in prior sexual relations—or even evidence of prior acquaintance or dating of the parties—may be used to infer a "continuous state of mind" or the "unlikelihood of a serious attitude of opposition."[49]

As has been previously discussed,[50] the jury is more likely to sympathize with the assailant, particularly when there is evidence of the parties having formerly had some sort of interaction. Male jurors are especially likely to be unsympathetic to the prosecution in such situations,[51] presumably because they can more easily identify with the male offender than they can with a female victim. Although prosecutors usually seek out women jurors, they may end up with mostly men, often because women ask to be excused because they feel they would not be objective.[52] Even if the prosecution can get female jurors, however, such jurors may find it difficult to empathize with a victim who has a bad reputation. Consequently, they may be just as harsh as their male counterparts.[53]

It is therefore submitted that jurors of both sexes may allow the reputation of the prosecutrix to influence them on issues other than consent. This would explain the fact that prostitutes stand little chance of obtaining a conviction for rape, even though they are often the victims of gang rapes.[54] It would also provide an explanation for the results in cases such as the following:

1 In a 1970 case, a woman was beaten, raped, and sodomized by four men in an apartment where she had been brought at gunpoint. The defense counsel won the case upon the grounds that both his client, who was the tenant at the apartment where the complainant had been raped, and the prosecutrix were sexual libertines. At the trial he destroyed the victim's reputation, revealing that she was a divorcee whose children were in a foster home, that she had had numerous affairs, and that she was living illicitly with a man at the time of the trial.[55]

2 In another case, three men seized a woman from the street at 1:30 A.M. and took her to an apartment where they brutally raped her. At the trial of one of the assailants it was revealed that the complainant had two illegitimate children and the defendant alleged that she was a prostitute without offering any evidence to that effect. The jury acquitted.[56]

3 The situation is even more extreme when the victim and the offender have previously had sexual relations since the reputation of the complainant as well as her assumption of risk are considered. In one case of "savage rape," the victim's jaw was fractured in two places. The jury

nevertheless acquitted because it found that there may have been sexual relations on previous occasions, and the parties had been drinking on the night of the incident.[57]

Although character evidence is admitted on the issue of consent,[58] its probative value is arguably low since the fact that a woman has consented to sexual relations with men in the past does not show that she has consented to intercourse with a particular man on a particular occasion. The probative value of character evidence on the issue of consent may also be outweighed by its prejudiciality to the victim. Such evidence should, in most cases, be excluded.

In some jurisdictions, the unchastity of the complainant may also be admissible on the question of her veracity.[59] Here again, prejudiciality is high and probative value low. Fortunately, character evidence is not usually admitted for this purpose.

More often it is evidence concerning the victim's psychiatric state which is admitted on the issue of her credibility as a witness.[60] According to Wigmore, the "social history and mental makeup" of the prosecutrix in a sex crime case should be examined before the charge is given to the jury.[61] Fortunately, no court has felt compelled to follow this,[62] although currently the mental stability of the complainant can be put at issue in a rape case.[63]

Since psychiatric evidence is highly prejudicial it should only be admitted when it clearly has bearing upon the issue of veracity. When the evidence is admitted, the judge should be careful to instruct on both the purpose to which the evidence is to be put and the weight which it is to be given. When it appears that the alleged purpose of the evidence is merely an excuse for its admission on another issue it should be excluded.

Resistance

Even if a victim does not precipitate the rape, has a good reputation, and is mentally well adjusted, her efforts to have her assailant convicted may nevertheless go unrewarded if the jury feels that she has not shown enough resistance. A dramatic illustration of this phenomenon is a recent case in the District of Columbia in which seventeen-year-old Santionta C. Butler was accused of raping a George Washington University student and forcing her and another female student to commit sodomy.[64] Although Butler conceded that he committed the crimes, his confession was not admitted at the trial due to technical reasons.[65] The jury, composed of four men and eight women, acquitted, according to one juror because the women neither resisted enough nor tried to escape.[66] According to testimony at trial, both victims were hysterical after the crime, and one was found by a physician to have at least ten sizable bruises on her body.[67] One woman, who had been beaten repeatedly on the head, said that she was afraid that Butler had a gun;[68] the other was described by her roommate, who saw her and Butler emerge from the washroom where the assault occurred, as being bruised and disheveled after the incident.[69] One of the complainants, who claimed to feel more like a defendant than a plaintiff, said, "I wasn't on trial. I don't see anything I did wrong. I screamed. I struggled. How could they have decided that he was innocent, that I didn't resist. It's preposterous."[70] Nevertheless, the jury did not find that "consent was induced by physical force, or by threats which put her in reasonable fear of death or grave bodily harm," as required by District of Columbia law.[71]

The victim is thus placed in a very difficult predicament. If she chooses to resist to the extent of her physical capacity, she is likely to incur serious injuries. In one case a thirty-seven-year-old woman required 120 stitches on her face and head after having resisted a man who attempted to rape her in Central Park at 7:30 A.M.[72] Detective Al Simon of the Central Park Precinct said of this case:

> We've been looking for this guy for a long time. Two years ago we picked him up for attempted rape, and it was a throw-out in court; no corroboration. Now we have this poor woman, who fought like hell and didn't get raped. The guy has been indicted for assault in the first degree. She's scarred for life. And you know what she says now? She says she wishes she hadn't fought, and maybe he wouldn't have cut her up the horrible way he did.[73]

If the victim does not resist, however, her assailant is likely to escape punishment and, due to the sadistic nature of the act, he may use violence upon her anyway. Furthermore, he may commit the crime again and may set an example for would-be rapists.

The Complainant's Ordeal

Reporting the Crime. Because of the bias within the system and the emotional trauma which accompanies the crime, victims often fail to report rape. According to the *Uniform Crime Reports,* rape is probably reported to the police less than any other Crime Index offense.[74] It is difficult to estimate the percentage of crimes which are, in fact, reported, but estimates run from a high degree of reportability to as low as 5 percent.[75]

Some women do not bother reporting rapes because they feel it would be useless. One past victim at the Rape Crisis Center in Washington, D.C., remarked that a woman must be "bruised, bloody, and damned near dead" in order for the activity to be considered not consensual.[76] Others do not report the crime because they do not wish to encounter additional stress and abuse.[77] Many victims feel the process through which they must go in order to even attempt to obtain a conviction may be worse than the crime.[78]

Victims who have received aid at the Rape Crisis Center in Washington, D.C., report a wide range of treatment by the police.[79] Some victims were satisfied with the treatment they received.[80] At the other extreme were complaints about the police having made snide remarks, such as "How many orgasms did you have?", "I know why you got raped," or "Didn't I pick you up last week for prostitution?"[81] Some of the police even linger over sexual details with relish—"How big was he?" and "What were you thinking about while he was doing it?" are questions victims have been asked.[82] One woman said that although the rape was really bad, the police interrogation was six times as horrible.[83]

The police in effect have absolute discretion as to whether or not any action is taken to obtain a conviction.[84] Often they will refuse to accept charges, especially when the victim is alone when she comes to file them[85] and when the charges are accepted, they may neglect to work on cases which they feel are unsubstantiated.[86] Often the police (and the court) may, due to a common socio-cultural orientation, see the situation from the offender's point of view rather than from the victim's.[87] Hence they may infer consent when none was given or think in terms of victim precipitation. As a result it is often both futile and frustrating for a woman to report the crime.[88]

The Investigatory Process. For those who wish to report rape, the first step in Washington, D.C., is for the complainant to call the police so that they can pick her up and take her to the precinct for questioning by the Sex Squad. Next she is taken to the hospital by the police, who leave her there alone. Since some hospitals are crowded and rape victims are not given priority, women may have to wait up to four hours before obtaining medical aid.[89] This can be extremely unpleasant since victims cannot cleanse themselves of any blood or semen which might be present.[90] The major problem, however, is that no one is concerned with the victim's mental state.[91]

The physical examination is used to prove that intercourse took place, since the crime is rarely witnessed. A blood alcohol test may also be taken since intoxication may be used to imply assumption of risk.[92] The woman is next undressed and her clothing is examined for blood and seminal stains and for any indications of violence. The presence of seminal stains on clothing, however, may merely indicate attempted rape. Tests for semen on clothing are nevertheless valuable since they may be effective even if several months have passed.[93]

The victim is next asked whether she has washed or douched, since either would be likely to destroy any evidence. She is then given a routine gynecological examination and tested for the presence of spermatozoa to see if intercourse did, in fact, occur.[94]

In Washington, D.C., the physician is required to fill out a form concerning the rape. The "mental health evaluation" consists of nine categories: apparently normal, lethargic, crying, agitated, angry, verbose, hysterical, unconscious, and "other."[95] The physician is also asked whether the evidence is most compatible with vaginal intercourse, forced vaginal intercourse, anal sodomy, or forced anal sodomy.[96]

Generally the victim goes home after the physical examination and returns to the Sex Squad the next day to make a complete report. Although after a wait in the emergency room the complainant may not be out until 5 A.M., she may still be told to appear before the Sex Squad at 8:30 A.M.[97] At that time she makes a formal statement and is shown photographs of potential suspects. Then she is sent away, often with the promise that she will hear from a "lawyer."[98] Usually she is not informed as to when there is to be a preliminary hearing, whether the charges have been dropped, or what action is being taken.[99] In order to find out any information, the victim must call the police herself.[100] This uncertainty only adds to the mental pressure which the victim is experiencing.[101]

The Trial. Even if a woman is able to convince the police and the district attorney that there is some possibility that she has been raped, her ordeal is not over. She must still endure a personal attack during private hearings before a magistrate, grand jury investigations, and a public trial.[102] In fact, an official at the San Francisco Sex Crimes Department stated that one of the functions of police interrogation in a rape case is to prepare the victim for the attack which she can expect from the defense counsel "to make sure the woman is not petrified, embarrassed, or driven to tears on the stand."[103]

The cross-examination in court can be grueling.[104] The accused rapist's attorney often initiates his case by inquiring as to the number of men with whom the victim has had intercourse.[105] He then makes her go over the details of the rape,[106] while insinuating that she is mistaken as to the identity of her assailant or that she consented to the intercourse. Although in the interests of justice a careful cross-examination is warranted in any type of criminal proceeding, the psychological side effects which a victim in a rape case must otherwise endure may justify the limitation of the amount of pressure used by the defense attorney. It should not be forgotten that the prosecutrix is the victim and, as such, should not be subjected to any more duress than necessary.

The victim in a rape case thus may find herself subjected to an ordeal as bad or worse than the crime itself if she does not choose to keep her victimization a secret. According to Pittsburgh Police Superintendent Robert Colville:

> Rape is the only crime in which the victim is doubly violated, first by the attacker, and then by society. It is the only crime in which social, religious, and cultural core attitudes of society turn upon the victim. In rape, society tends to blame or accuse the women.[107]

Alternatives

As has been shown, the present system is less than ideal. The best solution, of course, would be to effectuate a change in attitudes—to try to make men see the crime from the victim's point of view and to try to stop the victims from blaming themselves. Hopefully policemen eventually will sympathize with women to the point at which they will be able to refrain from making sarcastic or callous comments. Authors will hopefully stop thinking about such concepts as victim precipitation and assumption of risk and start thinking of the complainant as the helpless victim of an act of hatred and aggression. Jurors, too, will hopefully start following the law rather than their own ideas about sexual property rights and blame-worthiness.

Emotional support. These hopes are unlikely to materialize in the near future. There are, however, present schemes which are being used to alleviate the bias in the current system. The Rape Crisis Center begun in June, 1972, in Washington, D.C., has been a successful effort. The center provides information and services for women who have just been raped as well as support for women who have been raped in the past and either are having trouble adjusting emotionally or just would like to talk to someone about their experience. The center also provides lessons in self-defense. If a woman has just been raped, the center will provide another woman to go to the police with the victim as "a friend." This often makes members of the police force more careful in their treatment of victims. Sometimes the police assume an actual friend is from the Rape Crisis Center since they do not know all the names of the members.[108] Crisis Centers are beginning to be formed in other areas.

Another promising development is the chaplains' counseling service for rape victims—or "Code R"—which was begun at the University of Chicago hospitals and clinics in March, 1972.[109] After a victim arrives at the emergency room, a chaplain is summoned who takes the victim to a private consultation room where he attempts to assuage her anxieties. He then accompanies her while she fills out forms and waits for her gynecological examination, and he may even, if necessary, offer to help the victim break the news to her husband. Apparently this project has also been successful in changing the attitudes of the police. According to Dr. Peter Rosen, medical director of the emergency room at the University of Chicago's Billings Hospital, "They don't come into the emergency room any more and yell, 'I got a rape for ya, Charlie.' "[110]

An increase in the number of women on the police forces would also be helpful. More women would then be available both to take complete reports at the precinct and record the victim's initial complaint. Moreover, those policemen who are assigned to question rape victims should be discouraged by their superiors from making any remarks concerning the incident.

Suggested Legal Changes. Within the legal system itself, several changes should be made in order to obtain more equitable treatment for rape victims. The distinctions between rape victims and victims of other crimes should be abolished. Corroboration should never be required in order to bring a case before the jury since the jury itself is capable of determining whether or not the evidence is sufficient to support a conviction. The notion that the victim's character has an unquestionable bearing on the issue of consent should no longer be adhered to. Evidence of the victim's reputation and psychiatric state should only be admitted when probative value clearly outweighs prejudicial effects and the resistance standard should depend upon whether the victim's resistance was reasonable under the circumstances.

In order to partly compensate for the jury's concentration upon assumption of risk and victim precipitation,[111] the law itself should be changed in all jurisdictions to provide for different degrees of rape. The National Commission on Reform of Federal Criminal Laws has come up with a proposed federal law which would divide rape into different sexual offenses.[112] Such a scheme would prevent jurors from acquitting in situations in which they feel that the crime committed does not justify the punishment and stigma of a rape conviction.

Under the proposed federal statute, the sexual offense known as rape would include situations in which the victim was compelled to submit either by force or "by threat of imminent death, serious bodily injury, or kidnapping, to be inflicted on any human being."[113] It would also include attacks upon victims who were less than ten years old, or who were drugged or intoxicated by the assailant.[114] Rape would be a Class A felony if serious bodily injury were inflicted upon the victim, if the victim were less than ten years old, or if the victim was not a voluntary companion of the actor and had not previously permitted him sexual liberties.[115] Otherwise it would be a Class B felony.[116]

The crime of Gross Sexual Imposition, a Class C felony, would consist of intercourse with a woman whom the offender knows to have a mental disease or defect which "renders her incapable of understanding the nature of her conduct,"[117] whom he knows is unaware a sexual act is being performed upon her, who submits due to the mistaken supposition that he is her husband, or who submits because of "any threat that would render a female of reasonable firmness incapable of resisting."[118] The crimes of aggravated involuntary sodomy and involuntary sodomy would be analogous and have analogous penalties, but a person of either sex would be capable of being an offender or a victim.[119] The offense of corruption of minors would consist of intercourse or deviate sexual relations with a person less than sixteen years old when the actor is at least five years older than the other person.[120] Less severe sexual offenses would be covered by the sexual assault section.[121]

Another plan has been suggested which would provide Rape in the First Degree, Rape in the Second Degree, and Sexual Intercourse by Deceit.[122] Under this proposal, it is significant that the fact that the victim was not a voluntary social companion of the actor and had not previously permitted him sexual liberties would be irrelevant.[123] Actually such circumstances are, arguably, irrelevant since, from the victim's point of view, it is hardly more desirable to be abused by an acquaintance than by a stranger. To treat such factors as relevant is to adopt Amir's victim precipitation approach. However, from a more practical point of view it would be wise to adopt a distinction between "date rape" and "stranger rape" since jurors are likely to adopt such a distinction on their own. Whether such factors should be taken into consideration in legislative proceedings is beyond the scope of this article.

Conclusion

Temporary measures, such as crisis centers or legislative reforms, may be able to alleviate current atrocities, but until the time when the rape victim is no longer looked upon with suspicion and distrust, most rapists are likely to commit the crime with impunity. The bias against the rape victim in the United States today can only be dispelled if people become aware of the quandary in which she has been placed by a society which tends to adopt a male perspective. Exposing the defects in the present system is the first step in curing them.

NOTES

1. S. Rosenblatt, *Justice Denied*, p. 36 (1971) [hereinafter cited as Rosenblatt].
2. Although only forcible rape will be considered in this article, some of the discussion is applicable to statutory rape. Since in some states the penalties for statutory and forcible rape are identical, statutory rape is alleged because no force need be proven. J. MacDonald, *Psychiatry and the Criminal*, p. 235 (2d ed., 1969) [hereinafter cited as MacDonald].
3. See notes 4 & 5 *infra* and accompanying text.
4. Note, *"Criminal Law-Psychiatric Examination of Prosecutrix in Rape Case,"* 45 *North Carolina Law Review* 234 (1966).
5. Note, *"Corroborating Charges of Rape,"* 67 *Columbia Law Review* 1137 (1967). New York, for instance, previously required corroboration of the assailant's identity, penetration, and the application of force, but not longer does. In California, corroboration is unnecessary unless the testimony of the prosecutrix is "inherently improbable or unbelievable." 42 Cal. Jur. 2d § 97 at 286 (1965). In Texas, corroboration is required only when there has been a delay in reporting the crime. *E.g.,* White v. State, 478 S. W. 2d 506 (Tex. Crim. App. 1972); Thomas v. State, 476 S. W. 2nd 305 (Tex. Crim. App. 1972).
6. Rosenblatt, *supra* note 1, at 37; 3A J. Wigmore, *Evidence,* p. 736 (Chadbourne rev. 1970) [hereinafter cited as Wigmore].
7. A recent analysis reflects this attitude and comments upon it:
   False accusations of sex crimes in general, and rape in particular, are generally believed to be much more frequent than untrue charges of other crimes. A woman may accuse an innocent man of raping her because she is mentally sick and given to delusions; or because, having consented to intercourse, she is ashamed of herself and bitter at her partner; or because she is pregnant, and prefers a false explanation to the true one; or simply because she hates the man whom she accuses. Since stories of rape are frequently lies or fantasies, it is reasonable to provide that such a story, in itself, should not be enough evidence to convict a man of crime ... Normally our law relies on a jury to distinguish truth from falsehood after hearing evidence on both sides and giving weight to the truth that a man must be considered innocent unless proven guilty beyond a reasonable doubt. It is normally assumed, not that false accusations never occur, but that they will not mislead a jury into

convicting. When the crime charged is rape, it is unsafe to rely on this assumption.

Note, "Corroborating Charges of Rape," 67 *Columbia Law Review* 1137, 1138 (1967).

8. Wigmore states:

Modern psychiatrists have amply studied the behavior of errant young girls and women coming before the courts in all sorts of cases. Their psychic complexes are multifarious, distorted partly by inherent defects, partly by diseased derangements or abnormal instincts, partly by bad social environments, partly by temporary physiological or emotional conditions. One form taken by these complexes is that of contriving false charges of sexual offenses by men. The unchaste (let us call it) mentality finds incidental but direct expression in the narration of imaginary sex incidents of which the narrator is the heroine or the victim. On the surface the narration is straightforward and convincing. The real victim, however, too often is the innocent man; for the respect and sympathy naturally felt by any tribunal for a wronged female helps to give easy credit to such a plausible tale.

Wigmore, *supra* note 6, p. 736.

9. *Ibid.*, p. 737.

10. *Ibid.*, Despite the lack of evidentiary support for his conclusion, Wigmore is often quoted to substantiate the contention that fabricated stories may lead to convictions in rape cases. *See* Ballard v. Superior Court, 64 Cal. 2d 159, 171, 410 P. 2d 838, 846 (1966); Note, "Corroborating Charges of Rape," 67 *Colum. L. Rev.* 1137, 1139 (1967); Note, "Criminal Law—Psychiatric Examination of Prosecutrix in Rape Case," 45 *N.C.L. Rev.* 234, 235 (1966).

11. Rosenblatt, *supra note* 1, p. 39.

12. According to a Philadelphia study of 646 rapes taking place between January 1, 1958, and December 31, 1958, and between January 1, 1960 and December 31, 1960, less than 7 percent were interracial. (In 4.2 percent there were black offenders and white victims and in 2.6 percent there were white offenders and black victims.) Amir. "Victim Precipitated Forcible Rape," 58 *J. Crim. L.C. & P.S.* 493, 498 (1967) [hereinafter cited as "V.P. Rape."].

13. Murder of a white woman by a black person also causes much unrest in southern communities. A. Trebach, *The Rationing of Justice*, p. 6 (1964). After discussing a case in which 88 blacks were arrested in Odessa following the rape of a 19-year-old white girl, Trebach comments:

These dragnet operations frequently are ordered in response to crimes that shock the conscience of the community, especially the rape or murder of white women by nonwhite assailants.

14. H. Kalven and H. Zeisel, *The American Jury*, p. 249 (1966) [hereinafter cited as Kalven and Zeisel].

15. One girl who had been raped was asked by her assailant why she did not enjoy it. Margolin, "Rape: The Facts," 3 *Women: A Journal of Liberation* 9 (1972). Another, whose assailant was convicted, has been approached at parties by men who say, "I'll bet you loved it." Schurr, "Rape: Victim as Criminal," 4, *Know, Inc.* reprint of a series of articles published in the Pittsburgh Forum, beginning November 5, 1971 [hereinafter cited as Schurr]. Even a man who attempted rape is still told by other men, "You should have gone ahead and done it. Every chick wants you to do it." *Ms.*, December 1972, p. 23.

16. Slovenko, "A Panoramic View: Sexual Behavior and the Law," in *Sexual Behavior and the Law*, p. 51 (R. Slovenko ed. 1965) [hereinafter cited as Slovenko].

17. Note, "The Resistance Standard in Rape Legislation," 18 *Stan. L. Rev.* 680, 682, (1966).
18. The study is discussed in more detail at note 12 *supra*.
19. M. Amir, *Patterns in Forcible Rape,* p. 156 (1971) [hereinafter cited as *Patterns.*]
20. *See* notes 23-27 *infra* and accompanying text.
21. "V.P. Rape," *supra* note 12, p. 501. The explanation for this seeming paradox given by Professor Amir of the Hebrew University is that although the offender might believe the victim to be sexually accessible, he resorts to violence so that he will not have to risk not completing the act in case he is mistaken. *Ibid.* This explanation does not in any way absolve the assailant from guilt from the crime of rape since it shows his intention to have intercourse even without the consent of the victim.
22. *Patterns, supra* note 19, p. 254.
23. Note, "The Resistance Standard in Rape Legislation," 18 *Stan. L. Rev.* 680, 682 (1966).
24. Slovenko, *supra* note 16, at 52.
25. Women who accept a ride home from a casual tavern acquaintance, who walk alone in dark streets late at night, who accept modeling appointments and babysitting jobs in strange homes without prior investigation, or who associate with motorcycle gangs invite trouble. Girls who have a reputation for promiscuity may find that some men will use force when their expectations of compliance are not fulfilled.
    MacDonald, *supra* note 2, p. 238.
26. "V.P. Rape," *supra* note 12, p. 493.
27. Professor Amir describes his theory as follows:
    In the sexual sphere, a man can interpret verbal and nonverbal behavior on the part of a woman in such a way as being contrary to the expectations of appropriate female behavior or, even as conflicting with the whole image of a woman's propriety. She will be placed, then, in the category of a sexually available female. Thus, wrongly or rightly, a woman's behavior, if passive may be seen as worthy to suit action, and if active it may be taken as an actual promise of her access for one's sexual intentions. The offender then will react as seems appropriate toward such a woman.
    Ibid., p. 494.
28. This analysis, however, is not without its critics:
    It is a vain delusion that rape is the expression of uncontrollable desire or some kind of compulsive response to overwhelming attraction. Any girl who has been bashed and raped can tell you how ludicrous it is when she pleads for a reason and her assailant replies "Because I love you" or "Because you're so beautiful" or some such rubbish. The act is one of murderous aggression, spawned in self-loathing and enacted upon the hated other. Men do not themselves know the depth of their hatred. It is played upon by inflammatory articles in the magazines designed for morons with virility problems which sell for high prices in transport cafes: "Eager Females: How they reveal themselves," writes Alex Austin in *Male* and proceeds to describe a number of harmless mannerisms, like slipping a shoe off, and showing a hearty appetite (for food) which indicate concealed goatishness in women. Barry Jamieson describes the underhand tactics of "The Willing Cheater: Your Wife's Best Friend" in *Stag.* The object of such articles is to imply that the world is full of liquorish sluts in flimsy disguises, who will welcome the most unceremonious

advances despite their prissy denials. Such women are *available, easy, push-overs.* Whatever they get, they have deserved.

G. Greer, *The Female Eunuch* pp. 265-66 (1971).

29. *Patterns, supra* note 19, p. 22.
30. "V.P. Rape," *supra* note 12, p. 497.
31. *Patterns, supra* note 19, p. 252.
32. *Ibid.,* p. 235.
33. One author comments:

> Yet, even though the female sometimes unconsciously sets up the rape, the fact remains that she is the victim. The law's purpose is to deal with the act and responsibility of the offender. The victim may seek psychotherapy for masochistic tendencies, but that is a private matter. The law's task is to protect against victimization. The offender, not the victim, is the guilty party. There seems to be, however, more and more attention being given to the contribution that the victim makes to his injury ... True, individuals are responsible for their affairs, but it is the aggressor who acts out his feelings against an available subject, and he is legally at fault.

Slovenko, *supra* note, p. 54.
34. The law recognizes only one issue in rape cases other than the fact of inter-course: whether there was consent at the moment of intercourse. The jury, as we come to see it, does not limit itself to this one issue; it goes on to weigh the woman's conduct in the prior history of the affair. It closely, and often harshly, scrutinizes the female complainant and is moved to be lenient with the de-fendant whenever there are suggestions of contributory behavior on her part.

Kalven and Zeisel, *supra* note 14, p. 249.
35. *Ibid.,* p. 33. Sample I was from 1954 to 1955; sample II was from 1958. *Ibid.*
36. *Ibid.,* p. 45.

> As a matter of both theoretical interest and methodological convenience, we study the performance of the judge as a baseline. Our material is a massive sample of actual criminal jury trials conducted in the United States in recent years. For each of these trials we have the actual decision of the jury and a communication from the trial judge, telling how he would have disposed of that case had it been tried before him without a jury. In this sense, we have been able to execute the grand experiment of having each case, over the wide universe of contemporary jury business in the criminal law, tried by a jury and also by a judge, thus obtaining matched verdicts for a study. The result is a systematic view of how often the jury disagrees with the judge, of the direction of such disagreement, and an assessment of the reasons for it.

Ibid., p. 10.
37. *Ibid.,* p. 250.
38. *Ibid.*
39. *Ibid.,* p. 250.
40. *Ibid.,* p. 252.
41. *Ibid.,* p. 253.
42. *Ibid.,* p. 253. A hung jury was counted as ½ an acquittal for the study.
43. *Ibid.,* p. 253.
44. *Ibid.,* p. 250.
45. *Ibid.,* pp. 86, 87.
46. *Patterns, supra* note 19, p. 11. It should also be noted that due to the operation of the "slum sex code," some girls are more likely to be raped than others because of their relationships with boys. *Ibid.,* p. 249. This does not mean that

they give any sort of consent.

47. *Ibid.,* p. 14.
48. *Ibid.,* p. 23.
49. *Ibid.,* p. 23. Professor Amir uses the Philadelphia study discussed in note 12 to show that there is little truth to the common myth that most rapes are explosive crimes committed by strangers. In 42 percent of the cases the assailant was a complete stranger, in 10 percent the victim had some knowledge of him, and in 48 percent he was an acquaintaince or friend. *Ibid.,* p. 235. A Detroit study for 1949 showed that 57 percent of the victims were known to the offender, whereas 43 percent were strangers. *Ibid.,* p. 250. The Philadelphia study also showed that 75 percent of the rapes had been planned. Amir, "Forcible Rape," 31 *Fed. Probation* 51 (1967).
50. *See* note 34 *supra.*
51. Lear, *Q.,* "If You Rape A Woman and Steal Her TV, What Can They Get You for in New York? *A.* Stealing Her TV," *New York Times,* January 30, 1972 (Magazine) at 11 [hereinafter cited as Lear] .
52. *Ibid.,* p. 11.
53. Schurr, *supra* note 15, p. 4.
54. *Ibid.,* p. 4.
55. *Ibid.,* p. 5.
56. Kalven and Zeisel, *supra* note 14, p. 251.
57. *Ibid.*
58. *See* notes 47 and 48 *supra* and accompanying text.
59. Wigmore, *supra* note 6, p. 729
60. Note, "Corroborating Charges of Rape," 67 *Colum. L. Rev.* 1137, 1142 (1967).
61. Wigmore, *supra* note 6, p. 737.
62. Note, "Criminal Law—Psychiatric Examination of Prosecutrix in Rape Case," 45 *N.C. L. Rev.* 234, 235 (1966).
63. Note, "Corroborating Charges of Rape," *supra* note 60, p. 1142.
64. Smith, "The Rape Victim's Dilemma: How to React?," *Washington Post,* December 2, 1972. at E1, col. 2-3 [hereinafter cited as Smith] .
65. *Ibid.* at E1, col. 4-5.
66. Barker, "She Felt Like a Defendant," *Washington Post,* December 2, 1972, at E1, col. 6 [hereinafter cited as Barker] .
67. Smith, *supra* note 64, at E1, col. 2-6.
68. Barker, *supra* note 66, at E1, col. 7.
69. *Ibid.* at E1, col. 6.
70. *Ibid.* at E1, col. 5.
71. *Ibid.* at E1, col. 6.
72. Lear, *supra* note 51, p. 55.
73. *Ibid.*
74. F.B.I., *Uniform Crime Reports* 14 (1970).
75. *Patterns, supra* note 19, p. 27.
76. Television program, "Perspective," on WRC, Washington, D.C., November 12, 1972.
77. The woman's shame may be so great that she does not reveal the assault to anyone. Fear of rejection by her husband may seal her lips. Risk of newspaper publicity and embarrassment in the courtroom may deter the victim from informing the police. As many rapists threaten to kill their victims if they go to the police, fear of retaliation may also be a factor. Some victims do not report sexual assaults by close relatives or family friends.
MacDonald, *supra* note 2, p. 238.

Testimony in rape cases can be extremely embarrassing and humiliating, and our courts bend over backward to spare the victims any undue shame or strain. Often they are permitted to testify in secret and their testimony may later be suppressed or sealed. Even in secret testimony, naturally, the woman must speak before the jury and the court personnel, which fact sometimes may cause a woman not to press charges even when they are eminently justified.
Rosenblatt, *supra* note 1, p. 37.

78. MacDonald, *supra* note 2, p. 238. The Michigan Governor's Study Commission on the Deviated Criminal Sex Offender in 1951 recommended that police, district attorneys, defense counsel, and courts handle the victims of sex crimes, and children in particular, more carefully in order to reduce the traumatic effects of the entire experience. *Ibid.,* p. 238.

79. Interview with Brenda, member of the Rape Crisis Center, in Washington, D.C., November 20, 1972. This interview was supplemented by a simultaneous interview with Darlene, another member of the center, and an earlier interview with Karen, also a member, on November 14, 1972. The information obtained in the interview with Karen was verified by the later interviews. Since all three women have worked at the Rape Crisis Center in Washington, D.C., opened in June, 1972, they have talked to a large number of rape victims. Currently Darlene is working with other members of the center on a book about rape. (The last names of these women have been withheld upon their request, due to the fact that they are past rape victims, as are most of the members of the Rape Crisis Center.)

80. Interview with Brenda, member of the Rape Crisis Center, in Washington, D.C., November 20, 1972.

81. Interview with Karen, member of the Rape Crisis Center, in Washington, D.C., November 14, 1972.

82. *Ibid.*

83. *Ibid.* Many women at the Rape Crisis Center have complained that the interrogation was worse than the rape. Interview with Darlene, member of the Rape Crisis Center, in Washington, D.C., November 20, 1972.

84. Interview with Karen, member of the Rape Crisis Center, in Washington, D.C., November 14, 1972.

85. Kearon and Mearhof, "Rape: An Act of Terror," *Notes from the Third Year,* p. 80 (1971).

86. Interview with Brenda, member of the Rape Crisis Center, in Washington, D.C., November 20, 1972.

87. *Patterns, supra* note 19, p. 263.

88. [T]he main issue was ... whether a rape should ever be reported. On one hand, it can be argued that because of the rarity of rape convictions, the haranguing questions asked at the police station and in court, and the voyeurism exhibited by many police officers, a woman should be discouraged from reporting a rape—personal considerations aside, it just doesn't do much good. On the other hand if rapes are not reported, or if the rapist is not otherwise dealt with, this would mean that men can rape with full knowledge that nothing will happen to them.
D.C. Rape Crisis Center, *How to Start a Rape Crisis Center,* p. 7 (1972).

89. Interview with Darlene, member of the Rape Crisis Center, in Washington, D.C., November 20, 1972.

90. In one case a girl had managed to severely scratch the face of her assailant so that blood and flesh were present under her fingernails. She showed the evidence to the police, who told her they would not need it. The next day, after

she had taken a bath and destroyed the evidence, they asked her for it, and when she was unable to produce it they claimed they could do nothing since there was no evidence. *Ibid.*

91. Interview with Darlene, member of the Rape Crisis Center, in Washington, D.C., November 20, 1972.
92. Bornstein, "Investigation of Rape: Medicolegal Problems," 9 *Med. Trial Tech. Q.* 61, 63 (1963).
93. *Ibid.,* p. 68.
94. Motile spermatozoa are present 12 hours after coitus and nonmotile are present 48 hours afterwards. *Ibid.,* p. 65. Although there are no visible marks in a mature woman after normal intercourse, severe lacerations may be produced by violent rape, and there are usually visible lesions after a woman's first intercourse. These lesions are actually produced from a tear in the mucosa of the vulva rather than by the tearing of the hymen, as is commonly believed. *Ibid.,* p. 66.
95. "Medical Examination of Allegedly Sexually Assaulted Persons" Form P-4760.
96. *Ibid.*
97. Interview with Karen, member of the Rape Crisis Center, in Washington, D.C., November 14, 1972.
98. *Ibid.*
99. *Ibid.* One woman was not shown a lineup until months after the crime occurred. Her assailant had been detained and released shortly after the crime.
100. Interview with Darlene, member of the Rape Crisis Center, in Washington, D.C., November 20, 1972.
101. [T]he following pattern has been noticed from the women who have called the Center: the first few days is a period when the woman feels isolated and alienated from herself and others; the first year is a period when the woman is very much involved with fear—on the streets, at home, and among strangers; after the first year the woman is concerned with the effect the rape has had on interpersonal relationships.
     D.C. Rape Crisis Center, *How to Start a Rape Crisis Center,* p. 7 (1972).
102. Schurr, *supra* note 15, p. 5.
103. Margolin, "Rape: The Facts," 3 *Women: A Journal of Liberation* 21 (1972).
104. Schurr, *supra* note 15, p. 5.
105. *Ibid.*
106. *Ibid.*
107. *Ibid.,* p. 3.
108. D.C. Rape Crisis Center, *How to Start a Rape Crisis Center,* p. 7 (1972).
109. *Newsweek,* November 13, 1972, p. 75.
110. *Ibid.*
111. See note 34 *supra* and accompanying text.
112. National Commission on Reform of Federal Criminal Laws, *Final Report,* p. 187 (1971).
113. *Ibid.*
114. *Ibid.*
115. *Ibid.*
116. *Ibid.*
117. *Ibid.,* p. 188.
118. *Ibid.*
119. *Ibid.,* p. 189.
120. *Ibid.*

121. *Ibid.*, p. 191.
122. Note, "The Resistance Standard in Rape Legislation," 18 *Stan. L. Rev.* 680, 688 (1966).

A Model Rape Law

The following model statute was proposed by the New York University Law School Clinical Program in Women's Legal Rights, one of the first such programs in the country. As part of the program, Professors Anna Garfinkle and Kristin Glen and their law students counseled rape victims. Their proposal is a result of that work. Although the proposal was drawn up in response to the New York State rape law, it is applicable to any state statute. It is the kind of "neutral" law to which Jan Goodman refers because it treats rape like any other crime. It corrects seven of the most flagrant injustices now inherent in our legal system:

1. Eliminates corroboration.
2. Eliminates the need for a rape victim to be physically injured to prove rape.
3. Eliminates the need to prove lack of consent.
4. Lowers the unrealistic age of consent.
5. Eliminates as admissible evidence the victim's prior sexual activity or previous consensual sex with the defendant.
6. Eliminates the spousal exclusion in sexual offenses.
7. Defines rape in terms of degrees of serious injury.

—Editors' Note

STATUTE

We propose that Penal Section 130 be repealed and superseded by Amendments to Section 120.

Section 120.00. ASSAULT AND RELATED OFFENSES;
DEFINITION OF TERMS

This Section repeals Section 130.00

The following definitions are applicable to this article:

1. "Sexual intercourse" means contact between the mouth and the anus, the mouth and the penis, and the mouth and the vulva, or between the penis and the vulva and penis and anus, or contact between the anus or vulva and any artificial substitute.

2. "Sexual contact" means any intentional touching of the sexual or other intimate parts of a person.

3. "Obscene language" shall include, without being limited to, any language and/or any gesture which is sexually abusive and which places an individual in fear of physical contact or causes an individual to reasonably alter or abandon her or his lawful course of conduct.

4. "Serious physical injury" shall include, without being limited to, extreme mental anguish, pregnancy, disease, or loss or impairment of a sexual or reproductive organ, resulting from an assault.

5. "Mentally defective" means that a person suffers from a mental disease or defect which renders her or him incapable of appraising the nature of her or his conduct.

6. "Mentally incapacitated" means that a person is rendered temporarily incapable of appraising or controlling her or his conduct owing to the influence of a narcotic or intoxicating substance administered to her or him without consent or to any other act committed upon her or him without her or his consent.

7. "Physically helpless" means that a person is unconscious or for any other reason is physically unable to communicate unwillingness to an act.

These definitions will remain the same as they are in the present Penal Code.

Section 120.05 LACK OF CONSENT

This section repeals Sections 130.05, 130.25 (Rape in the third degree), and 130.30 (Rape in the second degree).

Whether or not specifically stated, it is an element of every offense defined in this article that the act was committed without consent of the victim. "Consent" is used to denote meaningful and knowledgeable assent, not mere acquiescence.

A person is deemed incapable of consent when:

1. She or he is less than twelve years old; or

2. She or he is mentally defective, mentally incapacitated, or physically helpless; or

3. If she or he is more than twelve but less than sixteen years old, and the party to be charged is more than five years older than she or he, there shall be a rebuttable presumption that, in fact, there was no consent. For purposes of determining the sufficiency of rebuttal testimony, the greater the disparity of age between the parties involved or where the parties share the same household, or are otherwise related by

blood or affinity, the weightier the presumption of coercion, abuse of authority and lack of consent.

Section 120.10 EVIDENCE

This section repeals Sections 130.10 and 130.15.

1. Evidence of prior sexual activity on the part of the victim or previous occasions of consensual sexual activity between the parties involved shall be inadmissible and immaterial to issues of consent and/or injury.
2. Marital relationship between the parties is no defense or bar to prosecution.
3. Evidence of earnest physical resistance to the assault by the victim is not required.

Section 120.15 ASSAULT IN THE FOURTH DEGREE

This section supersedes Section 240.25 (Harassment).

A person is guilty of *assault in the fourth degree* when, with intent to harass, annoy or alarm another person:
1. She or he strikes, shoves, kicks or otherwise subjects her or him to physical contact, or attempts or threatens to do the same; or
2. In a public place, she or he uses abusive or obscene language, or makes an obscene gesture *or sexual overture;* or
3. She or he follows a person in or about a public place or places; or
4. As a student in school, college or other institution of learning, she or he engages in conduct commonly called hazing; or
5. She or he engages in a course of conduct or repeatedly commits acts which alarm or seriously annoy such other person and which serve no legitimate purpose; or

(We amend this section to include)

6. *She or he subjects another to sexual contact, e.g., touching, pinching, goosing.* Assault in the fourth degree is a class B misdemeanor.

This section covers offenses formerly prohibited by the harassment statute. The only additions we have made are the inclusions of indecent sexual proposals and minor sexual attacks. We feel that these are not offenses against the public order, but rather assaults on individuals.

You will notice the reference to obscene language, which is presently undefined in the Penal Law. By this term we mean the uncalled-for and humiliating comments and remarks which invade the privacy and dignity of women every day on the streets of New York and put them in fear of physical contact. We think that comments such as "Baby, I want to eat you" are truly assaults.

Section 120.20 ASSAULT IN THE THIRD DEGREE

This section repeals Section 130.55 (Sexual abuse in the third degree), Section 130.60 (Sexual abuse in the second degree), and Section 130.65 (Sexual abuse in the first degree), and amends Section 120.00.

A person is guilty of assault in the third degree when:
1. With intent to cause physical injury to another person, she or he caused such injury, to such person or to a third person; or
2. She or he recklessly causes physical injury to another person; or
3. With criminal negligence, she or he caused physical injury to another person by means of a deadly weapon or a dangerous instrument; or
4. She or he subjected another person to any sexual contact which tends to immobilize or inhibit her or his freedom of movement however briefly.

Assault in the third degree is a class A misdemeanor.

This section covers situations in which a person is cornered or jumped on or grabbed and subjected to sexual contact. We are speaking of the many instances in which the assailant not only intentionally feels his victim's breasts or buttocks, but also prevents her or him from escaping such unwelcome attentions.

Section 120.25 ASSAULT IN THE SECOND DEGREE

This section repeals Section 130.20 (Sexual misconduct), Section 130.38 (Consensual sodomy), Section 130.40 (Sodomy in the third degree), Section 130.45 (Sodomy in the second degree), Section 130.50 (Sodomy in the first degree), Section 130.25 (Rape in the third degree), Section 130.30 (Rape in the second degree), and Section 130.35 (Rape in the first degree), and amends Section 120.05.

A person is guilty of assault in the second degree when:
1. With intent to cause serious physical injury to another person, she or he causes such injury to such person or to a third person; or
2. With intent to cause physical injury to another person, she or he causes such injury to such person or to a third person by means of a deadly weapon or a dangerous instrument; or
3. With intent to prevent a peace officer from performing a lawful duty, she or he causes physical injury to such peace officer; or
4. She or he recklessly causes serious physical injury to another person by means of a deadly weapon or a dangerous instrument; or
5. For a purpose other than lawful medical or therapeutic treatment, she or he intentionally causes stupor, unconsciousness or other physical impairment or injury to another person by administering to her or him, without her or his consent, a drug, substance or preparation capable of producing the same; or

6. In the course of and in the furtherance of the commission or attempted commission of a felony, or of immediate flight therefrom, she or he or any other participant if there be any, causes physical injury to a person other than one of the participants; or

7. *She or he subjects another person to sexual intercourse.*

Assault in the second degree is a class D felony.

Assault in the second degree is garden-variety rape, e.g., in any of our city parks a woman with a knife at her throat being forced to engage in sexual activity. We have broadened the definition of sexual intercourse to include acts done by both men and women. By incorporating it into the assault statute, the crime of forcible sexual intercourse would carry a sentence of four to seven or seven to fifteen years, depending on the degree of injury. Thus, it conforms with the penalties of the assault statute. We feel that by doing this, more convictions will be obtained, for the penalty will be more consistent with the crime. Rape is presently a class B felony, as are manslaughter and arson, with a maximum sentence of twenty-five years.

Section 120.30 ASSAULT IN THE FIRST DEGREE

This section amends Section 120.10.

A person is guilty of assault in the first degree when:

1. With intent to cause serious physical injury to another person, she or he causes such injury to such person or to a third person by means of a deadly weapon or a dangerous instrument; or

2. With intent to disfigure another person seriously and permanently, or to destroy, amputate, or disable permanently a member or organ of her or his body, she or he causes injury to such person or to a third person; or

3. Under circumstances evincing a depraved indifference to human life, she or he recklessly engages in conduct which creates a grave risk of death to another person, and thereby causes serious physical injury to another person; or

4. In the course of and in furtherance of the commission of a felony or of immediate flight therefrom, she or he or another participant, if there be any, causes serious physical injury to a person other than one of the participants; or

5. *She or he engages in sexual intercourse with another person which results in serious physical injury.*

Assault in the first degree is a class C felony.

Assault in the first degree occurs when the victim is seriously harmed. Thus it is consistent with the existing provisions of the assault statute which distinguishes between those assaults which result in serious physical harm and those which do not. In addition to the horrifying experience of rape, there are also residual effects which may remain with the victim for the rest of her life. She or he may never be able to enjoy a normal sexual relationship. She may never be able to have a child.

In conclusion, we would like to reiterate our opposition to the corroboration requirement for any sexual offense. It is the product of a prejudice which has no basis in fact. Eliminating the corroboration requirement is only patchwork reform. We need a reexamination of the entire law. We urge the legislature to seriously consider our proposal.

New York University Law School
Clinical Program in Women's Legal Rights

FIVE

Feminist Action: Women Must Begin Taking Responsibility at All Times for the Survival and Well-Being of Other Women

Introduction

In a letter to *Ain't I a Woman,* Ann Leffler writes: "There are three ways you can study rape. You can examine the rapist, depicting him as a weird deviant compelled to crime against the sentiments of proper society and good people everywhere. Unfortunately, evidence indicates he differs in no significant way from any other man. So much for that approach.

"The second way to study rape is to look at its victims. Here you might want to prove *they're* the weird ones; they asked for it, didn't fight back, came fifty-seven times, etc. *ad nauseam.* That's the conservative version of approach number two, and I assume we all know what's wrong with it. But there's also a liberal version of number two. This emphasizes the susceptibility of all women to rape, and instead of saying it's only bad girls who get raped anyway, says that—and here is the important part—since even nice women get raped (and feel free to translate "nice" into race, class, and age categories), and since rape victims suffer, rape is bad. These liberal studies direct their efforts to proving that nice women get raped and that rape victims (yes, George, your *very own* sister!) suffer. (If you catch yourself wondering why suffering needs to be proved, you just don't understand the meticulous attention to unnecessary evidence of the liberal academic mind. Remember how five years ago they wanted us to prove women are oppressed? Well, they grant that now; so now they want proof that women suffer from oppression.) The assumption behind the liberal approach is that the powers-that-be allow us to be victimized because they don't know how bad it hurts. So what we have to do is unite under the mass slogan, "Ouch." Once they understand the enormity of our pain, they will forsake their opposition to us, and moral decency will triumph. It's a communication problem.

"I trust we all know what's wrong with that approach.

"The third way to examine rape is to consider it an illustration of a more general problem: sexism. We know it is men who perpetuate sexism. We have reason to suspect all or most rules of the game they call justice are designed and administered in such a way as to protect them against us. The student of rape who holds these assumptions will be primarily interested in male responses to rape ... The feminist rape student would also observe some of these agents firsthand (hospitals, for instance) to see what happens and to support rape victims who want aid ... at least this third approach has the virtue of proving injustice, which angers us, rather than suffering, which merely depresses us. It has the additional merit of making the oppressors rather than the oppressed objects of study."[1] This quote is a long one, but Ann Leffler's analysis of what distinguishes a feminist analysis of rape from a liberal one explains why the issue of rape from the very first consciousness-raising discussions was not only a theoretical issue but a practical one. Raising the issue of rape was definitely not uniting "under the mass slogan, 'Ouch' " but an attempt to mobilize women to combat their oppression in a sexist society. But how can rape be stopped? Certainly it is not a matter of exposing the issue and then asking men to stop raping women out of the kindness of their hearts. Nor is it a matter of locking up those rapists who are caught—our society is structured so that men continuously exploit women whether it is called rape, prostitution, or marriage.

The question of how to combat rape is a much larger one and how we can organize politically to fundamentally change the structures of power. When the New York Radical Feminists held their conference on rape, a list of short- and long-range goals was presented and many of the participants outlined plans of action.* Yet three years ago these goals seemed utopian and idealistic; we recognized that goals in themselves are not an answer to the question of how to organize. First, we had to recognize that some solutions were false ones that misdirected our energies. Even now when some women first become involved in the rape issue, they advocate a "get the rapist" philosophy. This attitude must be respected because it is an expression of anger and a declaration that men, and not women, are responsible for rape, yet it must also be recognized that vigilante justice is not a solution to rape. First of all, it is not a sustained political action, and second, it focuses too much attention on the individual rapist rather than the institutions that encourage rape. Every rapist should be held responsible for the crime that he commits—he is not innocent because he is merely acting out the dictates of sexist society—but the larger society is also responsible. While vigilante groups may happen upon an attempted rape or may become aware of a rapist in the neighborhood, they cannot patrol a whole city nor help a woman who is too frightened to inform them that she was attacked. Another questionable solution is the suggestion that women should arm themselves. In response to an article advocating that all women should own a gun, the Washington, D.C., Rape Crisis

*See Appendix IV.

Center Collective wrote a letter stating, "The possession of weapons does not give us the mind-set to use them; if taken from us, we are left not only undefended, but also in an even more vulnerable position by virtue of the fact that the weapon may be used against us ... Women have been kept powerless through isolation, thus having to develop individual solutions to their oppression. *You do not have to do it yourself!* Collectively, we are creating solutions to rape."[2] Like vigilante justice, weapons only deal with the rapist, and not the roots of the rape psychology. Very often self-defense techniques are viewed as only a "humanitarian" version of this individualistic solution, but in actuality it involves transformation of our "mind-set," of learning how to be strong from each other and with each other.

But when women began to act, the problem was not only the confusion on our part, but a lack of resources and organization. For instance, one of the goals presented at the conference was that all schools should give self-defense courses for women, yet three years ago there was not one course being offered on self-defense in any school in New York City and the planners of the conference had to search for months before they found women who could demonstrate self-defense techniques at the conference. Feminists who enrolled in judo and karate courses often met hostility and derision from their teachers and male classmates. Now it is no longer considered unusual if a woman takes up the martial arts, and some judo and karate classes are made up mostly of women, and some women are themselves teaching other women how to defend themselves. Similarly, though one of the goals was to change the rape laws, no women's organization had been involved in lobbying the state capital on women's issues. A year later, because of the threat of a restrictive abortion law, N.Y. NOW and the MWPC both developed effective lobbying strategies and programs, and both are now actively lobbying for the repeal of corroboration as well as for other changes. Three years ago there were no women's groups who had an emergency "hot-line" for rape victims nor any counseling skills. Now there are two rape groups in Manhattan and we expect that other rape centers will be established in the other boroughs and in the immediate suburbs.

Also, three years ago we knew that the white male establishment used rape as a political tool against the Third World—branding black men as rapists while ignoring the rape of black women by both black and white men. Yet we realized that the issue of rape still had racist connotations that were difficult to overcome despite data that most rapes are intraracial. Many women felt that the accusation of rape could still be used as a weapon again Third World men. A special study group was formed but quickly disbanded. This still remains an open question, but now black feminist organizations are forming, and they are dealing with the issue in their own communities and in the context of a combined fight against sexism and racism. A measure of progress has been that three years ago feminists were often told that rape laws should not be changed because black men would be falsely accused of rape. In short, women were once again being told, this time by "Liberals," that the possibility of falsely convicting a man was more important than a fair trial for women. Now it is possible to talk of justice for black women as well as white. The more that the myths of rape are exposed, the more the real motives for the lynching and execution of black men in the South will be exposed.

Many of these problems of lack of resources and confusion are behind us, and across the nation the women's movement—from small groups of less than ten women to national organizations of thousands of women—is focusing on rape and how to stop it. But unlike the women's movement of fifty years ago, the "second wave" of feminism is multi-issued, partly because we learned through painful disillusionment that there is no one solution to our oppression, just as there is no one source of our oppression. What this means is that we must combat rape on many different fronts. We have organized the following section into five smaller sections which deal with one aspect of the struggle, though each aspect involves overlapping forms of feminist action. Each action taken by itself—whether it is self-defense, changing emergency ward procedures, or starting a rape crisis center—is an attempt to reform the system, but when they are combined they are a series of demands for a radical change, for ultimately we are not demanding better treatment of rape victims or more protection, but an end to rape and other forms of sexual abuse and exploitation. No one reform will succeed if women continue to be viewed as objects or possessions, which is why we must continue to fight on every front.

NOTES

1. "Sisterhood Strikes Again . . ." *Ain't I a Woman?*, Vol. 3, No. 5, July 20, 1973, p. 5.
2. "Our Sisters Speak, Rape: The Response," *Women: A Journal of Liberation*, Vol. 3, No. 2, p. 69.

Rape Crisis Centers

Rape crisis centers are a unique grass-roots phenomenon that developed with the rape issue. In 1971 feminist groups in Washington, D.C., New York, Detroit, and California began rape centers with little or no knowledge of each other. Yet, despite their different locations and the different problems they had to confront, they all share essentially the same general orientation and perspective. Rape centers that are now being started all around the country do not differ from these "pioneer" centers except that they have the advantage of drawing on the experience of the Washington, D.C., Rape Crisis Center collective.* Indeed, what is surprising is not the similarities between the centers, but the fact that they have so quickly realized what were only abstract projections of what feminists should do to combat rape. In this section we have included a workshop report from the NYRF conference which outlined six goals for community responsibility. Two years later there are rape crisis centers all around the country attacking these problems and sometimes solving them. What we thought might be particular problems of women in large urban cities have turned out to be the same ones that women in suburbs and small towns are facing.

While rape centers have emerged as a response to the issue of rape, they have sought to monopolize it—and in fact their existence has led to even more interest and involvement in the issue on the part of the feminist community. Instead of setting themselves up as "experts," their research and their accumulating experience are being shared with other feminist groups who want to work on legislative programs, pamphlets, or other actions. And while every center has concentrated on educating the general public on an informal basis, they also continuously educate the feminist community on new aspects of the rape problem that they are becoming aware of in their day-to-day contact with rape victims, the police, lawyers, and city agencies. They are serving as liaison between feminist groups and the larger community. In some cities the police and the hospitals are beginning to rely on feminist groups for information on

*See Appendix III.

the rape problem, simply because there are no other knowledgeable sources of information. Also, given the media's interest in rape, the rape crisis centers are raising broad feminist issues whenever they talk to reporters about the problem. Thus, the rape centers perform many more functions than those they have been set up to do. In many respects they have served to sustain the issue of rape and to help mobilize women around it.

Because they are such a new type of organization, it is too early to predict their future with certainty. Hopefully, they will not become so involved with their services to rape victims that they cease becoming political action groups. In New York women who were involved in abortion counseling and referrals were so busy they did not have time to lobby against bills that threatened to make abortions illegal again in New York State. The Boston Labor Pains Collective, a group that is actively involved in the child-care movement, reports, "In their own ways, the many cooperative play groups and nurseries which grew from the women's movement are as unlikely a base for a child-care movement as are the federal programs. The most obvious problem is that the parent's time is tied to running the cooperative center itself. Money for staff, space, and supplies is scarce, so that keeping the center open, rather than the political change, naturally becomes the priority."[1] So far, each center's struggle for survival has not been so overwhelming that it has totally absorbed the energies of the women involved, and they have not lost sight of basic changes in the system that have to be made. Possibly one reason why rape crisis centers can continue to be political groups while at the same time providing a service to rape victims is that their ultimate objective is to eliminate the need for that service.

While so far the problem of being exclusively service-oriented has not developed, by and large most rape groups are facing the same serious dilemmas that are confronting all feminist organizations, the problems of structure and funding. Collectivism is an ideal that most feminist groups believe in, but making it a reality is often a painful process which demands self-criticism, self-motivation, and sustained effort. Being a collective means not falling into a pattern and not taking things for granted, both of which seem attractive short-cuts when a group is trying to accomplish some sort of organization. Collective decision-making takes time, sometimes too much time, because as individuals we have different points of view, and collective action takes even more time because we have different skills. One of the more honest discussions of the problems of trying to be a collective is an issue of *Second Wave* by the women who make up the Female Liberation Collective.[2] They came to realize that much of the work was performed by only a few women—partly because they were so overworked that they did not have the time to teach other women their skills and partly because their overwork served to frighten other women from becoming involved in the production work. Of course, with any organization, women have different amounts of energy and time that they can contribute, but what was becoming increasingly evident to the women in the Female Liberation Collective was that those women who were shouldering most of the workload were being "burnt-out," while new members felt isolated and useless. In order to end this countercollective and counterproductive pattern that had developed, the women organized themselves into task groups. This vital reorganization took time, and the magazine came out later than planned. Several of the rape center collectives, which are described in the following article by Cassandra Wilson, have also formed task groups in order to cope with this problem. But again, it may be too early to evaluate whether this division of labor is a real solution to the problem of a collective structure.

The other problem, funding, is a two-edged sword. The Female Liberation Collective writes, "We grew up with a social ethic that expected women to do volunteer work, not take paying jobs (much less make a go of a serious, independent enterprise). And we are also part of a political movement that, whether intentional or not, reinforces the notion that one should sacrifice one's self for her cause."[3] Yet as women's consciousnesses are raised, we begin to realize that this volunteer ethic stems in part from the sense of our own worthlessness—that our hard work is not worth money. Also, this ethic, however noble, has several negative consequences for women's groups such as magazine collectives, child-care centers, and rape crisis centers. First, since these activities demand a great deal of time, only women who have a certain level of income or leisure can become fully involved in the group. And second, even women who do have some financial security can only devote one or two years to full-time work and then they must return to their careers, unless they are independently wealthy, and few women in the movement are. A "revolving-door" system where some women give up a few months or years of their livelihood on a rotating basis creates a lack of continuity and a residue of resentment by women who have had to make these economic sacrifices. On the other hand, funding poses massive problems for any collective. Even when the grant is large, there is rarely enough money to put everyone in the collective on the payroll, and usually only one or two women are selected to receive a salary. Having a few full-time, salaried workers and a large number of volunteer workers creates a definite split in the collective and might be the beginning of a hierarchical structure. Even when no one is put on a payroll, funding entails added paperwork and responsibility, and those women who devote more of their time and energy may resent the fact that though the group allocates money for rent and material, their own time and work are not rewarded.

There are no simple solutions to these problems, but in our interviews with women who are involved directly with rape centers we found that their political commitment to the issue of rape is so strong that these problems are still minor ones. These women expressed no uncertainty as to what had to be accomplished to combat rape—public education, a change in the courts, responsible law enforcement, and a change in hospital procedures. Since these women come into day-to-day contact with the victims of rape, they are constantly reminded of what has to be accomplished and that in a very real sense women have only women to turn to for emotional and political support. In the future, when other issues emerge, new types of crisis centers may develop. Even now, women in New York are thinking about halfway houses where women who have recently been divorced can live for a short period while making the sometimes difficult transition from being psychologically and economically dependent to being independent. Certainly, rape crisis centers have proven not to be utopian pipedreams, and their very presence is a radical achievement of the women's movement.

—N.C.

NOTES

1. Marnette O'Brien, May Pardee, Marie Schacter, and Sheli Wortis, "Labor Pains II: A Collective Evaluation of Child-Care Politics," *The Second Wave,* Vol. 2, No. 4, p. 37.
2. "From Us," *The Second Wave,* Vol. 3, No. 1, pp. 2-3.
3. *Ibid.,* p. 3.

Workshop Summary*

Reported by Mary Ann Manhart

COMMUNITY RESPONSIBILITY AND SURVIVAL NOW: FINAL STATEMENT

The community of women must begin assuming responsibility for preventing and prosecuting acts of rape by the FORMATION OF A FEMINIST RAPE PROJECT . . .

1. Establish a central number which women would call in cases of rape or attempted rape for information and moral support.
2. Establish a "protection squad" to accompany the victim to the police station—to see she gets appropriate health and legal services—and for women to accompany the victim to the courts—to act as proxy during the pictorial procedures. Women rape victims must be helped through the entire situation.
3. Organize transportation for women late at night by accompanying women to and from public transportation facilities.
4. Demand preventive and prosecuting actions from the community agencies which already exist. Force the police to be responsive to the problem of rape. There should be policewomen and women detectives on all rape cases. Community centers should offer free self-defense courses to women.
5. Educate the community. Hold seminars on rape which provide an opportunity for all members of the community to share experiences of rape. All social centers should have available existing information on rape. Block associations should have women's tables where women can organize citizen's committees to demand safety measures in the community. Public hearings should be held to raise the consciousness of the whole population on the issue of rape.
6. Insist that schools provide psychological and physical self-defense education for children.

Women must begin taking responsibility at all times for the survival and well-being of other women.

---

* This workshop summary from the 1971 NYRF rape conference reflects the concerns and politics which led to the formation of rape crisis centers throughout the United States.

Rape Groups
Cassandra Wilson

In an attempt to help women understand how rape groups are organized and function—so they too can start their own rape group—we interviewed[1] five rape groups across the country. It is our hope and the hope of the groups surveyed that women who live in a town where there is no rape group will benefit from the experience of already existing groups. We have included information that in some cases might be damaging to the individual group but beneficial to other groups or groups yet to be formed. For that reason, when necessary, we have not mentioned the name of the group that supplied us information about their internal problems or their candid attitudes toward the institutions and agencies that they have to work with. In addition to the five interviews, we have quoted from an excellent pamphlet by the Washington, D.C., Rape Crisis Center.[2] The five rape groups are located in eastern, central, and western states, but to us and to you, the *How* is more important than the *Where*.

Motivations

We asked each group about their original motives in forming a rape group. One group formed because one woman was so incensed about the treatment her daughter had received at the hands of the police and hospital— "she was treated like a piece of meat"—that she got two of her friends interested in forming an anti-rape group. The original motives of the other groups were more diffuse. Although individual members had been thinking about the problem for a long time and had connected with their anger, they did not act collectively until one woman initiated a meeting, or a series of incidents occurred. One woman described how she got involved.

> I was really thinking about rape a lot and then two of the three roommates I had at the time both were attacked within a month of each other on the same exact spot on the street near our apartment.

So that really got me thinking about it; I started getting all these different ideas. What I first thought of was just somehow getting a radio show on that could publicize the different bad areas in the city to sort of warn women. That's sort of a bad thing because it's keeping women from being free, but it would help. I started talking to other people and I put up a sign in the women's center and within the same week someone else put up a sign saying if anyone is interested let's start up a group. So the two of us got together and within a couple of weeks we had a meeting with about eight women altogether.

The original members of another group had been to a rape conference, had participated in consciousness-raising groups and in forums on rape, but did not get started as a formal group until a woman speaker suggested forming a "militant gang of women roaming the streets." Yet, when the group was formed, they did not become a "militant gang," and they gained a new focus:

The militant gang idea really didn't pan out that way, but other people came gradually and formed themselves around the idea of rape counseling.

Though some women become seriously involved in the rape issue because they themselves have been raped, we got the impression from our interviews that most of the women who organized themselves into groups were feminists and belonged either to a feminist organization or were part of a feminist community. The experience of rape in itself did not motivate individuals to join together, instead they responded largely out of a political commitment to feminism and the hope that somehow rape could be prevented.

Organization

All groups surveyed started with from three to fifteen women. All groups gained in numbers, but generally never reached more than thirty members. As one anti-rape group member surmised, "I think that somehow we all have remained in small groups simply because it is a difficult issue for all of us. We do things that are easy for people—like signing petitions—and we don't expect a hundred women to show up at a meeting. The issue, especially for women who are not feminists, is difficult to wrestle with. If women can do that, then they can face an awful lot of things and very strongly."

All groups meet regularly, usually once a week. In Washington, D.C., a group of seven women, who formed the rape crisis center, met for the third time:

> At that meeting several basic but important decisions were made. It was decided that meetings would be held weekly from 7:30 to 10:00 P.M.[3]

Focus for any group is extremely important. From the first or second meeting of a few women, an anti-rape group does heavy consciousness-raising and collects data and articles on rape so that there is a common understanding of what the group fosus will be. Inevitably, the group's feminist base leads them to focus on the needs of the rape victim. The Detroit Women Against Rape quickly focused on a public examination of these needs. In the space of three months, eleven women got together by word of mouth, researched, wrote and published one of the first handbooks to counsel women about rape.[4] Soon after, they initiated public conferences to reinforce the information in their handbook. The handbook is now in its second printing, so great was the need for this kind of information. The Washington, D.C., Rape Crisis Center quickly focused on telephone counseling of rape victims. Discussions at their second meeting prompted them to write a working paper outlining and clarifying their interests so that by their third meeting the group was able to identify their focus as " . . . counseling and serving the needs of rape victims."[5] Other groups focused more slowly, but nevertheless continued to evolve a feminist viewpoint on rape.

> We talked to a lot of women who had been raped, the group consisted primarily of women who had been raped, and I guess the approach is what you would call consciousness-raising. We got to-gether magazine articles, whatever articles were available, and we worked on a pamphlet that would help women who had been raped. We researched medical care, but we never actually published it. We learned a lot from our research though and we may still be able to publish it. And then we started having more public forums which we publicized and invited women to come and tell their experience. We got into more of the problems of women who had reported the crime and had had difficulties with the police. So we started getting involved with the police and the courts. And then the group broke in half. We decided to get another focus. Right about that time we were joined by four new women who had been in a c-r group together and who had decided in their c-r group that they would like to work on repeal of the rape law. So in terms of our history, the

first thing was this militant anti-rape squad business and then the rape counseling and more recently political work.

Organizational Problems

When we asked each group, "What are the pitfalls?" their response was energetic and detailed. In a sense, they were measuring their successes by what they had had to overcome. For the most part, their problems are organizational: decision-making, funding, politics, splits, space, telephone, publicity, seasons, and new members. They are very sensitive to these personal and political blocks because rape continues to be a serious problem and their services are more and more in demand. Their mere existence gives increasing numbers of rape victims the courage to come out into the open and release their fear, guilt, and anger. Consequently, the groups could tick off on their fingers each problem and immediately tell us their solution or projected solution. We had the feeling, naturally, that the more successful groups are those that are good at problem-solving because they never lose sight of their focus.

Collective decision-making is considered very important by all groups. This means that the group structure is nonhierarchical. Any woman is a member so long as she does the work deemed necessary by the group. All decisions, big and small, are made by the group. There are no officers responsible to the organization. Each member is responsible to the group, not to any individual.

> We tried to do everything completely collectively, we tried to make every little decision collectively and you'd be sitting in this room with twenty women, it would be packed, and every little idea we'd consider and we'd vote on it and it was just ridiculous after a while. Plus each of us had come for different reasons that made it harder too . . . we had a couple of good women who really had a lot of time to spend . . . there's a whole lot of running around you have to do.

This particular group solved the confusion sometimes inherent in a collective. They simply put more organization into the collective. The broke themselves down into what they call "task groups." These are subcommittees responsible for certain activities of the group, i.e., medical information. So, despite their initial hassles, this group, with funding under $500, opened a rape crisis center based on the Washington, D.C., guidelines six months after two women put up a notice on the local women's center bulletin board. In the Washington, D.C., group every member is responsible for staffing the crisis phones. This is the one activity the group believes absolutely essential to being an involved member because it is closest to the group focus. Any other specialized activity is encouraged, but only if a member feels "comfortable."[6]

Funding in the form of grants appeals to all the groups for one reason: members begin to feel overburdened by voluntarily doing "shit-work jobs"[7] and this in turn puts a strain on group unity. Most of the groups with small funds feel that certain positions should be salaried if the funds were available. However, one anti-rape group recently received a large grant and is approaching the future with extreme caution.

> That is one thing we would warn other groups about. We're a collective, but we are finding it difficult to function as one with the grant. A small amount of money doesn't usually change a group, but massive funding demands some sort of structure. The question we are wrestling with now is how to have a nonhierarchical structure. With this amount of money the foundation wants certain people to be responsible administratively. That's okay, we can see their point, but it's difficult to combine that sort of setup with a collective. Let's just say that foundation grants, or any large grants, require a lot of administration. Is this compatible with a collective? We don't know.

Some groups function on very small incomes, usually through contributions. They find their autonomy less threatened. Other groups carefully review their policies toward funding.

> In the beginning we saw the need to keep our expenditures small. We felt that if our needs were small they would be easier to meet and the survival of the Center would be more secure. But after a year we realized that while survival is important, growth is equally essential. New projects require money . . . we feel a definite need to have paid staff members. With a paid staff we would not be limited to women with enough privilege to be able to do volunteer work.[8]

Politics. The same group that feels the large grant threatens to destroy the collective nature of their organization has also discovered that their feminist focus may be shifted.

> It keeps coming up at our meetings. The thing is, if we are mainly a service organization, how can we include consciousness-raising as part of our service? Right now there is a push to have more political

discussions about what our views are about the legal system, the police and the rapist. But then we are so busy doing different things that we have less and less time to *analyze* the system and to talk to other women about it. And yet we still feel we need to carry on political work as feminists.

Other groups have discovered that their work, in itself, is political and their political base becomes stronger with time.

Amidst all this diversity few conflicts arise. It is necessary, of course, for all the women to feel a deep commitment to working with women ... For the most part, after working at the Center for a period of time, attitudes toward established institutions tend to become less diverse. It is hard to deal with problems associated with rape for any period of time without getting angry. As long as this continues, it can be expected that the possibility of serious political conflicts will decrease.[9]

Splits. A large portion of group energy can be spent on discussing a unified approach to the police, hospitals, and courts. These are important political decisions that must be made in every group. We have observed that a group can be totally drained by its efforts to relate to disinterested and sometimes hostile institutions. In several cities the original group broke in half over just this issue. One of the groups that had split now focuses on different areas of rape, but their political attitudes toward established institutions never changed. Their present goal—"a fairly modest process"—is to repeal one legislative loophole. However, the group does not attempt to work with the legislators, but to challenge them.

Other groups have found the split to be based upon the "gay/straight debate," an issue still unresolved in the women's movement. One group handled it through a delicate political maneuver.

We divided up into two groups. One was the Rape Crisis Center which has a meeting once a week and is concerned with keeping the center going, staffing, paying bills, and fund-raising. Then the Women Against Rape would meet separately and those were women who were interested in working out ideologies and maybe writing them down.

Still another group had a big fight over the cost of their pamphlet. This is another political issue in the women's movement that is unclear: is making money evil? The group split over this issue, and efforts in that city are now divided between counseling and publishing.

Space. Important to all rape group organization is a private space to work. The Detroit Women Against Rape had a room in the YWCA until recently when they moved to the new Women's Resource Center. Another anti-rape group is based in the local women's center. Unfortunately, the space is a political football and the center is in constant threat of losing the space to other community groups. This threat of evictions was one of the many problems the group had to contend with:

> There we were at that Women's Center which was in terrible condition and it was getting cold and there was no heat and you would freeze if you were there for several hours. You were subject to all kinds of interruptions because this was the Women's Center and we did not have any way of barring people from entering our rape speak-out, so it was hardly confidential. Well, you can't do counseling on that basis. In fact, we weren't getting anywhere.

Other groups were luckier. The Washington, D.C., Rape Crisis Center is located in a commercially zoned townhouse which was donated for use by a member. Another had better luck with their local women's center.

> The thing that delayed us was that we were trying to find a room—a place for the center to be in. And at first we thought it should be out of the women's center, but then we figured it would come to too much money to do that. Then we were given the children's room in the women's center and we felt kind of bad about that but it's just a little room anyway and we took it over . . . spent a lot of time working and cleaning it up, sanded the floors and painted it, getting a filing cabinet. . . .

From this small room a very well-organized rape crisis center operates daily. Donated space, however, sometimes has a way of backfiring and affecting group morale. One group discovered too late that the bug-infested space donated to them had to be shared with another community group and that they were not allowed to remove the white-elephant furniture that cluttered up the little space they had to work in.

Telephone. Sometimes a group finds the space, but has difficulty in staffing or acquring a telephone. Staffing a rape crisis phone at all hours can be handled in various ways, either by women who stay at the center in shifts, or by a rented tape-recorder, or by a hired answering service that notifies "on call" women. Of course, a staffer answering the phone is desirable, but if the group has a "skeleton crew," the other two methods work well. When the staffer is able to answer the phone at the center (sometimes only a room), several groups find having two phones enables the staffer to keep the crisis call on the line while calling the police, the hospital, a transportation woman, or any other person who might be helpful to the victim. The Boston Rape Crisis Center keeps a record[10] of every incoming call "except crank calls." These records can be used to analyze the group's service: how many calls are emergencies, how many referrals, how many are for general information, the times calls are most active, how often women request accompaniment, transportation, or lodging, and the geographical areas covered by the service.

Acquiring a telephone for an anti-rape group may test its problem-solving ability. Unfortunately, it is not always funds that present the problem. One group related to us that the telephone company refused to establish a special rape crisis number one week before their center was to open.

> You can't pre-order a phone number, so we just went through the phone book and called everybody who had 7273 (RAPE) in their number until we found a family who were quite willing to give us their number. We had them write it down on paper and we went to the phone company. They said it was against phone company rulings for this district to give out a number that spells out something. We were really angry because we weren't trying to sell anything. We called different supervisors and when that did no good we went to the phone company three at a time for appointments. Then we started noticing all over the city phone numbers spelling any product—you name it. We went back to the phone company and they said that the ruling had just come in recently. Finally, a lawyer who was willing to help us went to them. We didn't get the specific details, but he threatened to sue. We got the number within two days.

If a group is involved in action other than telephone counseling it is still necessary to have phone contacts because as one group discovered when they were without a phone for many months—"every lead we had to people was severed."

Publicity. Every group learns how to handle publicity by the use of leaflets, posters, press releases, and media interviews. Publicity has two purposes. First it encourages women to call the rape group. "I would say that the more publicity we get the more often we get calls from women who have just been raped," one woman told us. This is important not only because the victim is helped to relieve her anguish, but also because, if she is given accurate information by the group, she will be better prepared to report the crime and possibly have a better chance to prosecute. Second, publicity raises the rape issue in the community.

> Looking back, we can kind of see that some of the things we did helped raise the issue, like we made enough of a noise that we were available when other things made rape an issue. Once the law enforcement agencies began to get concerned that rape was running away and becoming a real menace to law enforcement and when they started casting around for quickie solutions, there we were trudging around saying all these bad things. At that point it had already been documented that police treat women badly, that their snide disrespect for women had deterred women from reporting. It's a big deal for police to get women to testify and they're having to rely on the feminist community who had developed a line of reason for why women don't report and why women don't testify in the first place. Pointing to the very obvious corruption in the system helped. Plus, we were by that time going around to a lot of schools and talking to classes. We had had isolated contacts with the press, so that when every TV show and every newspaper or magazine did their rape article we were available and better informed than anybody else. There was a big spate of publicity on the rape issue last spring and I think there was a pyramiding effect.

Seasons. Planning actions should realistically take vacations and holidays into account. Usually, the flow of people follows the school calendar. "During Christmas and holidays we got bogged down. It's sort of like the summer—people lose energy, they have other things to do." Since the summer months have the highest incidence of rape, groups who find themselves decimated during these months have difficulty functioning.

New Members. Because the number of women fluctuates, it is not always easy to welcome new members unless a definite plan has been discussed and tested.

> Initially ... we tried to have orientation sessions. These never did work, primarily because they ended up in the middle of summer floods ... Usually, a woman is asked to come in ... approximately four hours for training; hopefully this activity helps overcome the problems caused by being thrust into the middle of a highly active group.[11]

All the groups find that it takes a while for new members to understand the group focus. There can be misunderstandings and interruptions at meetings when new members have not been oriented. One method of orientation developed by the Boston group is to acquaint new members on a one-to-one basis.

> A new staffer will come in when an experienced staffer is working. They do role-playing. Somebody is the rape victim and somebody is the staffer. (You really have to learn how to think fast, think quickly, know what to do because it is a crisis.) We always do roleplaying with the phones to make sure new staffers get the information right.

Another method of orientation is to have a written statement of purpose and copies of the minutes available at all meetings for new members. Rap sessions held during slow periods for women interested in working in the rape group can also be helpful.

Types of Rape Groups

Rape prevention has many sides. Whatever a rape group calls itself, it has generally found its focus after one year of trial-and-error. New problems always arise, of course, but for the most part, the focus has settled. We see three types of rape groups emerging. One is the type of group we will call clearinghouse groups. They have not only reached their local communities, but have also reached other communities. The Washington, D.C., Rape Crisis Center and the Detroit Women Against Rape, two of the most well-known rape groups in the country, are examples of this type of group.

> Because we were the first Center of our kind and because we are in contact with so many similar centers, we have become a national clearinghouse of information and referrals . . . Since we're no longer staffing twenty-four hours a day, our new hours free more of our time for other activities we consider important: organizing self-defense classes, speaking and publishing.[12]

The Detroit group continues to publish their handbook. They also travel around the state giving conferences and helping other groups organize.

The second type of rape group is what we would call multiple centers. They are organized around staffing a rape crisis phone twenty-four hours a day, but they are also involved in efforts to inform the community about rape. One such group briefly outlined their current activities.

1. Maintain twenty-four-hour crisis phone.
2. Legal, medical, and police referral.
3. Rap groups for women to discuss their rape experience.
4. Sensitivity training sessions with police, district attorneys, hospital emergency room staff, law students.
5. Advise local university on rape prevention.
6. Lecture at local public schools.
7. Advise new rape groups.
8. Talk to media.
9. Post street sheets.
10. Sell bumper stickers.
11. Attend rape trials or pre-trial hearings to support rape victims and to learn defense attorneys' tactics for advising women what they can expect in court.

The bumper stickers can split-second consciousness-raise and publicize. The street sheets are used when the group gets a lot of calls from women who live in one area or whose attacker seems to be one man. They post these sheets on telephone poles warning women of the area that there is a suspicious character hanging around. They are very careful about the warning, of course, so that they aren't sued for libel.

The third type of group we'll call the expertise groups. These groups function as liaison between the feminist community and the community at large by focusing on one aspect of rape, such as the courts. They become knowledgeable about that particular area of rape. One example of this type of group is the New York Women Against Rape who now concentrate on court watching as well as rape counseling.

I think where we're going to have to dig in finally is the matter of having the woman questioned on the facts of the case and not being led by questioning into revealing her sexual life or any other parts of her life that have nothing to do with the case.

This same group has been successful in demonstrating against judges who prejudice cases by calling the victim "lady of the evening" or district attorneys who allow plea bargaining for rapists who have confessed to multiple rapes.

Conclusion

From our survey of the six rape groups across the United States, we discovered that although they are of different types (clearinghouse, multiple, and expertise), the organization of each group is essentially similar. The most interesting similarity is that they are all collectives with a strong sense of feminist history and ideals.

Neither those involved in the rape groups nor we as observers can yet judge the effectiveness of this type of political approach to rape, but women can feel proud of their efforts to reach out to and be responsible for their sisters. As one rape crisis staffer told us, "For a long time I was kind of disgusted with the group itself for my own reasons. I did actually drop out for a little, although I'm back. And I knew that September would bring with it a lot more women to help us out, and it really does help when you're getting bogged down to get new energy. But I'm beginning to feel good about the group. Like it's really something that's alive, it's there, it's part of the community. I've heard a lot of feedback. I think more and more people are beginning to know about us and use us."

Perhaps, as one woman expressed it, " . . . we are in a line that is bent on obsolescence. When the time comes that a woman doesn't feel lonely when she's raped, when she can go to her mother, her sister, her friends, her father, her boyfriends and, if she's treated sympathetically all along the line, she won't need us. And so it is really a great case to try whether women are really as valuable as men. And if we ever win that case, it will be an utterly revolutionary new world in every respect. We will be confining ourselves to the rape issue even though we know that the roots go far deeper and much wider than rape."

NOTES

1. Interviews conducted by Noreen Connell and myself in the fall of 1973.
2. "How to Start a Rape Crisis Center," Washington, D.C., 1972. (See Appendix III.)
3. *Ibid.*, p. 2.
4. "Stop Rape," Detroit, 1971. (See Appendix III.)
5. "How to Start a Rape Crisis Center," Washington, D.C., 1972, p. 2. (See Appendix III.)
6. *Ibid.*, p. 22.
7. *Ibid.*, p. 23.
8. Supplement to "How to Start a Rape Crisis Center," Washington, D.C., 1973.
9. "How to Start a Rape Crisis Center," Washington, D.C., 1972, p. 22.
10. See Appendix V and VI.
11. "How to Start a Rape Crisis Center," Washington, D.C., 1972, p. 23.
12. Supplement to "How to Start a Rape Crisis Center," Washington, D.C., 1973.

GUIDELINES FOR ORGANIZING A RAPE GROUP

1. Members

    a. *Definition.* A member could be any woman who comes to a meeting. She could be someone who shares in the responsibility of a particular task, i.e., staffing the phones. A member could also be someone who volunteers her car for crisis work but cannot attend meetings.

    b. *Responsibility.* If you are running a phone service or planning an action, it is important that the time volunteered by a member is realistic. No guilt tripping is allowed. Volunteer only the time you can afford to realistically give, then stick to it. One hour a week is better than no time. Then the group can set a schedule of activity based on the volunteered time.

    c. *New Members.* Be sure to include them somehow in the activity. Have a set method to make them feel welcome and also to maximize their usefulness to the group. Washington, D.C., Rape Crisis Center keeps minutes not only to brief new members on current activity but as a form of organizing discussion and backlog of information. Another group immediately involves new members by training them as phone staffers. A new member will sit with an old member while she answers the phone. They do role-playing. One plays the caller and one plays the staffer to learn effective crisis methods.

2. Meetings

    a. *Frequency.* Weekly until focus has been reached, then re-discuss.

    b. *Length.* Three hours tops!

    c. *Notes.* See 1.c. (above) for importance.

    d. *Focus.* Discuss at the first few meetings. Get to know individual motivations, c-r on rape, discuss any written material available on rape, i.e., *How to Start a Rape Crisis Center* by the Washington, D.C., Rape Crisis Center and *Stop Rape* by the Detroit Women Against Rape (see Appendix III).

3. Task Groups

When focus has been reached, divide work into subcommittees. Report by task groups at each meeting. A task group could investigate the local hospital procedures for rape victims while another group works on making contact with the local police.

4. Funding

Very little money is needed in the planning stages. A group may never go beyond a "tithing" system.

a. Member contribution

b. Community solicitation

c. Speaking engagements/handbooks/brochures

d. Self-defense classes

e. Public or private grants

f. Use your imagination

5. Self-Defense

This is really a task group activity, but it is a crucial activity. Either have a member who knows a martial art teach classes or research a list of reliable teachers for referral. Encourage all women to learn self-defense tactics. Publish a pamphlet.

6. Publicity

Let everyone know about you. Be persistent.

7. Advisors

Have an advisor, if possible, for medical, legal, psychiatric advice, someone who is sympathetic to the rape victim.

8. Space

Anywhere as long as it is private.

9. Telephone

A must for any type of group. Crank calls and media will be your main callers until the furor dies down.

GUIDELINES FOR ORGANIZING RAPE GROUP ACTIONS

The success of a newly formed rape group depends upon a group choosing a focus that is realistically workable by the women involved. No type of group is more successful than the other. Success for a rape group means (1) helping the rape victim, (2) helping all women, and (3) educating the community. The following are activities suggested by our talks with the six rape groups. Your group could do one or all of these, depending on the needs of your community.

1. Helping the rape victim

   a. Research and write pamphlets/handbooks/mimeographed papers on how to prevent VD and pregnancy, police procedures, hospital procedures, district attorney procedures, anything that you feel will help a rape victim in your community. Do not assume that women know this information. Make sure the pamphlet is available to the police, hospitals, and district attorneys. Pamphlet can be on all aspects or one aspect of rape.

   b. Crisis counseling by phone or in person

   c. Rap groups or c-r groups

   d. Legal, medical, psychiatric, and law enforcement referrals

   e. Transportation to hospital, police, court, your center, friends

   f. Support as "friend" at hospital, police HQ, court

2. Helping all women

   a. Same as 1 above, only add pamphlet on self-defense. Give women any information that will prevent rape.

   b. Self-defense classes

   c. Rape conferences

   d. Rape speak-outs

   e. Hospital survey—expose lax procedures

   f. Court watching—expose criminalizing the victim

   g. Street sheets—expose the rapist

   h. C-r groups

   i. Formulate task force that will include police, hospital and legal institutions in your community to discuss and improve treatment of rape victim

j. Formulation of rape unit on police force

k. Formulation of rape unit in DA's office

l. Train women in crisis-counseling

3. Educating the community

a. Publish pamphlets, distribute

b. Speak to community groups, schools, businesses

c. Sensitivity training for lawyers, judges, police, emergency ward personnel, law students, psychiatrists, any person who will be in contact with the rape victim now or in the future

d. Publicity-picket, lobby, radio, TV, magazines, newspapers, posters, stickers

e. Liaisons with police, DA, hospital, mayor, all legislators in your area

f. All activities in 1 and 2

Medical Issues

Women all over the country have been trying to understand what hospitals have against rape victims. The consensus seems to be that rape victims are a bureaucratic nuisance—either they have to evade the whole issue by directing the victim to another hospital or they have to call the police, calm the "hysterical" woman, fill out reports. Stress must be placed on the treatment of rape victims in hospital emergency rooms. For too long women have trusted the medical establishment to use thorough and safe medical procedures. Sadly, in rape cases, this trust has often resulted in pregnancy, venereal disease, prolongation of the emotional trauma, and lack of evidence if the case gets to trial. It is necessary, therefore, that women's groups in every city and town investigate their hospitals' emergency room policy for rape victims. If the resultant investigation indicates little or no uniform policy, as Sarah Lydgate's report documents, it is suggested that the *ACOG Technical Bulletin** be obtained and posted in all hospital emergency rooms, given to hospital administrators and professional staff, posted in all police stations, and distributed to all law enforcement officers. Then, because the *ACOG Bulletin* is written in technical language, an information bulletin similar to the one written by the Boston Women Against Rape should be widely available to all women. This bulletin should explain the importance of physical evidence in rape cases—if a victim wants to press charges later she should go to the hospital immediately *as is,* without bathing, washing, douching, combing hair, changing clothes, or throwing away clothes. The bulletin should also explain the side effects of the "morning-after" pill and venereal disease prevention.

The Manhattan Women's Political Caucus and the New York Women Against Rape have updated the medical issue to include their discoveries concerning the coordination of information between the hospital, police, and district attorney's office. Your investigation in this direction should

*See Appendix III.

prove valuable for women in your area if you ask such questions as:

1. Does the hospital release medical information to the district attorney's office and the police department only by subpoena even if the consent has been obtained from the victim?
2. Is there statewide training for all medical personnel who come in contact with the rape victim?
3. Is there mandatory notification by hospitals to the police department when a rape victim comes in for treatment?
4. Is there a mandatory form to be completed by the examining physician that provides the necessary information for the compilation of corroborative evidence?
5. Is there psychiatric referral of rape victims, with their consent, expenses to be covered by a Crime Compensation Board (if it exists in your state)?
6. Are all expenses incurred by the rape victims as a result of the rape paid by the state in a special budget allocation to reimburse victims of crime (i.e., Crime Compensation Board)?
7. Is the rape victim directly informed of the results of the hospital examination or does the hospital subject her to the indignity of only allowing a "family physician" access to this information to then be passed on to the victim.

As the MWPC and the New York Women Against Rape point out, the very need to ask these questions is a direct result of the disinterested and uncooperative attitudes of the hospital hierarchy.

These attitudes have prompted women to action on several fronts. Efforts have been made to involve hospitals in task forces on rape composed of all institutions that come in contact with rape victims. If hospitals are not interested in this type of action, it is suggested you pressure the hospital board to form a committee on rape to investigate the issues. A list of these issues should be drawn up and implemented. Questionnaires should be sent to all hospitals in your area inquiring about their procedures in rape cases and their interest in forming a task force. Gross hospital negligence should be exposed whenever possible through a media blitz or organized letter writing and telephone campaigns to pressure hospital administrators. Liaison with hospital emergency room personnel has been effective in getting the hospital to inform rape victims of rape support groups and calling the group if victims request it. And most helpful to the immediate need of the rape victim is a hospital referral list. This list should reflect your investigations into hospital procedures and also local rules, if they exist, in regard to treatment by precinct or locality. Rape support groups should not be afraid to warn women of the worst hospital emergency rooms or doctors. Also of importance to the victim at the time of the rape is the availability of women to accompany the victim to the hospital if she requests it. The woman who accompanies the victim can give emotional support while at the same time serving as her advocate.

—C.W.

Workshop Summary*

Reported by Sarah Lydgate, Chairwoman, Medical Issues Committee

The Medical Issues Committee attempted to determine answers to the following questions about hospital procedures for rape victims in New York City hospitals:

1. What is the emergency room procedure for rape victims?
2. Are there tests for the presence of semen?
3. What procedures are used to prevent pregnancy, if any?
4. Is the victim interviewed by a psychiatrist, or is such help offered?
5. What procedures are used to determine damage to sexual organs?
6. Is there a different procedure used for the treatment of minors who are victims of rape?
7. What is the attitude of attending personnel toward the rape victim?
8. Are tests performed for venereal disease or are prophylactic measures given?
9. Are there any follow-up procedures for rape victims?

In attempting to answer the above questions, committee members met with noncooperation, evasion, and outright hostility in all but one instance, a voluntary, nonprofit hospital with which one committee member had a prior working relationship and was thus able to obtain accurate information.

The New York Health and Hospital Corporation was contacted as the policy-making body for all New York municipal (city) hospitals. From

*The following report is the result of research done in preparation for the workshop entitled "Medical Aspects of Rape," by the Medical Issues Committee of the New York Radical Feminists Conference on Rape. The report also contains conclusions reached as a result of workshop discussions.

them it was learned that no standard procedures are followed by city hospitals in cases of rape; indeed no policy had been set by Health and Hospital Corp. for such cases. It took the threat of public disclosure at a press conference to gain this information.

Several hospitals were then contacted individually, both city hospitals and voluntary hospitals with an ambulance service. For purposes of clarification, generally speaking, rape cases which are reported to the police are taken by them to city hospitals; rape victims who are unable or unwilling to call the police often go to voluntary hospitals seeking treatment. For this reason both kinds of facilities were contacted for information.

In all but one case, replies were evasive or noncommittal. Attempts were made—often at the same hospital—to speak with directors of the emergency, administration, gynecology, and nursing departments. Often such calls were transferred to the office of public information, with little result.

One committee member talked with an RN supervisor in the gynecology department of a large city hospital who indignantly reacted to the suggestion that her department would have any knowledge of medical procedures for rape victims.

Another city hospital representative flatly stated he was not allowed to release this information to the public. The only information the hospital would divulge was that women under eighteen years old were handled differently (as minors, different laws apply in rape cases).

A voluntary hospital contacted admitted it had no written policy or special medical-profession training for treatment of rape victims but that it followed a loose set of unwritten procedures as follows: (1) Call police if the patient is not brought in by police (this is obligatory in assault cases); (2) Check for bruises; (3) Get sperm count. This hospital refused information on procedures to prevent VD or pregnancy. Tranquilizers were prescribed if the patient was hysterical, but followup visits to the out-patient psychiatric clinic were not offered or suggested.

A doctor spokesman for the Medical Center for Human Rights gave the same informal set of procedures.

This author, with ten years' experience in the health and medical public relations field, contacted a voluntary hospital with which she had formerly been connected in a professional capacity and was able to gather information. The hospital is not required by law to take "off-the-street" victims of crime but will treat rape cases, if accompanied by a policeman, in its emergency ward, as well as women who enter the ward on an emergency basis. This hospital, under the direction of its medical director for the department of obstetrics-gynecology, follows the procedures outlined in a bulletin published by the American College of Obstetricians and Gynecologists (*ACOG Bulletin* #14). A copy of this bulletin was provided the committee, and it outlines in great detail medical procedures to be followed. However, it is written in technical and medical language, difficult for any patient to understand, and is intended for medical personnel. The OB–Gyn director with whom I spoke also indicated that the use of the bulletin was to prevent legal suits and was a safeguard against "difficulties."

As a result of the committee's findings and the discussion at the Medical Issues workshop, the following actions were suggested:

1. A demand for written, uniform city hospital policy for emergency room procedures for rape victims.
2. That copies of the American College of Obstetricians and Gynecologists *Bulletin* #14 outlining medical procedures for rape victims be made available to hospital personnel and be conspicuously posted in emergency rooms of city and voluntary hospitals.
3. That hospital procedures for rape victims—written in easy-to-understand language—be made available, in both English and Spanish, to all rape victims.

At a press conference held during the rape conference weekend, this author made the following statement before television cameras and the press:

We demand that the New York Health and Hospitals Corporation, which is the policy-making body for New York City's public hospitals, immediately develop uniform, written emergency medical procedures for rape victims. This policy must be printed in both English and Spanish and given to each alleged rape victim who enters a city hospital's emergency room.

We further demand that this policy be made after consultation with members of New York Radical Feminists' Conference on Rape and other women's groups.

Suspected Rape*

1. PURPOSE

The purpose of this Technical Bulletin is to provide proper procedures for protection of patient and doctor as well as in the interest of justice in cases of alleged or suspected rape or sexual molestation.

2. DEFINITIONS

Rape is coitus without the consent of the woman.

Statutory Rape is coitus with a female below the age of consent. This is usually 16 but differs in the various States or Provinces.

Sexual Molestation is non-coital sexual contact without consent.

3. CONSENT

To protect the physician, written and witnessed consent for the following procedures should be obtained if possible:
  a. Examination
  b. Collection of specimens
  c. Photographs
  d. Release of information to proper authorities.

4. CAUTIONS

The physician must protect the interests of patient, of justice and of himself. Every instance is a potential court case, and the physician should expect to be subpoenaed to justify his statements. Whether rape occurred is a legal matter for court decision and is NOT a medical diagnosis.

Principal cautions are as follows:
  a. GET CONSENT
  b. GET HISTORY IN PATIENT'S WORDS
  c. RECORD EXAMINATION FINDINGS
  d. GET LABORATORY WORK
  e. SAVE CLOTHING
  f. MAKE NO DIAGNOSIS
  g. NOTIFY POLICE
  h. PROTECT AGAINST DISEASE, PREGNANCY AND PSYCHIC TRAUMA

5. HISTORY

A good history must be obtained and written down as quotations in

---

*Reprinted with the permission of The American College of Obstetricians and Gynecologists. ACOG Technical Bulletin No. 14 (July, 1970).

the patient's words. The time, place, and circumstances should be recorded. The patient's emotional state should also be noted (e.g., hysterical, alcoholic, stoic). Has the patient taken a bath since the alleged assault?

6. EXAMINATION

Get consent to examine from responsible person. Is it legal in your jurisdiction to examine the presumed victim before she has been seen by a police surgeon or similar official? Often the evidence needed to establish guilt or innocence in a case of suspected rape has been thoughtlessly destroyed by a well-intentioned physician.

   a. General appearance: bruises, lacerations, torn or bloody clothing and condition of patient (e.g., alcoholic, hysterical, punch-drunk) should be recorded.

   b. External genitalia: evidence of trauma.

   c. Speculum examination: inspect cervix and vagina with a non-lubricated, but water-moistened speculum. Vaginoscope may be useful.

7. LABORATORY SPECIMENS

The following specimens SHOULD be taken:

   a. SWAB from vaginal pool, and from any suspicious areas about the vulva. Protect in test tube. These can be examined by police laboratory for:

      (1) acid phosphatase

      (2) blood group antigen of semen

      (3) precipitin tests against human sperm and blood

   b. WET MOUNT of material from fornix examined immediately for motile sperm.

   c. Separate SMEARS from vulva.

   d. CULTURE for Neisseria in appropriate medium such as Thayer-Martin.

Laboratory specimens should be obtained by a responsible physician in the presence of a witness, and personally handed to the pathologist or technician. They should not be sent to the laboratory by routine messenger service. Unless specimens can be positively identified, they prosecuting attorney may have difficulty in submitting the reports in evidence. Clearly label slides by etching the patient's name on them, using a diamond pencil.

The use of diagnostic tablets will aid in the immediate diagnosis of the presence of acid phosphatase, indicating semen.

8. CLOTHING AND PHOTOGRAPHS

Stained clothing, photographs, and any other potential evidence should be retained by the physician and personally turned over to the proper police authorities in return for a detailed receipt.

9. OBJECTIVE STATEMENTS

The record should contain the

patient's statements. It should give descriptions of the physician's findings and what he did. It should state to WHOM he delivered specimens, clothing or photographs. The physician should express NO conclusions, opinions or diagnoses to the patient or others. NO conclusions, opinions or diagnoses should be written in the record.

NEVER say or write in the record an opinion concerning whether or not the patient was raped. The phrases "suspected rape" or "alleged rape" may be used when necessary.

The physician should remember that both he and the record may be subpoenaed and that he may be required to testify. All information should be exact and detailed to avoid any misinterpretation. Negative findings are as important as positive ones and may assist in the protection of an alleged assailant who has been falsely accused.

10. CARE OF A CHILD

The protection of a child is an important duty of the physician. Pyschosexual trauma must be recognized and minimized. Emotional support and gentle sympathetic understanding of both child and family are very important. The physician must be tactful and kind.* The parents should be given reassurance and guidance. They should be warned specifically against magni-

fying the situation. They should be told to avoid such terms as "ruined," "violated," "dirty," or "lost her innocence" lest the child develop severe guilt feelings and anxiety. It has been shown by many psychiatrists that the child's emotional reaction to sexual molestation is far less damaging than that arising from imposition of adult values upon the episode.

Lacerations should be repaired under general anesthesia. Fine catgut should be used and care taken not to reduce the size of the introitus. Tetanus toxoid may be indicated inasmuch as these wounds may contain dirt particles and may become infected.

11. PREVENTION OF DISEASE

The attacker may have a venereal disease. For this reason, with the written consent of the family, some physicians customarily give prophylactic antibiotic therapy. In the absence of a penicillin allergy the patient may be given 2.4 million units of benzathine penicillin G (Bicillin®) or an appropriate dose based on age.

12. PREVENTION OF PREGNANCY

The possibility of pregnancy should always be considered. Should exposure occur near midcycle, the administration of large doses of estrogen within 5 days ap-

*Editor's note: It would be helpful if doctors were as concerned with the possibility of psychosexual trauma in adolescent and adult women.

pears to be effective in preventing implantation.

Widest experience has been with diethylstilbestrol 25 mg. twice daily, or 50 mg. of stilbestrol diphosphate (Stilphosterol ®) once daily, for 5 days. Success has also been reported with ethinyl estradiol 5 mg. daily for 5 days. The only significant side effect appears to be nausea which occurs in approximately half the patients. This can be lessened with concomitant prochlorperazine (Compazine ®) 15 mg. spansules once or twice a day. Less nausea is encountered if intravenous Premarin 25 mg. a day for 3 days is used, but experience with this method is considerably less than with stilbestrol.

As estrogens are more properly post-ovulatory than post-coital contraceptives, patients should be carefully questioned about prior exposures in the cycle and warned to avoid subsequent unprotected exposures in the same cycle. A basal temperature chart may be useful in determining whether the patient has ovulated. Temperature will usually decline while on estrogen. If the patient does not have a period within 3-4 weeks of treatment, a D&C should be done.

If a pregnancy occurs as a result of rape, its interruption is indicated.

13. FOLLOW-UP OF PATIENT

All patients should be followed to be certain that they do not develop a venereal disease, or become pregnant. The possibility of delayed psychologic effects on child and parents must be remembered. The family physician or a trusted pediatrician is best suited for patient follow-up. In an institutional milieu, one physician should accept the responsibility for supervision and guidance.

14. LOCAL LAWS AND REGULATIONS

The physician must familiarize himself with local laws, regulations and customs. The requirements for police notification vary. If the patient alleges rape, there is usually a duty to report immediately. If rape is suspected, but not stated, "an authorization for release of information" should be obtained.

In some states a physician may not examine a patient until she has been examined by a police surgeon or other authorized medical personnel.

If the child is less than eighteen years of age there may be a duty to make an immediate verbal report to designated officials under the "battered child laws."

. . . .

To assist in obtaining the necessary authorizations and data, a standardized form is of great value.

On page 208 is a suggested "Suspected Rape" form.

. . . .

Emergency Medical Needs of the Rape Victim*

Rape Crisis Center
Boston, Massachusetts

There are several basic medical needs that every woman should have attended to immediately after she is raped. They include the prevention of pregnancy, prevention of VD, and care of general body trauma. The following is a description of these needs and their treatment in more detail.

1. General Bodily Injuries and Trauma

These injuries may be in the form of lacerations, stab wounds, bruises, etc. Surgical care, X-rays, dressings, and medication may be necessary. If so, you can expect to be seen by a number of hospital personnel, and you can expect to spend time waiting.

2. The Police.

Most hospitals will routinely report a possible rape to the police if the victim hasn't already. The police should be informed as soon as possible if you want the rapist arrested or to collect evidence in case you later decide to prosecute in court.

3. The Possibility of Pregnancy

If there is a chance that you are pregnant as a result of a rape, there are only two possible alternatives to avoid pregnancy—the "morning-after" pill or an abortion.

A. Diethylstilbestrol ("morning-after" pill)

Many facts must be taken into consideration before a woman decides to take this notorious drug. This estrogen is given in large doses to prevent the implantation of a fertilized egg in the lining of the uterus. The treatment is commonly 50 milligrams a day by mouth for five days and must be initiated within twenty-four hours of the rape. It is necessary to take the full course of medication for it to work correctly.

*Reprinted with the permission of the Boston Rape Crisis Center. This article is from their pamphlet entitled *Rape, Medical and Legal Information.*

MEDICAL REPORT   Date
Suspected Rape

(Hospital Name)   Brought by:
Receiving Ward

Name of Patient   Birthdate

Address   Age

AUTHORIZATION FOR RELEASE OF INFORMATION

I hereby authorize_____to supply copies of ALL medical reports
(Hospital Name)
including any laboratory reports, immediately upon completion, to the Police Dept.
and the Office of the District Attorney having jurisdiction.

Person
Examined_____

Address_____
Parent or
Date_____ Guardian_____

Witness _____ Address _____

MEDICAL REPORT   Time arrived   Date & Time of Alleged Rape

History (as related to physician)

_____

EXAMINATION   Date_____ Time_____

General Examination (include ALL signs of external evidence of trauma)

Laboratory Specimens Collected   **Pelvic Examination** (include All signs of trauma,
size, and development of female sexual organs)

Yes   No
(Mandatory, or explain absence)   Vulva

Hymen

Date_____ Time_____   Vagina

Smears _____ Vulva   Cervix
_____ Vagina
_____ Cervix   Fundus

Adnexa (right)
Saline
Washings _____ Vulva   Adnexa (left)
_____ Vagina
Rectal

(Laboratory Reports Attached)   Examining Physician

I hereby certify that this is a true and correct copy of the official_____
(Hospital Name)
Records concerning the examination of the above named patient.
Date   Title

The important hazard of diethylstilbestrol is that it is a *known potent carcinogen* (cancer-inducing ingredient). It has been banned from beef in this country and it has been banned for use as an antimiscarriage drug in already pregnant women.

Its effects take years to determine; only recently has it been discovered that some daughters of women who took DES in the 1940's and 1950's have vaginal cancer. There is as yet no proof that the woman who takes the "morning-after" pill will get cancer.

The choice is yours to make, but be certain of the following facts before you consider further.

(1) Ask your mother if she took an antimiscarriage drug when pregnant for you. If the answer is yes, we strongly recommend not taking DES yourself. You should follow up this knowledge by having an iodine stain test done of your vaginal walls and a Pap smear taken every six months to screen out the possibility of cancer.

(2) Ask yourself whether you may be pregnant already at the time of the rape. If so, have a pregnancy test done to be sure you don't take DES after pregnancy has begun. It *won't* stop the pregnancy.

(3) Be certain that your medical history is taken to screen out any contraindications to DES such as:
    —any family history of cancer or diabetes
    —diseases of the liver, kidneys, lungs, or heart.

(4) Be aware that the side effects of DES are severe nausea and vomiting. Therefore you should take some antinausea pills. Other effects may be vaginal spotting, diarrhea, breast tenderness, insomnia, and skin rash.

(5) There is a possibility that after the "morning-after" pill treatment you will have greatly increased fertility. Therefore be careful to consider contraception.

B. Abortion

In six weeks after your last period a pregnancy test will show for certain if you are pregnant. Legal abortion can be obtained in Boston for $150, or for a sliding scale fee in New York.*

If you don't wish to wait as long as six weeks, menstrual extraction can be done four weeks after the last period. This actually is an abortion procedure, but is done without positive knowledge of pregnancy. Menstrual extractions are obtainable in New York for $30-$50 and some private physicians do them in Boston, probably for a higher fee.*

Be aware that any pregnancy test done in the emergency room will only determine if you were already pregnant when assaulted.

*Check abortion clinics in your area.

4. Venereal Disease

   A. Testing

   Emergency rooms generally do VD testing of rape victims. As with pregnancy testing, this VD testing determines only if you already had VD at the time of the rape. Therefore it is up to you if you wish to be tested at this time. (Take the extra cost into consideration.) A vaginal culture for gonorrhea and a blood test for syphilis would be involved.

   It is essential for your own welfare that you do get diagnostic tests for VD at some point after the rape. We recommend six weeks after the rape because:

   (1) the gonorrhea culture can be taken one week to three months after contact;

   (2) the syphilis blood test can be taken as soon as three weeks after contact.

   A negative VD result six weeks after exposure does not mean it won't read positive at a later date. In other words, regular VD testing at six-month intervals is essential. VD clinics are state-run and do free testing. Most large hospitals have a VD clinic. A good resource material for further information on VD is the Montreal Collective's free *VD Handbook.* *

   Note: Women on birth control pills are said to have an increased susceptibility to gonorrhea.

   B. Treatment

   Preventive penicillin treatment can be given to the rape victim in the emergency room to prevent possible VD infection from the attacker. This treatment is effective if administered correctly, but keep in mind that you will never know for sure whether or not you would have had VD. Later testing should of course prove negative.

   1. The type of penicillin used should be (*Procaine*) *Penicillin G* and no other kind (i.e., not Benzathine penicillin, or PAM-Penicillin with Aluminum Monostearate). This is because gonorrhea must be treated only with fast-absorbed penicillin and only Procaine Penicillin G is fast-absorbed. You can expect one shot in each buttock.

   2. In a large coastal city such as Boston, very often there will be penicillin-resistant strains of gonococcus. Probenecid is then given along with the penicillin. Probenecid is an oral medication which increases the absorption of penicillin from the injection site.

   3. You can receive an oral form of penicillin for gonorrhea called Ampicillin. It is usually given with Probenecid and should be taken on an empty stomach. Avoid eating for an hour after. These precautions are because food in the stomach and especially milk products greatly decrease the absorption of the medication.

*See Appendix III.

4. Allergic reactions to penicillin are rare, but do happen. They occur five to fourteen days after treatment and may be a red skin rash or a fever. They will disappear, but you should notify the doctor who prescribed it.

5. People with a known allergy to penicillin receive instead Tetracycline in oral form every six hours for about four days. Take it with the same precautions as for Ampicillin. Side effects most commonly experienced are heartburn, nausea, vomiting, and diarrhea. The only antacid you should take for heartburn here is sodium bicarbonate. Report the symptom of diarrhea to a doctor.

6. One fact women should be aware of with any antibiotic therapy is that it may disrupt normal existing vaginal bacterial organisms by allowing an organism foreign to the area to grow. The result can be a new vaginal (nonvenereal) infection with accompanying symptoms of unusual and/or increased discharge, etc.

5. Pelvic Examination

There are two reasons for having a gynecologist examine you soon after the rape: (1) to determine if you have been injured internally; (2) to obtain possible evidence of sperm in the vagina for the police if you should decide to prosecute.

The American College of Obstetricians and Gynecologists advises physicians to obtain written and witnessed consent for:

1. the examination
2. collection of specimens
3. photographs
4. release of information to the authorities.

The examining doctor is at all times urged to be as objective and non-judgmental as possible since both the doctor and medical record can very well be subpoenaed in court. In any case you can tell by your treatment whether any judgments have been made.

The following is what the doctor should note:

1. General body appearance—presence of scratches, lacerations, bruises, etc. (Photographs taken for evidence should be of nongenital injuries.)

2. Condition of "patient"—whether she appears to be "hysterical" or "drunk," etc.

3. Clothing—whether it is torn or bloody. The doctor may request to keep an item of clothing as evidence. (Or you can request it.)

4. Any evidence of trauma to the external genitalia.

The vaginal examination will involve insertion of a speculum as in a routine exam. But after you've been raped this part of the exam will be particularly distasteful and it would help to have a sympathetic nurse present. A nurse *must* be there, but we all know it's no help to have the nurse reiterate "just relax, dear" as the doctor himself will often say.

Most doctors will be uptight about allowing a friend to be present during the internal exam, but if you do want someone with you, ask. She could stand by your head.

Once the speculum is inserted, the doctor will take a swab from the vaginal pool and put it in a test tube for the lab to detect evidence of semen. One slide will be made for immediate examination for sperm, and another swab may be taken from the vulva.

Most hospitals are required to label slides and specimens as "? rape" and this or the medical record is released to no one, not even police, without the victim's consent.

6. Emotional Needs

That a rape victim is very upset is one important aspect of rape which is often unrecognized or even denied by hospital personnel, both male and female. It's ironic—how can a woman gain sympathy when her claims of rape are not even believed? So in this crisis a woman will need support from someone she knows will be sympathetic. The most desirable person to have would be a close friend. Another alternative is a woman who will come just because you talked to her on the phone after the rape (from the Crisis Center). The point is to get support. Support means strength and with strength you can insist on the humane medical treatment you deserve. Support means also that you can better recognize your rage. It means you may better deal with the guilt that society and you may impose on yourself.

Concerning medical treatment, a sympathetic physician may prescribe a sedative for short-term use. Don't be afraid to ask for it.

7. Follow-Up

The rape is not always over a few hours after the actual experience. You may experience more mental and emotional distress for a period of time. We feel that a large part of this distress is valid anger which, if recognized, can motivate you to take positive actions in your life.

We'd like for you to keep in contact with us to let us know how you're doing. We want to bring women together to discuss in groups their feelings about their rape experiences and possible things that could be done about rape. We don't recommend it, but if you feel psychotherapy is necessary, we'll try to refer you to a sympathetic therapist. Most of all we want to see the feelings of isolation, guilt, and helplessness dispelled from the mind of the woman who has been raped.

For further peace of mind, please follow up on later medical needs caused by the rape, that is, VD testing and pregnancy testing.

8. Cost

What you pay the hospital is a very real concern. A woman who's with you in the emergency room could find out, and we also have information on the major hospitals. If you have no money, a couple of alternatives are Medicaid and the Massachusetts Victims of Violent Crimes Act which legally makes the state responsible for your medical bills (if the rape is reported).

Self-Defense

Self-defense, on the surface, may appear to be a short-range and individualistic solution, but in actuality self-defense is one of the means by which all women can combat the myth of their defenselessness and essential passivity. This society sets us up to be victims. We are told that "little girls don't fight," we are not given physical fitness courses in schools that train us to use our bodies, and we are advised that the best way to avoid attack is to not go out at night without a man. The result is our trained incapacity to defend ourselves and fight back. Like the women in ancient China whose feet were bound so that they could take only the smallest steps, we are socialized to be cripples, to see our bodies in terms of beauty rather than strength.

What follows is a report from the self-defense workshop at the NYRF Conference on Rape. While just reading the report might help you to remember some techniques if you are assaulted, the report was intended to suggest ways of practicing self-defense techniques with friends or a group. An excellent guide to more techniques is "Fighting Back" by Cate Stadelman in *Stop Rape*.* Only steady practice with other women will help us overcome situations that tend to freak us out. Self-defense practice has its limits and if women want to increase their strength, coordination, and self-dicipline, they should enroll in a martial arts course. But the key to self-defense, whether it is self-taught in informal groups or it is learned through martial arts courses, is both *psychological* and *physical* practice in sizing up the situation, in discovering our strengths and weaknesses, and in being prepared to fight back. Learning to use our hands and feet as

*See Appendix III.

weapons and learning the vulnerable parts of the human body are useless unless we change our body image and our mind-set. Sarita Cordell describes this transformation of consciousness in a Tai Kwan Do class:

> It was a time to go beyond individual practice and to tell what it's like to have something more than air at the end of a punch or kick. We lined up in facing pairs and listened intently as Carole, our instructor, explained what to do and how to prevent accidents. Go! Mady and I looked at each other, grinning a bit uncertainly; out shot her arm. I froze. An extraordinary rush of images and feelings flooded me. "Stop that! Ladies do not hit!" said my mother. "Did you see the muscles on Susan? Ugh!" said a high-school classmate ... Most immobilizing of all, my gut reaction was undiluted fear. What if she hit me? I'd never known what it's like to be hit since my mother slapped me when I was thirteen; the memory of that slap had festered for years. The thought that hitting could be other than traumatic hadn't entered my head until I stood there looking at Mady; feeling utterly confused.
>
> Suddenly I saw in my mind an incident in a playground many years ago. My son was about five; I was wiping the blood from his cheek after his tussle with another boy, and he pulled away from me to return to the fray. "I actually think he's *enjoying* it," I had thought, perplexed. I hadn't remembered that incident until it jumped into my head in the class and set off a mind-blowing explosion of awareness. He *did* enjoy it! He was getting stronger; that's how he tested himself. The other boy needed and wanted that play-practice, too. If an arm shoots out at *him*, he's got a set of well-practiced reflexes. I turned to Mady, and I felt myself grinning with excitement as I told her it would be okay, I was ready to try again. And spar we did; grunts and laughter punctuated the atmosphere all over the gym. I began to remember what I had done in previous classes, and to notice what changes I needed to make, what I was doing right. It felt great, even the blows I didn't block. I wasn't destroyed by a hit![1]

As individuals, self-defense courses can help us when we are attacked, but if we want self-defense to be one of the means of combatting rape, both the physical act and its psychological and social causes, then we must work collectively so that all women can defend themselves.

1. Many rape crisis centers offer martial arts courses for a nominal fee or have referral lists of nonsexist instructors so that women can develop skill in a supportive environment. If there are few martial arts experts in the area, women's groups should encourage women in their community to

form self-defense practice groups. They should also put pressure on schools, organizations, and agencies to offer these courses for a nominal fee. Self-defense should be seen as essential training for women's psychological independence.

2. When women speakers talk about rape and how to stop it, they should point out that self-defense begins early and at home. Parents must be encouraged to show their daughters, as they do their sons, how to defend themselves. Playful rough-housing between girls or girls and boys should be tolerated. Brothers should not be stereotyped as their sisters' protectors, and instead little girls should be praised if they are independent and assertive.

3. Women's groups should demand that gym classes at all educational levels be integrated and taught by both sexes. Since short and weaker males are not excluded from boxing and wrestling classes, there is no reason that females should be automatically denied the knowledge of combative skills. Body contact between the sexes should not be restricted to sexual contact, but should involve other types of interaction.

4. Feminists should develop special methods of self-defense for women. Martial arts training is structured on the male body, and those areas where a woman's body might be stronger are ignored and left undeveloped. Cate Stadelman has found that judo and jujitsu require more weight and body strength than karate. There may be a method or a combination of methods that would greatly increase a woman's combative skill.

—N.C.

NOTES

1. "Self-Confidence/Self-Defense," *The Second Wave,* Vol. 2, No. 4, pp. 38-39.

Report from the Workshop on Self-Defense

Mary Ann Manhart

Rape is not an act of sensuality, pleasure, or an expression of an enormous sexual appetite. It is an act of hostility. And in a time of increasing violence in both cities and suburbs, women must have enough respect for their bodies and lives to defend themselves. Rape and violence in America are institutionalized—and yet women think that the average rapist is a foaming maniac. The fact is that he is an average man. Women are raped by the average American soldier in times of war and are being raped by the average man today in our society. We must change the image that men have of women as passive, delicate sex-objects upon which they can take out their frustrations and anger.

Since you are living in a jungle, be self-reliant; don't expect men, whether relatives, boyfriends, or policemen, to help you. Better laws for prosecuting the rapist, better police protection and attitudes *are* important since there is little concern about whether we are raped or not. But let's not get raped in the first place.

Look strong, walk with courage, don't look like a victim. Think ahead of what might happen in your own apartment and in the areas that you travel to and from. Have an action plan. Get in shape. Wear sensible clothing and shoes when traveling. You must be able to run, yell, swear, and speak in a loud, aggressive voice. Take a self-defense course, and if you can't do that right away, practice running, practice techniques suggested here, get books on the subject, and practice with friends. Or carry a weapon. *Your will to survive should override any damage you may to do your assailant.* Everyone has a tiger inside of her. *Defend other women.* At least go get help or call the police. If there is a test case in court when a woman is being tried for defending herself and harming her assailant, go to court, show your support.

Street Tactics

Street tactics are no substitute for a defense course, but women's time is not their own, and the simplest of defenses can often avert disaster. The training and dress of women have left them virtually without defense against violence; we hope by street tactics to avert some of the immediate consequences, and make the ordinary woman less defenseless against society. A surprise offensive move on your part will throw your attacker off guard. Jump at him, feint a blow, and *yell to scare him* (and get your adrenaline going). This may give you a chance to run. But if you must fight for your life, here are some suggestions.

Weapons*
Legal weapons. Any defense object that is primarily used for another

*But *remember*—your weapon can be taken from you and used against you by your attacker.

purpose: ice pick, large hat pin, large skating lacer, baseball bat, old-fashioned corkscrew, kitchen knives, artist's knife, large screwdriver, hammer, large scissors, crowbar, monkey wrench. *Noisemakers:* Invento Palm Size Alarm, police whistle, pocket alarm. *Common weapons:* pocketbook (weighted, if possible), hardbound books, rolled newspapers or magazines, umbrella, cane. Guardian Spray, sold over the counter as of 4/17/71, is also legal. If you have a hunting license, you can carry a switchblade.

Illegal weapons. New York City laws prohibit the following deadly weapons: tear gas gun or pen, billyclub. New York State prohibits the following: spray devices, brass knuckles, billyclub, sandbag, sling shot, bludgeon, stiletto, blackjack, dirk, dagger, toy gun that looks real.

Dogs. They are one of the most effective deterrents. Most dogs will instinctively defend you. Large dogs will be the most effective. You can send or take your dog to a training school. German shepherds, Doberman pinschers, and Airdales are used as attack dogs. Attacker must deal with dog before you, giving you time to escape.

Weapons that may anger and not deter your attacker: small hat pin, lit cigarette, cigarette lighter, rattail comb, powder in face, metal nail file, small screwdriver, Exacto knife. Use your own judgment. Any close-range weapon must be used on vital areas such as eyes and throat, and you just get one chance.

Vulnerable Areas
Avoid muscular areas and concentrate on bones and vital organs. Strike hard and repeatedly: nose, eyes, throat, solar plexis, knee, groin, and shin. Use thrusts and blows with objects, chops with side of hands, fingers straight on elbows, and kicks. Kick or knee the groin, box the ears with the heels of your hands, elbow into the solar plexis, jab fingers into the windpipe and eyes. A chop to the side of the throat is more difficult. If attacked from behind, bend knee, kick backward into shin or kneecap, breaking away at the same time.† It is easier, however, to bring your heel down *hard* onto the instep. In a frontal attack, kick the shin or smash your foot down hard onto the instep. The heel of your hand, thrust up under the nose, can be fatal—USE ONLY TO SAVE LIFE. Fist with second joint of second finger protruding—grind into vein on the hand if held over your mouth or into Adam's apple or hollow below.

How to Use Common Weapons
Pocketbook: Never hit the person over the head with it; instead jab or thrust into face, groin, or solar plexis.

†But *remember,* if you are attacked from behind, he may have a weapon or other men may be behind him. Size up the situation. If he uses both hands, chances are he does not have a weapon.

Umbrella or Cane: Hold with both hands and use as a bayonet—jab point first. Choose for strength. Smash up into chin, jab to stomach or groin. Whenever possible, use whole body thrust behind attack of any kind.

Newspaper or Magazine. Use it tightly rolled as a jabbing stick. Hold firmly and jab into side of face, eyes, up under chin, solar plexis, groin.

Hardbound Book: Try to use both hands and jab into vital areas.

Garbage Can Lid: Can be lifted off and pushed into the face of an attacker. It can also be used as a shield if you are being attacked with a weapon.

MAKING A CHOP

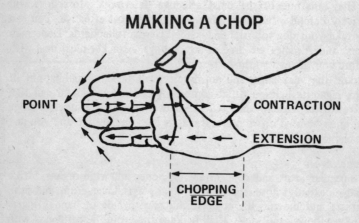

POINT

CONTRACTION

EXTENSION

CHOPPING EDGE

MAKING A FIST

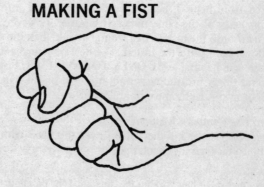

TARGETS OF SEVERE PAIN

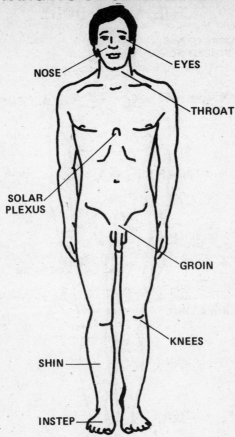

NOSE

EYES

THROAT

SOLAR PLEXUS

GROIN

KNEES

SHIN

INSTEP

Apartments

One of the myths of rape is that it occurs on the street late at night. Don't be fooled, be prepared at all times. Know your apartment building and make your own apartment as safe as possible. Entrance halls should be well lighted; if not, don't hesitate to bring a flashlight. Know the floor plan and exits in the building. Ask the super to show you how fire escape ladder releases on the bottom to give you access to the street in case your attacker has entered your apartment. This knowledge will also help you if a fire breaks out.

VITAL SPOTS OF THE MALE BODY

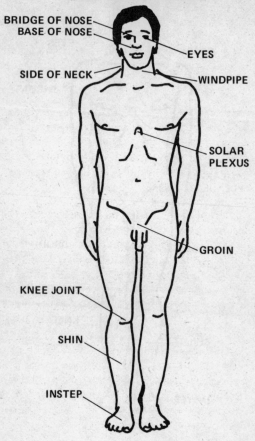

BRIDGE OF NOSE
BASE OF NOSE
EYES
SIDE OF NECK
WINDPIPE
SOLAR PLEXUS
GROIN
KNEE JOINT
SHIN
INSTEP

Doors
Know who is on the other side—let visitor identify self—do not open to unknown, unexpected callers, i.e., repair or service men. Have telegrams or messages slipped under door; have packages left outside door; a chain on your door is especially effective at this time. Your viewer should be large enough to see the hallway outside your apartment; if not, change viewers.

Locks

Have both types A and B on your door. (A) Segal lock: Ring and Bar Pin Tumbler or Fox Police Lock. The best tumbler and key are Sargent Radial Lock and Key. (B) Bar or chain lock. Has no outside tumbler, can't be picked. Never pass out extra keys. Change lock tumbler at regular intervals, especially if your pocketbook is stolen, or if you are suspicious of your landlord, doorman, super, ex-roommate, boyfriend, or friend.

Windows

Keep your doors and windows over fire escape or possible access windows locked at all times. Use window screws or key locks. Bars or grates over the windows are effective, but they can be a fire hazard—have easily accessible key. Booby-trap windows with bells, mobiles, bottles, hanging plants, chimes, etc. Put up curtains so that no one can see who is inside.

Other Precautions

Get a night light, but not in the room you are sleeping in. Get a separate extension of telephone in the room you sleep in or a long extension cord. In a large apartment or house it is best to have a security room. You can then give your warning, go in there, lock the door, and call the police. This room should have locks on the inside door, weapons, and a telephone. Locks on the doors inside your apartment, even a small one, are also a good deterrent. If you can afford a burglar alarm system, buy one.

Police Number

Know your local police precinct number and try to obtain their telephone number from information. If you're unsuccessful, tape the central switchboard number to your telephone and in an emergency call this number and ask for your local precinct. If you're too nervous, dial 0 and give the operator your name, address, and local precinct. If you don't have time, dial 0, yell "Help," and leave the phone off the hook.

Apartment Break-ins

If you hear someone breaking in through your now fortified door or windows, call out in a gruff voice, saying that the police have been called and you have a weapon (you should be able to back this up). In most cases the intruder will be a burglar and will vanish after your warning. Do not hesitate, however; immediately call the police. Begin to barricade your door, or window, pull all the furniture you can push or carry in front of the door. If the person breaks through or picks your lock and you have a chain on, he will no doubt put his hand through to try to unhook it. Slam the door on his hand and try to get the door closed again. A dog is very helpful at this time, since even a small dog can sound ferocious. When someone is climbing through a window, he can easily be bombarded while he is busy getting in. If attempted entry continues after warning, run out the door if the person is on the fire escape, or vice versa. You can proceed down the fire escape, knocking on windows for assistance. If the intruder breaks through and you're still in the apartment, don't cower or hide, hit him with everything you can get your hands on: chairs, lamps, small tables, etc. Attack him first. If you have a firearm, threaten him with it and be prepared to shoot if necessary. The important thing is to get out of your apartment, and if you can't, then be on the offensive rather than the defensive. Don't let yourself be trapped.

If someone breaks in while you are asleep or preoccupied in another room, the situation is critical. If you are awakened, a night light will allow you to see what is going on outside your bedroom. Never turn the light on in your own room. He probably doesn't know where you are or if you're even at home. If you hear someone approaching, get your weapon and wait in the dark to strike or run out of your room for a surprise attack. Obey your instincts and use your own judgment. This is the situation where a weapon, a telephone, and a noisemaker by your bed will help you. If you awaken to find someone burglarizing your room, pretend to be asleep until you find out if that's all he wants. If you're caught and he has a knife at your throat, you may want to reason with him until you can get him to put it away. Then try to make a run for it or get to your weapon or improvise one. But if you fear for your life, defend yourself. If you're not alone or have a roommate, don't be afraid to gang up on the intruder. Don't let yourselves be talked into becoming separated or tied up. Remember the eight nurses killed by Richard Speck in Chicago.

Traveling

When traveling home late at night alone, call the person you left to inform them that you have arrived home safely. When on the street at night, try not to walk alone, but remember if we all start staying inside off the streets, we make it more dangerous for other women and cut down on our own freedom. Walk quickly and close to the street, away from buildings. Be observant and aware of street action. *Scared?* Walk in the street. Avoid cars—don't flag them down, you may find more trouble. *Followed?* Obey your instincts. Don't hesitate or debate for blocks. Act quickly. Turn around, confirm your suspicions, cross the street immediately, go toward the most populated, well-lighted area, even if it means going in the opposite direction. Don't try to be cool: look, run, scream. Ring fire alarm or police call box. Don't hesitate to seek aid of policeman or security guards.

If you are walking in the suburbs, walk near the street or in the middle of the street at night. Stay away from shrubbery. If followed, run to the nearest lighted house and ring the doorbell. Even if they won't let you in, ask them to call the police. Keep standing by the door so that the attacker will think that you are being assisted. If you are forced to put up a fight on the street, try to get your back up against a solid object such as a wall, post, or mailbox.

Avoid telephone booths in subways and deserted streets. Never use them at night unless people are around you. They are soundproof and a tight trap.

Subways

Avoid lonely stations without attendants, if possible. Avoid pedestrian tunnels and passageways alone or accompanied at night. Wait outside turnstile near attendant until train pulls into station at night. As the train approaches, go through the turnstile and walk toward the car you wish to enter. Avoid ends of platforms and benches not in view of attendant. The attendant won't come out of the booth to help, but he or she could phone for assistance. If you get off the train to make a transfer, follow the same rule and stand by the turnstile. If the platform is on another level, go upstairs and wait for more people.

On the train, know where the exit is, if possible, at the destination stop. Get in the first car with the motorman or the car with the conductor or TA policeman. Near your stop walk toward the car closest to your exit. If you are wary of someone who gets on, change cars. Try not to be alone in a car or with a single man or group of men. If the train approaches a station and a gang is about to get on, prepare to get off just before the door closes so they can't change their mind and follow you. Push your way off if necessary or run to another door. If you are attacked, don't pull the emergency cord, as you want the train to proceed to the next station to obtain help. Bang on the door of the motorman or conductor (who probably won't come out) to signal ahead or call out of his cab for help. Try to get your back against a door for support to fend off your attacker. Defend yourself!

Stairways

Go up and down them as quickly as possible. Have your key ready. Be prepared at each turn for the unexpected. Turn and look if you hear someone. Be aggressive if someone is behind you and they come at you. Do hit them with whatever you have, shove or kick them down the stairs. Your surprise attack may save you. And remember, you are at an advantage if you're above them. If you see someone waiting for you and you're suspicious, do run down the stairs and out of the building. Don't hesitate to scream. Yell Fire, not Help. You may want to knock on doors, if you have the time, otherwise run out into the street.

Elevators

In a suspicious building, use the stairs if possible. If this is not practical, check the mirror; stand by the door; know where the alarm button is. Test the one in your own building regularly to know how it sounds and that it works. Ride alone if possible. Get off if you don't like what gets on. Don't be afraid to push your way off, and make noise at the same time. If you can't tell when an elevator is going to the basement, and it does so late at night, press the emergency button to alert whatever help is available or to stop the car between floors. Do this also if you suspect someone is waiting for you on another floor. If someone attacks you in the elevator, press the emergency button and scream. If he has a weapon, use your own judgment, but think twice before you quietly let someone take you to the basement or roof.

Cars

Travel with your doors and windows locked, particularly, in strange, isolated places, day or night—keep them locked when stopped. Only park your car in conspicuous, well-lighted places. Be especially careful of airport and shopping center parking lots. Check back seats for unwanted passengers upon entering. If your car breaks down, be wary of accepting help. Use accepted auto safety rules, and stay in your car, getting out only to attach white cloth to car identifying it as an auto in distress (always report at first opportunity any car displaying such a signal). Other distress signals are three blasts on car horn and blinking lights at night. *Don't run down your battery;* stay in your car all night if necessary. Talk to would-be rescuers from crack in window.

If someone forces his way into the car, *never* allow yourself to be driven or forced to drive to a secluded area, it may mean your life. If you are forced to drive, RUN a light, slow down, and run car into the curb—attract attention in any matter you can. Example: Drive into a gas station and honk your horn. If he is driving, turn off the ignition and throw out the keys. If you can't reach them, try to jump out as the car starts. Make a racket, this may be your only chance to save your life.

Hitchhiking

Don't go alone or at night. Don't get into a car that has more men than women. Don't sit in the middle of the back seat with two men or in the back seat of a two-door car. Don't be afraid to say no to men who offer rides. Hitching alone is dangerous, but use your own discretion. Do accept rides with women; couples are usually safe. Check where the door handle is and keep your hand on it; carry a defense weapon. Know where you're going and the route you should be taking. If the driver turns off route, ask why immediately and ask to be let out. *Trouble:* Grab keys and turn off the ignition, put your foot on the brake to slow down the car, jump out. Heavy shoes are important if you need to kick. Picking up hitchhikers is dangerous. Don't do it alone. Don't be outnumbered. Don't take them off the main roads. If any trouble develops, use same tactics as when someone forces their way into your car.

Motels and Hotels

They are often dangerous and do not have secure locks on doors and windows. Find out how to call the office or some other assistance from the room telephone in case of emergency when you check in. Try to avoid places that do not offer this security. Check all locks for safety. Barricade door. Booby-trap windows with noisemakers. Get travel locks for doors and windows.

SOURCES

New York City Police Department—Interview, 1971.
How to Defend Yourself, Your Family—Your Home, George Hunter, David McKay Co., New York, 1967.
The Womanly Art of Self-Defense, Chester W. Krone, Jr., Award Books, New York, 1967.
Articles by chief-policewoman in *Ladies Home Journal,* 1969, Margret Disco.
New York Magazine—"The Urban Strategist," Nancy Lyon.

The Sexual Abuse of Children

As Shulamith Firestone stated in *The Dialectic of Sex,* "We must include the oppression of children in any program for feminist revolution or we will be subject to the same failings of which we have so often accused the men: of not having gone deep enough in our analysis, of having missed an important substratum of oppression merely because it didn't directly concern us."[1] Clearly the sexual abuse of young children is surrounded by the same myths that women are now trying to destroy. Menachim Amir's study indicated that the largest group of rape victims are young and between the ages of eleven and nineteen. Since these figures are based on reported rape, an even larger number of rape victims might be children. What follows is a list of recommendations formulated by Florence Rush. We wish that we could also include a description and list of what women's groups are planning or doing, but to be honest, we have not yet heard of any directed action. Possibly one explanation is that the effort to change the way in which institutions deal with rape would help child victims as well as women. But, on the other hand, there are special problems associated with child abuse.

Unlike adults, children must depend on the willingness of their parents to report the crime; and too often they have been raped by a close relative or a family friend. Other adults who may be aware of the incident are reluctant to become involved if the parents show no interest in reporting the incident. Women medical students at one New York City hospital have reported that when young girls are brought to the emergency room with injuries indicating that they have been raped, the doctors treat them without reporting the incident either to the police or the child protective agencies. When it is not a matter of rape, but sexual abuse, children are often accused of lying or the act of confronting the offender seems to be of greater concern than the continued abuse of the child. Children have few if any civil rights, and they are completely dependent on the good graces of adults. This would seem to suggest that initially women's groups should try to educate parents and other interested adults as to the scope and seriousness of the sexual abuse and exploitation that children experience. A long-range solution would be to end the total powerlessness of children by giving them certain fundamental civil rights.

Another serious problem is that it is commonly assumed that the sexual assault of children is not a frequent phenomenon since only severely psychotic males would attempt to rape or seduce a child. Social agencies, police departments, and the media seem reluctant to expose the extent to which child abuse is widespread. Part of this reluctance can be explained as an attempt to avoid the uglier aspects of our society, yet it might also be true that our major institutions do not want to reveal the degree to which some children are victimized. The child molester/rapist is very often not the suspicious stranger lurking in the shadows, but a doctor, dentist, social worker, or a relative or friend of the family. Another problem is that agencies that have been established to deal with child abuse are for the most part understaffed and under-financed. Despite the "child-centered" myths we hold about ourselves, children come last when it is a mtter of national priorities. Women's groups must raise the issue of child sexual abuse just as they raise the issue of rape through conferences, speak-outs, research, and writing, and then work to make all institutions responsive to the real needs of children.

–N.C.

NOTES

1. Bantam Books, 1971, p. 104.

Recommendations and Proposals for Victims of Child Abuse

Florence Rush

What can we do about the problem of child abuse? The following suggestions are for parents, guardians, all those who care for and work with children and anyone else, no matter how young or old, who can read and is interested in helping victims of child abuse.

1. If a family or young woman decides to report an incident of sexual abuse to the police, please be aware of how difficult the law makes it for the victims. Do not let the victim go alone. Get help and support from your local women's movement and from those aware of the sexist implications. If you can, get a good lawyer, preferably a woman who is familiar with sex discrimination and the rape laws.

2. If a child reports a molestation to you, believe her story. If she names and knows the molester, and chances are good that she will, take the child, if she wishes to confront him—*no matter who he is and no matter how close a family relative or friend.* For example:

> *Child:* Mommy, Cousin Charlie just put his hand up my dress and touched me and looked funny.
> *Mother:* What! Please tell me what happened.
> *Child:* We were playing hide-and-seek and when it was my turn to hide, he found me behind the curtain. He said he loved me and thought I was sweet and that is when it happened. He told me that it was a secret and not to tell anyone.
> *Mother:* I'm going to talk to him about this at once. Do you want to come with me?

With this attitude on the part of the parent, my guess is the child will go along. Assured she did nothing wrong and with the support of her mother, she will be able to face Cousin Charlie. But if the child cannot face him, do not insist. The important thing about believing the child, and an expression of anger against the act, is the support the child will get, particularly where it concerns the right to control her own body. One reason girls and women think so little of themselves is because they know that almost all of society sees them as objects for sexual pleasure and this is implicit in the sexual molestation of children.

3. Fathers and mothers often ask how they can raise their sons not to be sexist and not to abuse or exploit females either sexually or otherwise. Often, even for the best-intentioned families, this is difficult since it is so hard to combat attitudes of male superiority and aggression that boys pick up in school, on TV and other communications media. However, the effort should be made. In some situations it may mean the difference between a male sensitive to the feelings and exploitation of women or one who uses and exploits them. Please compare the following reactions:

> *Father:* Why were you rude to Nancy?
> *Son:* I hate girls.

Father: I guess that happens to boys when they reach a certain age. You'll get over it when you grow up.

or

Father: But you were playing with Nancy yesterday. You mean she didn't do anything to you and you just don't like her because she's a girl?

Son: Yeah. You know how it is.

Father: No, I don't know how it is. If you dislike someone you must have a reason, and being a girl is not a reason. I don't buy it, and I don't like it.

Another situation:

Father: What is Nancy screaming about?

Son: Oh, I was kidding and pulled up her dress. It makes her mad.

Father: I did the same at your age. She'll get over it.

or

Father: If she doesn't like it, why do you do it?

Son: You know . . . it's fun.

Father: No, I don't know. How would you feel if someone pulled down your pants. Don't ever do it again, and apologize to her at once.

4. The sexual abuse of children should be openly discussed in families as a danger and violation of human rights with strong and definite disapproval of the offender.

5. The subject should be openly and frankly discussed in schools, churches, social agencies, and all groups that work with or are concerned with children.

6. The subject should be discussed in all women's movement groups, in consciousness-raising groups, rap sessions. Women and young girls should be encouraged to tell their experiences, their feelings and events that surrounded the incident. It will become clear that the problem is not a personal experience of one little girl who had the misfortune to meet up with a sick old man, but a political problem which is used to undermine and intimidate female children and prepare them to be submissive to men all their lives. The women's movement can lead the way in making the political connections and exposing the crime for what it is.

7. Many feel that if what we say here is true and we must tell children about how men treat women and girls, then girls will grow up to hate and fear men—even their fathers! It is my opinion that avoiding the truth is

much worse than facing it. If the father of a young girl recognizes that females are regarded as sex objects he will be better able to cope with this reality for himself, support his daughter in her own sense of self-value and esteem, and perhaps protect her or at least help her should sexual abuse occur. I would predict that a young woman with a father, brothers, or male relatives and friends who openly face and deal with sexual abuse of females as a reality will approach the world better able to protect herself and with a more positive attitude toward men than the child who, insulted and abused, has had no experience with a man she can trust.

8. Bring all these problems to your women's groups for discussion, help, and support. Let's bring the problem out into the open and talk about the fact that men do sexually molest female children. The offender should be exposed and the child victim believed and taken seriously. Silence does not protect the child; it protects the offender. Let us stop feeling ashamed and guilty for crimes that have been committed against us and let us expose and identify our offenders and abusers and let us support and help the child victims of male sexual aggression to do the same.

Political Action

A common critique is that American political groups tend to be either reformist (Naderism) or anarchistic (Yippies), both of which may fail to transform the basic structures of power. Part of this dichotomy is reflected in the women's movement. There are women's groups who feel that their main interest is equality between the sexes and that problems, such as rape, can be solved by legal reform alone, and there are separatist groups who feel that the problem of rape can be solved if women learn to fight back. However, these are only extremes of the spectrum, and most women's groups—even those who see themselves as being primarily re-formist or radical—share many of the same goals, though they place different emphasis on them within their own organizations. Those initially interested only in the legal aspect have come to realize that rape laws are the end result of myths that men hold about women, while those who advocate working completely outside the political system recognize that rape laws must be changed.

In the following section is a short summary by Roz Pulitzer of the involvement of her organization, the Manhattan Woman's Political Caucus, <u>Manhattan Woman's Political Caucus,</u> *MWPC* with New York Women Against Rape in a campaign to raise the issue of rape in the larger community—New York City—and to pressure the city agencies to be responsive to the needs of rape victims. The campaign was supported by other feminist groups as well, such as NOW, New York Radical Feminists, the National Black Feminist Organization, the New York Women's Anti-Rape Group, and the Household Technicians of America, but the MWCP and NYWAR did most of the hard work. It has been one of the most successful feminist campaigns in New York City since the women's movement's emergence in the late sixties. It was able to catch the attention of the press and T.V. for several months so that large numbers of people became aware of the issues. Key city agencies were forced to become involved, if only to defend themselves against mounting public pressure. District Attorneys' offices and legal groups which had been largely noncommittal about their attitude toward the rape laws became advocates of their repeal. By far the most important victory of the campaign was that the corroboration requirement was eliminated from the state penal code. This represented ten months of intensive lobbying by the members of the MWPC—they not only contacted all the legislators on the Assembly and Senate committees when the bills were submitted, but they followed the bills' progress on the floors of both houses, where they were passed unanimously. Their final lobbying effort was a letter-writing campaign to the governor when the bill was sent to him for his signature.

A large measure of the success of the caucus campaign rests on a number of factors: the orientation of the caucus was already political, and as an organization it is committed to working within the established system; they had experience in lobbying; they had a publicity team of women who knew how to write releases, organize press conferences, and catch the attention of the media; the New York State rape law was clearly one of the worst in the nation; and, of course, since rape had been an issue in the New York feminist community for over two years, the caucus knew what they wanted changed. Not all groups have these advantages, and their campaigns are often preceded by an internal struggle for a common focus and for a common goal, long discussions on strategy, and, sometimes, effort-wasting actions which do not succeed. For feminist groups who do not work within the established system, a strategy for political action against rape may be more difficult to develop. Also, since they take a radical stand, the media is more likely to distort their actions or not report them at all.

One persistent problem that women have encountered when they become politically active in the rape issue is that very often they are accused of racism. In New York City, one of the first attempts at political action was undertaken by the Feminists, a radical group of women, in September, 1971, five months after the NYRF conference. They had come to a sentencing hearing of a sixteen-year-old boy who had confessed to rape and even boasted about it, but who had been charged with a lesser crime because under the law there was no corroboration as to identity. His accomplice, a thirteen-year-old, was remanded to a juvenile center. The sixteen-year-old was facing a sentence of ninety days in jail, but it was suspected that it would be suspended. Colette Price described what happened in *Woman's World*: "At 9 A.M. Tuesday the 28th, women began to gather in front of the Criminal Court Building at 100 Center Street. The turnout was small, maybe fifteen to twenty women, which was somewhat surprising. It wasn't until later on in the morning that we got wind of the fact that there were objections by women to the action. It seems that after a WBAI radio announcement to publicize the action, there was mention made of not getting involved in the prosecution of a minority group member—Medina is a Puerto Rican. Feminists feel that he is a rapist first by demonstrated actions, a Puerto Rican merely by birthright. If he rapes women, we want him prosecuted to protect *our* lives. Another objection stemmed from the fact that Medina was so young. The raped girls were only eleven and fourteen—not too young to be raped."[1] What was involved in this episode was a nearsighted liberalism which ignores the plight of minority women who have never come under the protection of the white male legal establishment. On the other hand, The Feminists apparently focused their action on the prosecution of Medina, rather than on raising broader issues. A much more serious and divisive incident was described by Kathy Williams in *Aint I a Woman?* When feminists attempted to distribute a poster directed to Third World men about rape, they lost the support of Third World women and the Lower East Side community. The poster, which read, "Raping a woman does not make you a man. Rape does not make you a revolutionary brother. Rape is a political crime against our sisters, mothers, and daughters. We have so many things to deal with in this community . . . we have to deal with these things together. Rape divides us and destroys women. Rape destroys our own people," was never actually put up. But it gave the impression that it had been written by Third World women, which it hadn't, and that all rapists were Third World men. Another proposal, which was to put up a poster addressed to women, everyone agreed to, but the work was never done. Kathy Williams ends her long and detailed letter with suggestions as to how women can eliminate their unconscious racism.[2] One may question, however, whether racism was at fault in all the misunderstandings between the white and Third World women or whether the idea of directing a poster to men reveals a far more complex confusion of strategy and goals. No campaign is structured to ask men, Third World or white, to stop raping women—it is structured to *force* them to stop. Secondly, no poster will counteract the structures of power which tolerate rape, and its only usefulness would be if it were to be used as a means of organizing women into political action and theory. An assumption is made by some liberal and Left groups that they have to organize Third World and working-class communities, but this assumption is an issue among feminists. While some feel that we must begin to organize a broad-based movement from the beginning, others feel that Third World and working-class women will organize themselves around their particular needs and then unite with other sections of the women's movement around unifying goals.

What follows is an interview with Essie Green Williams, a Manhattan Women's Political Caucus member who has been involved in the National Black Feminist Organization, which was formed in August, 1973. Since feminism has just begun to make an impact on black women, she is concerned with the problems facing black women who must combine two movements—she does not feel that there are any easy solutions to what often becomes a conflict of loyalties. However, she does begin to outline the ways in which women can work in coalitions. Essentially, the Caucus, a less radical group than the Feminists or the Lower East Side women, was able to create such a coalition because it focused on positive issues of the elimination of the corroboration requirement and on fourteen demands for preventing rape. These demands served to expose the fact that the city agencies were doing little to prevent rape and, in fact, were unconcerned about the problem. They were able to present their point of view with clarity, and conflicts with other groups did not develop over misunderstandings. Thus, when NYWAR and the MWPC held a demonstration to protest the low bail that one judge had imposed on an accused rapist who murdered a woman on his release, they drew public attention not only to this one incident but also to the New York rape laws and to the bail structure. Even though their lobbying effort to eliminate corroboration was highly effective, it is still too early to know whether their successful campaign will also lead to fundamental changes in those institutions—the police department, hospitals, and courts—which can help rather than hinder the rape victim and which, ultimately, might take an active role in rape prevention.

One of the immediate results of publicizing the fourteen feminist demands was that a Mayor's Task Force on rape was formed and the Caucus along with NOW and several other feminist groups, was invited to work out improvements and innovations with representatives of city agencies. The following interview was conducted in November, 1973, and at the time Roz Pulitzer could not foresee two major setbacks. First, after the inauguration of a new mayor of New York City, the Task Force on rape has been unable to effect any meaningful action from the new administration. The second setback is that for all intents and purposes the Rape Investigation and Analysis Unit, which had been representing the police department on the Task Force, has been disbanded. Its establishment at the end of 1972 was viewed as a general improvement of the police department because rape victims would not have to face hostile or skeptical policemen but instead could go directly to the Unit, where they were not only better treated but were assured a proper investigation of their case. In December, Lieutenant Julia Tucker, a highly effective administrator and policewoman, and six other women were transferred to other posts without explanation. Indications are that the police department has shifted the emphasis of this unit to that of a statistical analysis unit. Significantly, the name has been changed to the Sex Crimes Analysis Unit. Although this unit has a telephone number, it has never been publicized. Rape victims must now call their local precincts and talk to police officers who have had little training in rape investigation. When Lieutenant Tucker was transferred, the MWPC and NYWAR held demonstrations to have her returned to her previous position, but at present the police department, now under a new commissioner, has been unresponsive. However, the caucus is still actively involved in pressing for all fourteen demands, and given their previous successes, within a few years may achieve all of them.*

So far most political action has been on a local level, but possibly feminists could launch a national one. Currently there is a bill in the Senate (S.2422) responsored by Senator Mathias (R-Md.) that would establish a National Center for the Prevention and Control of Rape and that would authorize funding (up to $10,000,000) for studies on state rape laws, the causes of rape, and programs for its prevention, and feminist organizations would be eligible for these research grants. If passed—it is proposed as an amendment to the National Mental Health Act—this legislation would enable feminist groups in every locality to make the same recommendations that the Washington, D.C., Task Force and the New York Mayor's Task Force have made to their respective city governments. But even if this bill is defeated in the 1973-74 session, possibly feminists should begin to think of a nationwide campaign to create such a National Center for Rape Prevention so that local feminist groups that are actively involved in the rape issue can begin putting pressure on all levels of

---

*See Appendix III for the Washington, D.C., Task Force on Rape Report, which several feminists worked on and which is an excellent in-depth study and analysis of all the aspects of the problem. As with the New York City Task Force, there is no way of knowing whether its recommendations will be accepted.

government. Rape is not only a local issue, it is a national problem which reflects the prejudices of the whole society toward women and their worth as human beings.

—N.C.

NOTES

1. "Bringing Rapists to Trial," *Woman's World*, Vol. 1, No. 3, November-December, 1971, p. 6.
2. "What to Do about Rape in a Third World Neighborhood: A White Woman's Self-Criticism," *Ain't I a Woman?*, Vol. 3, No. 5, July 20, 1973, pp. 6-9.

Interview with Roz Pulitzer of the Manhattan Women's Political Caucus

Roz Pulitzer of the Manhattan (New York) Women's Political Caucus* talked to the Editors, Noreen Connell and Cassandra Wilson, about the caucus's work on the issue of rape. She described the attitudes and problems that the caucus encountered when it became involved in the issue. The actions described are meant to be suggestions for what other women can do.

Our involvement with rape started with a lobbying effort. We went to the state capitol in May of 1973 to pressure for legislation on women's issues. We had prepared a legislative program which, among other important issues, called for the elimination of corroboration in rape cases. While talking to the legislators about our program, two women recognized that the legislators were consistently interested in our opinion on the rape

*Roz Pulitzer is on the Coordinating Council of MWPC which is its governing body. She is liaison to the MWPC Legislative Action Committee and a member of the Mayor's Task Force on Rape of New York City. MWPC describe their objective as: "... to work on a multipartisan basis to insure the representation and active participation of women in every level of political and governmental activity, particularly at the decision-making level." They are affiliated with the National Women's Political Caucus whose headquarters are in Washington, D.C.

issue. These two women undertook to research and prepare a legislative memo outlining MWPC's arguments for eliminating corroboration.

A few weeks later, at MWPC's Legislative Action Committee meeting, these women told us what they had learned. One of the first things they told us was that the summer months have the highest incidence of rape, and so we decided to make our plans to publicize the issue in August. After various ideas were batted around, we hit upon declaring August as "Rape Prevention Month" and decided to talk to the mayor to see if he would make this official. We'd invite all kinds of legislators and the mayor to a press conference and see what happened.

Everybody started taking assignments. I spoke to the mayor's assistant. She said that she would speak to the mayor about it, and meanwhile we could give her our proposals. We had worked up fourteen demands that we felt had to be addressed. The mayor was basically sympathetic to us, but he didn't want to declare August "Rape Prevention Month." That would call too much attention to the whole thing, he felt. But we were very insistent and just took it upon ourselves to declare "Rape Prevention Month" in a press conference.

Press Conference

The mayor was out of town at the time of the press conference, but his assistant read his statement announcing the formation of a Task Force on Rape to deal with the fourteen demands. The MWPC asked other women's groups to join and support them. New York Radical Feminists, New York Women Against Rape, and NOW accepted. Just from a personal point of view, one of the things that excited me most was the support the women's groups gave us during the press conference. At the last minute we had to change the location because somebody had requested the wrong permit. It had already been advertised in the feminist press and it was too late to reach all women. So the New York Radical Feminists, at the same time the press conference was going on downtown, gave a small demonstration at the original press conference location so that any woman who came there not knowing of the change still found a demonstration going on, which was fantastically supportive.

All the TV and *all* the newspaper and radio reporters were there to cover us. We had sent out a tremendous number of press releases beforehand to a good mailing list.* Also, we called all our women friends in the press. We're still getting follow-up requests by the way, for speakers. Publicity has been coming from everywhere.

*See Appendix VII.

Task Force on Rape

On the Task Force we had to fight very hard for feminist representation. The Mayor's Office wanted someone from each of the departments of the city, such as the health and hospitals department, corporation counsel, etc. We made very strong recommendations for people who were in these departments and who we knew were active feminists. These women got the appointments. At first, the Mayor's Office wanted only two women to represent the women's movement because they didn't want the Task Force to be too heavily weighted with feminists. But we insisted on more and we got more. We were insisting, by the way, even in the case where candidates to represent the various departments weren't people whom we knew to be feminists and active feminists, that they should at least be women. In the majority of instances, we did get just that. Fortunately, even the police are represented by a woman, Lieutenant Julia Tucker, head of the New York City Police Rape Investigation and Analysis Unit.

Other interested parties attended Task Force meetings, such as the chief of detectives of the police department whom Julia Tucker once brought along. He was surprisingly sensitive to the problem, and apparently he was the one who first got Julia Tucker interested in the issue of rape, and he also got her interested in setting up her own department. I was really very surprised at his attitudes. He's very aware of the issues. The police department as a whole is more sensitive and more responsive and more eager to accept criticism and make changes than some other city agencies. Whereas you would expect a greater sensitivity on the part of physicians, etc., it's coming from the police, where you would least expect it.

The whole hospital situation is a real trauma. Evidence isn't being collected properly. Even if the need for corroboration is removed from the law, that doesn't mean that evidence doesn't make your case stronger. Very few hospitals have a form with a checklist of possible evidence in rape cases. This is a procedure that should be set up regardless of changes in the law. We've developed such a form. But even if a hospital has done this, they don't have any kind of central rape filing system, and when the DA's Office goes to get the information, it's often lost or misplaced. In addition, the feminists on the Task Force are very insistent about extending city guidelines to the voluntary hospitals as well as to the municipal hospitals.

We want to send invitations to the phone company to come and sit in on a meeting with us and discuss how they can help us. We want all the public phone booths to have the Police Rape Unit number. But we're having problems with the phone company. Julia Tucker has had to move her Rape Unit office, and the phone company wouldn't let her keep the same number. So the Task Force intervened and the Task Force chair-woman, representing the mayor, spoke to the phone company asking that they please allow the Rape Unit to retain its current number. It was explained that a lot of time and effort had been expended on informing the public of the Rape Unit number, that it was very important the number stay the same. The phone company said no. They absolutely refused to do it. They said that by law they were not required to transfer a number, and they just wouldn't do it. And I think we're going to have problems too in getting the phone company to list the rape number as a separate number. They have this kind of attitude—well, if you're going to make rape a separate thing, then why not a special number for murder, and why not a special number for any type of crime. They're a difficult group, especially considering the number of women they employ who must come home late at night. They've had, as you know, suits against them for all kinds of discrimination. They've had to pay back wages to women, etc. They won't do anything without a suit.

Since Lindsay is a lame duck mayor, we've asked Mayor-elect Abe Beame if he would consider continuing the Task Force in his administration. He said yes. Now, I don't know whether this is a campaign promise or not. It just depends on how strong the tide keeps going, how much pressure the women can pull together and put on him, because he also promised that nothing would happen to the women's center and two weeks later he, as controller, went to a budget meeting and supported the sale of the women's center. I don't know that we're going to get all fourteen demands; we went for broke and we're going to try to get as many as we can.

Legislation

Our chances this year of getting a fair rape law passed are greater because of our efforts, I think. A packet went out to all state legislators in New York City saying what we had done, giving them copies of our press releases from the press conference, and asking for a statement of support from them on the issues. We are collecting the statements and then we plan to present them to the legislature. When the legislature opens in January we hope to do some lobbying, possibly even getting some kind of visual presentation to show two or three times on a given lobbying day and invite the legislators to come and see it. We found through experience that although very often you can get a great deal of men to sympathize with the problem, they still find it difficult to relate emotionally to rape. They just really can't relate to it or fully understand it.

We've received a great deal of support from the legislator who has proposed the repeal of the corroboration requirement from the law. Another legislator has suggested that perhaps we'd want to support a bill proposing reducing rape to degrees of assault. He suggested he could get his party to back such a thing, and swing it through the legislature this term. Everybody seems to be jumping on the bandwagon now that we've made a splash of it.

A state joint legislative committee is holding hearings on the rape law. People are being asked to testify from all kinds of groups. These hearings give us an even better chance of getting corroboration off the law books.

At a recent caucus general meeting, held the day before the New York City joint legislative hearings, we debated rape legislation positions. There were arguments either to remove the corroboration requirement from the law or to write degrees of assault into the rape law. We had as speakers in the debate a very heavy panel of good women. They all know the issues right down to the technicalities of law. At the end of the debate, the caucus had a general membership vote to determine our position. We voted, at this time, to support the removal of the corroboration requirement.

The more women we get in support of our position the better, and the more women who testify at the joint legislative hearings, the more we can get accomplished. It's just a question of women getting together and making our positions heard.

Speakers Bureau

We are setting up a rape speakers bureau in coalition with the New York Women Against Rape. It was decided to hold a speakers bureau workshop at which we will show the National Educational Television tape "No Tears for Rachel," broadcast on Bill Moyers Journal last year. Then we will break up into workshops to train women to go out and speak on the issue. We've had some requests to speak already. We want to do a mailing to all the community organizations and block associations, and try to hit the hospitals, high schools, and anywhere that we can do the most good. I think community organizations, block associations are excellent groups to reach because people who go to those meetings tend to have a social conscience and tend to be somewhat active. So, if we can turn them on to an issue, they are likely to respond with action.

We will be prepared to speak on how women can prevent rape. We will talk about the importance of self-confidence as well as practical methods

of self-protection. We will talk about what to expect and what to demand
from the police, the hospital, and the courts. We will discuss how to
change society's attitudes. We will counter with facts the myths that are
responsible for the oppressive guilt that a victim of rape experiences. We
will discuss how to change the law, the injustice of the existing rape law,
and the proposal presently in the legislature for changing that law. Because
of the steadily increasing number of attacks on women, we consider it of
paramount importance to convey our message to the public. We are
particularly anxious to talk to young women, because many rape victims
are between the ages of eleven and nineteen. By raising awareness through
the cooperation of schools, community groups, and other organizations,
we can not only decrease these numbers, but at the same time lessen the
burden for women forced to cope with the victimization of rape. We are
asking women from all groups to join us in the speakers bureau.

Brochure

We've received, to date, since the press conference, over 700 requests for
our rape brochure.* This is from women all over, many of whom are not
part of the women's movement. They're the kind of women we've been
trying to interest in the movement, so it's been a perfect outreach. We can
continue to print the brochure for ten cents, but that only covers the cost
of mailing. It doesn't cover the cost of printing. So we hope to cover the
printing cost through the speakers bureau, just to make the brochure
self-perpetuating. We are also having the brochure translated into Spanish.
    As women begin to perceive this particular problem on other levels and
in other terms, they begin to see all women's problems in a different light.
We're trying to call women into the movement. Women can't ignore
studies that claim, as a recent study did, that the majority of rapists had
mothers who sexually molested them. A man did this study. This was his
interpretation. You pin it on your mother. Psychology has made the gross
mistake of placing the entire burden of all kinds of mental problems on
the mother. This is a distortion, and we've got to rethink a lot of this stuff.
That was much too convenient a conclusion. They stick a woman in the
home and tell her this is all she can do, and then they hurl all kinds of
accusations against her for having done a terrible job.
    Changing attitudes and combating myths is a slow, drawn-out process,
but change is possible.

*See Appendix III.

Manhattan Women's Political Caucus
Fourteen Demands

1. Declare August "Rape Prevention Month."
2. Launch a publicity campaign to make the 577-RAPE number as well known as the 911 number.
3. Twenty-four hour staffing of the Rape Investigation and Analysis Unit, seven days a week.
4. Referral of all rape calls to the Rape Unit.
5. Issue portable composite units to the Rape Unit.
6. List the 577-RAPE number with other emergency telephone numbers in all phone booths and telephone books.
7. Put policewomen on patrol in plainclothes in areas where rape is likely to occur.
8. Give refresher courses in self-defense to all policewomen on patrol.
9. Put in better lighting in all city parks.
10. Put more police officers on patrol in high-crime areas in August.
11. Set up a special clinic in one municipal hospital in each borough to treat rape victims, to provide supportive psychiatric care, and to help victims establish corroborative evidence.
12. Assign a woman assistant district attorney in each borough to prosecute rape cases and avoid plea bargaining.
13. Provide sensitivity training and seminars for hospital personnel, police officers, and legal officials working on rape cases.
14. Provide self-defense classes in junior and senior high schools for women students, taught by women.

Interview with Essie Green Williams*

Do you think that rape is a unifying issue for black women?

To be absolutely honest, it hasn't been so far. On the one hand there are black women who have been victims of rape and it has been a

*Noreen Connell and Cassandra Wilson interviewed Essie Williams who has been involved with rape issues with the caucus and the NBFO.

destructive experience for them; but on the other hand, black women can also look at rape in its political context as just another desperate act among many—a way in which to act out hostility, frustration, and anger. I think black folks over the years have felt rape to be so much a part of their everyday lives, so when you talk to a black woman about rape, it's crucial, but so many other things are crucial—at least you're still alive. Unless it's an issue which is a matter of life or death, then I think issues such as rape will not have priority for the black woman, unless she is a very articulate black woman who's been raped and who then begins to see it in its feminist context. But so many of our young women have been raped and abused that it is almost an assumption in some black communities that a woman is to be abused. She does not dare go into a bar and sit, without someone feeling she is there "to be had" whether she wants to or not. And this is the kind of attitude that we have to deal with in our communities. And it has been the attitude not just of the police but of the community that when a woman is raped she must have done something wrong. And this causes the victim of rape unnecessary pain when facing her peers, her family, and her community. You see, black women rarely get the kind of response that they need when they've been raped.

As for the police—why bother going to the police? I don't know the percentage, but I'd say the majority of black women don't even bother notifying the police when they've been raped or abused. You know if the police put down a white woman what happens when a black woman walks into the precinct. The attitude of the police is that it's just another black person who has been hitting on another black person. You know, "Ho-hum, they're at it again." So black women don't report rape. The police look at you and say, "What did you do, anyway?" The basic assumption is that if you're black, you did something. So that's another issue.

Rape is a very emotionally destructive experience, but when it happens to a black woman—you say, "Oh well, let me get myself together and keep on going." I mean, so many other things in our life are destructive. These are things that are very difficult to address. Trying to deal with the rape issue when there are so many other issues of survival in the black community—it becomes a matter of priorities. Maybe other issues of survival in the black community—it becomes a matter of priorities. Maybe the abusive treatment they get in the streets. They will ask, "Why can't I walk down the street looking the way I want to look without being abused? I don't attack men on the street, so why should I be abused?" Not many women in the black community have asked these questions. The issue of their survival as women has been kind of put down because of the larger issue of the survival of our race—day to day survival, you know? But it's coming, and there are going to be some very sharp clashes. Rape is one of the issues that are going to have to be addressed in the black community as more women become aware of what the movement is all about, but as an issue it is going to touch on some aspects that you don't want out there. It will be very difficult, very painful to address, because what you're talking about is violence against each other. What happens when people are oppressed is that they take it out on each other instead of against the oppressor. Not everybody is going to make that political connection, and so some people in the black community will feel that the whole issue of rape is a put-down and that these problems within the community should not be exposed.

Do you think black feminists will be working with white feminists around the issue of rape?

No, not really at this stage. I think black women's involvement in the movement is still a recent kind of thing. The split between the concerns of white women and our concerns was so great that strategically we had to have a black organization to give the women's movement credibility in our own communities. Every group must go through its period of self-identity—of getting together and hashing out things between ourselves. You have to feel comfortable before you can bear to let out some of the skeletons, you know? And certainly you have to go through this process before you can talk about merging with the main force. We have to find out what black feminism is all about, because we lead different lives from most white feminists.

Just a few years ago there was the feeling among blacks that the women's movement was usurping some of our energies and that it was just another way to avoid dealing with the real issue of racism. We used that cliché that "black women were already liberated." But actually, I think it is still difficult for black women to openly come out and say there is some validity in the women's liberation movement. That's why, I think, Margaret Sloan thought it was crucial to form the National Black Feminist Organization. But it's going to be a long time coming. Black women still are concerned with survival issues and see the women's movement and sexism as a bullshit issue. The black group will allow us to be honest with each other. But you know it's very hard for us to be out with our white sisters and at the same time to deal with problems that are at home, problems that we have because we are black. I mean, one of those problems we have at home is relating to whites, and then to go out and join with white women can pose a conflict. That's my feeling.

But even though most black women haven't fully realized it yet, the women's movement has developed more of a consciousness in black women, which is why we've had to deal with ourselves as women and form our own groups. And we're beginning to address some of those issues which we weren't openly dealing with before. Also, you begin to look at other alternatives and make plans for your self in terms of what is best suited to your needs as a woman. Even black women who respond negatively to the women's movement are at least responding to it as a real movement now. When anyone starts responding on that level their consciousness is being raised whether they like it or not because they're forced to formulate some sort of ideas of their own. As I said, just a short time ago the women's movement was dismissed because we thought we didn't need it, and now for some of us it's come down to a matter of choice of where to put our energies or a matter of what should be accomplished first. Maybe that choice isn't too real, because it isn't that simple a situation, but it's a measure of the extent to which the women's movement has affected women who at first were totally unsympathetic to what the women's movement was saying.

I think that the women's movement is a powerful force and that most people, black or white, don't recognize the significance that it has both now and throughout our history. The participation of women in shaping history—I mean social work, the whole idea of services to a community and to children was started by women in the nineteenth century—must be taught. For black people the historical perspective is a new part of our lives, since most of us have had to deal with crisis. But the more we get into history the more we'll see that the issues of racism and sexism have overlapped. The women's movement and the black movement at certain times fused together or had the same interests. I think we have to begin recognizing our past.

But I also think that black women have a lot to learn from the women's movement because it has been so successful in studying the power structure and the political processes. Most black women don't have the time to participate in the women's movement since other things, basically living, are more crucial than this or that meeting or committee on rape. That's what I mean when I say that we are into this crisis bag. We don't have the time or the energy to develop strategies, so we find ourselves responding to one crisis after another instead of making long-range demands. It's this sort of expertise which black women can begin to draw on and develop in their own groups so that we can also begin to address ourselves to problems that are not immediate but need to be dealt with. White women have been able to really understand the system and use it to their advantage. I really don't think that most people, even women who are in the movement and doing this kind of analysis and strategy, fully realize the political sophistication women have acquired in such a short time. But, you know, white women were always on the sidelines, watching and knowing what was happening. They just didn't use that knowledge until the women's movement developed. Now black women never had ringside seats—we weren't wives of politicians, or secretaries— so it's more difficult for us to understand the subtleties, the underlying dynamics. I think this is an area where black feminists are really going to be helped when they get involved in feminist issues. Even though at this stage black women will be coming from their own groups and focusing on their own communities, they will not be working in isolation because the larger women's movement is laying the foundations and developing new issues and new styles of political action. Our sisters will be getting the word out, and black women can go on from there.

What changes do you think will happen in the black community now that black women have begun to form their own organizations?

For one thing, you start seeing our young women not tolerating a lot of stuff that I tolerated for the civil rights movement. The movement is for black people, and I'm a black woman, and so the movement is also for my personal liberation—that's the kind of connections that young women are making. And it's valid, and we all sensed it all along but just didn't have the guts to say it. What black women are saying now is that we're competent and individuals and that that doesn't affect the black man's thing. We ought to be able to pull together and still do our separate thing. I'm not really in favor of an exchange of one form of oppression for another. I do want to see a more egalitarian form of life style. But it's a strained kind of position to be in with our men, because you're saying there's a lot of validity to what the women's movement is about and you know it in your heart. And the conflict is not about who does the dishes. At the same time that the black woman does not want to be another foot on the black man's head, she is trying to point out that a lot of the interactions that go on between black men and women are very oppressive. It's a very difficult situation to deal with. You're caught up in the reality of these things being wrong, and you're caught up in the reality that it is a racist society too—it's almost as if you have to take sides. And there is really no one side to be taken, I think, if the issue of injustice is really dealt with.

There just aren't supposed to be black women out there pushing, but we are, and I don't know how its going to be resolved. There's a larger proportion of black women coming to the forefront and pushing for new directions in the civil rights movement. Now, the civil rights movement is largely led by men, so when more women get involved it is viewed as competition. I think that's one of the attitudes that black women's groups must deal with to create some sort of understanding so that we can work together. But I'm also aware that this might put a stronger wedge between us. I've heard comments such as, "All those bitches need is a good fuck," you know? And from people I happen to like. One of the concerns of many black men when we were lobbying for the change in the rape law was that accusations of rape was one of the ways of hanging black men. They wanted to know what kind of protection would be left in a new rape law. Some black men say that if they were to take out a white woman she could scream rape whenever she became angry. I won't say that this isn't a true concern for black men, because they do not expect to find justice in the courts, especially when they are accused of a crime against a white person. But in dealing with the statistics you find that most rapes are not interracial—that most black women are raped by black men and white women by white men. And it's still going to be really difficult to prove rape, so that affords some protection for black men. But I think if we keep on pushing, a lot of brothers will become more aware of how feminism is a part of the struggle for the liberation of all people and how these issues such as rape work into that pattern. But I don't have any feeling that right now there is a meaningful acceptance of these ideas and attitudes being developed in the larger black community. So we will have to keep on pushing.

What will black women do in response to the issue of rape?

At the first National Black Feminist Organization Conference, I held a workshop on rape where we discussed that question in terms of our individual attitudes toward rape, our role as black feminists, and the tone and atmosphere of the black community. What I tried to center it around was that the very fact that women were in the workshop meant that rape was an issue for black women. There was a sharing of different political perspectives and our emotional experience. One woman said she thought rapists should be hung, and some women in the workshop were not prepared for that kind of anger. We were trying to deal with a lot of these feelings more than anything else, and I still feel that they should be explored further. As for the second question, our role as black feminists, I asked whether we should become an arm in the white women's groups and work with them or start our own groups. But the very existence of the National Black Feminist Organization means that we want to do our own thing right now. But certain questions still have to be asked, even though we have started our own groups. Are we going to implement our own kind of services, or do we form coalitions with some white groups and then push for the same kind of counseling services in the black community—because there are very few in the black community?

I have really strong leanings toward the idea that members of black feminist groups who have the time or the commitment to the whole issue of rape should get involved with the New York Women Against Rape and the Manhattan Political Caucus to get the experience of rape counseling and public education as a preparation for setting up these same services in the black community. Black women should capitalize on what has already been accomplished by white women and go on from there. Of course, black women have to first know that these services exist. Last semester I taught a class in which a group of white students set up a rape hotline service in one semester—set it up in one semester! And I was glad my black students saw it being done so quickly. This particular group of students took a concept that already existed and built on it for their own needs. I think that a lot of things that have been built in the white feminist groups can be carried over. The whole concept that I presented to the NBFO workshop on rape was that we can take what we want from the existing groups and that a lot of the work has already been done. We can take that experience and apply it to our needs, make it relevant to our needs. And if we take the time to really work at this, we can find people in the black communities who will be willing to make a commitment to that kind of project because it is serving them and it's a protection for them.

I'd like to see a center in every hospital for rape counseling, especially in the poor neighborhoods. A whole unit can be set up in a hospital where most of the people are served anyway and which would allow all aspects of rape to be coordinated, that is, medical treatment, therapy, and criminal investigation. But there again, for that to happen, rape must become a priority in the black community. That can be accomplished by work and pressure by black feminist groups. How effective a rape service would be in a black community would depend on this pressure, because black communities have to demand the services they do get—we simply aren't offered these services. And there are black communities that do demand proper health services and get them—so the real problem is making black communities recognize that rape counseling is an important service and should be provided. That educational process has not really gotten off the ground in these communities. Black feminists need to bring the rape issue to the public through newspapers and television because the more the facts are presented so that people will listen, the more the problem will be recognized. For example, a very high percentage of rape victims are black and the persons committing the crime are black also, so what is the black community going to do about this? Rape is an issue that may have been started by white women, but it is an issue that addresses itself to our community. When we have that kind of thinking, rape will become a more acceptable issue among blacks and it will not be thought of as a white trip that has no relation to the black community. But that attitude comes from a constant bombardment with facts and a constant reminder of the real situation in our communities. How that comes across is really the job of the black feminist group.

But you have to have had some success to be able to feel that you can achieve something. The tendency is to be pessimistic and to think that nothing is going to happen anyway, that you're not going to get any support so why bother. Black women have to begin to see that women have gotten their thing together, that they have educated their communities and gotten support from community, city, and state government—because black women have never experienced this type of success and they have to know that it's possible. And we also have to know *how* it is possible—it's a process of constant work and planning. It's not just sitting down and talking rhetoric about what has happened and what is going to continue, but it's actually getting out and pushing. You learn through the experience of success, and I think this is the kind of experience that I'd like to see more black women become familiar with. Then when we know the process as well, we can really start talking about a coalition.

A good example of this learning process is the Mayor's Task Force on Rape. I was asked to serve on the Task Force and I made that commitment because I thought that we were going to talk about planning and establishing services in hospitals across the city. Apparently that wasn't what the committee was about, because it never got off the ground, even though we did talk about counseling services. Being a member of the Task Force was a learning experience for me, part of the educational process. Feminists could have gotten hung up with dealing with the Task Force and doing nothing else. You know, a task force can be a way of deterring you from what you have to do. I think the politicians really got a shock with the issue of rape, so they handed us a task force to keep us busy. One of the key things I've learned is that you really don't start achieving things until you know your enemy as well as he knows you. When he calls you by your first name, you should be able to call him by his first name. When they give you a task force to play around with, you should know what that means and go out and do another thing. And you know, that's what we did. Maybe the Task Force on Rape will meet again and something will be accomplished, but so far I feel that feminists have gotten something valuable from the experience in that they learned the name of the game pretty quickly and kept on pushing.

Conclusion

Earlier in the book we stated that the initial step in the feminist process is consciousness-raising and the final step is political action, because we wanted to describe as simply as possible what we and our sisters had experienced. There are different stages of awareness and action, but they do not necessarily follow one another as we have outlined them here. Consciousness-raising is a political act, and in turn, political action becomes consciousness-raising. But the process of radicalization is not circular; once it has begun, our involvement leads us to new levels of awareness and further involvement. It has been said that feminism is both personal and political, but this fusion occurs in every true social movement. We do not speak on behalf of an oppressed group nor is our struggle based on abstract principles, because as women we all have a concrete understanding of our own oppression. Even when we are simply reviewing our childhood in consciousness-raising sessions we often propose tentative plans and strategies of how women can change their situation—because in analyzing our past we realize that things *could* have been different. And now that we are gaining political power, every victory reveals just how much more has to be done. In reality, there is no "final step" or "last stage" to feminist consciousness and action.

When women first began to form feminist groups, much of our intellectual and physical energy came from anger. Consciousness-raising, speaking-out, and theory were means of exploring and exposing our oppression, and, as a result, rape became one of the issues. In the last few years the issue is no longer theoretical, we are acting on it. In many ways, we are now at a critical point of transition where our anger and the realization of our oppression are not enough—we need to know how to work together and how to fight our oppression. One of the best discussions of this transition is "The Tyranny of Structurelessness," in which a Chicago feminist, Joreen, writes, "These problems are coming to a head at this time because the nature of the movement is necessarily changing. Consciousness-raising as the main function of the women's liberation movement is becoming obsolete. Due to the intense press publicity of the last two years and the numerous overground books and articles now being circulated, women's liberation has become a household word. Its issues are discussed and informal rap groups are formed by people who have no explicit connection with any movement group. The movement must go on to other tasks. It now needs to establish its priorities, articulate its goals, and pursue its objectives in a coordinated fashion."[1] But while organizing consciousness-raising groups may no longer be our main function, we can still use consciousness-raising to evolve a new understanding of ourselves in the movement by analyzing how women relate to each other. From an honest recognition of where we need to direct our energies, we can begin building a national movement that will fundamentally alter the structures of our society.

Raising the issue of rape is just a beginning. If we stop at this point, rape will remain just that, another "liberal" issue. As Joreen makes clear, we must not be satisfied with only raising issues. "Given a certain amount of interest by the media and the appropriateness of social conditions, [feminist] ideas will still be diffused widely. But diffusion of ideas does not mean they are implemented; it only means they are talked about. Insofar as they can be applied individually they may be acted on; insofar as they require coordinated political power to be implemented, they will not be."[2] The institutions that we are now criticizing for their treatment of the rape victim might indeed reform themselves—our laws may change, the police might establish special rape squads, and our hospitals might examine rape victims efficiently and with sensitivity—but these reforms alone will not prevent rape, even though they would represent some change in the attitude of these institutions. If the avenues of power remain closed to women, then we will continue to be dependent on men to protect us from other men—Colette Price calls it "the male protection racket."

In a sense, rape is not a reformist but a revolutionary issue because our ultimate goal is to eliminate rape and that goal cannot be achieved without a revolutionary transformation of our society. It means a transformation of the family, of the economic system and the psychology of men and women so that sexual exploitation along with economic exploitation becomes impossible and even unimaginable. We cannot achieve this goal unless we continue as a movement to make increasing demands on the social system, to remain critical of minor reforms because they are minor reforms, and to constantly raise new issues that expose the sexism that pervades our lives. This is what we mean when we say that there is no "final step" or "last stage" to feminist consciousness and action. We must continue to analyze ourselves and our political situation and to devise new forms of political mobilization so that we will not be co-opted by media recognition and superficial reforms. We have passed beyond the stage where we have discovered that rape affects all our lives, we must now go on to eliminate it.

—N.C.

NOTES

1. *The Second Wave,* Vol. 2, No. 1, p. 25
2. *Ibid.,* p. 25

SIX

Appendix I–X

Appendix I
(1970)
An Introduction to the New York
Radical Feminists

Dear Sisters,

The following represents the basic philosophy, structures, and techniques of the New York Radical Feminists. We hope this information will help you in understanding the position of radical feminism in the women's liberation movement and will assist you in setting up small groups for the purposes of consciousness-raising.

The Philosophy of Radical Feminism

Radical feminism recognizes the oppression of women as a fundamental political oppression wherein women are categorized as an inferior class, based upon their sex. It is the aim of radical feminism to organize politically to destroy this sex class system.

We believe that the purpose of male chauvinism is primarily to obtain psychological ego satisfaction, and that only secondarily does this manifest itself in economic relationships. We do not believe that capitalism, or any other economic system, is the cause of female oppression, nor do we believe that female oppression will disappear as a result of purely economic revolution. The political oppression of women has its own class dynamic, namely, the politics of the ego.

As women we are living in a male power-structure, and our roles become necessarily a function of men. The services we supply are services to the male ego. If we do not choose to perform these ego services, but instead assert ourselves as primary to ourselves, we are denied alternatives wherein we can manifest our self-assertion. Our creative efforts are *a priori* judged not serious because we are females, our day-to-day lives are judged failures because we have not become "real women."

The oppression of women is manifested in particular institutions, such as marriage, motherhood, love, and sexual intercourse, constructed and maintained to keep women in their place. Through those institutions the woman is taught to confuse her biological sexual differences with her total human potential. Biology is destiny, she is told. Because she has child-bearing capacity, she is told that motherhood and childbearing are her *function*, not her *option*, and her function is to marry and have the man economically maintain her and make the decisions. She is told that sexual intercourse too is her function, rather than a voluntary act which she may engage in an expression of her general humanity. In each case *her* sexual difference is rationalized to trap her with it, while male sexual difference is rationalized to imply access to all areas of human activity. Love has been used politically to justify an oppressive relationship between men and women, but there can be no genuine love until the need to *control* the growth of another is substituted by the love *for* the growth of another.

It is politically necessary for any oppressive group to convince the oppressed that they are inferior. It is through the destruction of women's egos that they are robbed of their ability to resist.

We must begin to destroy the notion that we are only servants to the male ego; we must construct alternate selves that are independent and self-assertive. It remains for us as women to develop a new dialectic of sex class—an analysis of the way in which sexual identity and institutions reinforce one another.

Structural Approach of the New York Radical Feminists

As established by its founding cell, the Stanton-Anthony Brigade, on December 5, 1969, we hereby set up New York Radical Feminists in answer to the largely unmet political and organizational needs as set down below:

We are dedicated to a revival of knowledge about our forgotten feminist movement. We define this roughly as: the whole American Women's Right Movement until 1869, the Stanton-Anthony group thereafter (National Women's Suffrage Association), and much later, the revived militant tradition associated with Harriet Stanton Blatch in the U.S. (the Congressional Union, later the Woman's Party) and with the Pankhursts in Great Britain (the Women's Social and Political Union). We also include various feminist independents such as Simone de Beauvoir.

We are committed to the building of a mass-based radical feminist movement. To this end we have proposed a structure, consisting of small, closely coordinated groups: nuclear, leaderless, structureless groups of no more than fifteen, where women, over a period of time, develop a personal intimacy, a political awareness, and a positive group experience.

We suggest the following schedule of activity as a period of preparation and development which has proved useful to beginning groups:

1. *Consciousness-raising—For a minimum of three months.*

   a. to develop personal sensitivity to the various levels and forms that opression takes in our daily lives;

   b. to build group intimacy and thus group unity, the foundations of true internal democracy;

   c. to break down in our own heads the barriers between "private" and "public" (the "personal" and the "political"), in itself one of the deepest aspects of our oppression.

2. *Reading and discussion of current literature—for a minimum of six weeks, on the women's movement, both feminist and nonfeminist.*

   a. to acquaint each person with the broad spectrum of politics already apparent in the women's liberation movement;

   b. to discuss the position of radical feminism within the spectrum.

3. *Intensive reading and discussion of feminist history and theory—For a minimum of six weeks.*

   a. to acquaint each member of the group with her own history and to give her a sense of continuity within the feminist tradition;

   b. to give the group a good foundation in basic theory on which to build their own analysis;

   c. to give the group some basis on which to choose its name. This period of preparation should lead the group to an understanding of the character of action which it will undertake, e.g., research, theory, action, theater, etc.

Appendix II
(1972)
How to Organize a Small Consciousness-Raising Group

Select a topic. A topic is usually selected at the previous meeting so that those who wish to may have time to consider it. The suggested list of topics that follows is meant as a guideline and not as a questionnaire. Refer to the list when you need to, and include what you like. Sometimes you may even wish to spend an entire meeting on a single aspect of a topic. It is a good idea to discuss Background Experiences before moving on to Adult Experiences, etc. This is invaluable for developing trust and intimacy within the group. If you plunge into a "heavy" topic, such as marriage or lesbianism at your third session, there may be women who will feel threatened or defensive, as you will still be relative strangers to one another.

Go around in a circle. This creates a kind of "free space" where women can talk about themselves in a way they may never have before. Going around in a circle enables women who are more reticent to have the same opportunity to talk as more aggressive women. It also helps us to listen to each other and breaks down feelings of competitiveness among us.

Always speak personally, specifically and from your own experience. Try not to generalize, theorize, or talk in abstractions.

Don't interrupt, except to ask a specific informational question or to clarify a point. If someone else's experience reminds you of one of yours, you might take notes so that you remember what it is you wish to say when it is your turn. Everyone will get a chance to speak.

Never challenge anyone else's experience. Try to accept that what another woman says is true for her, although it may seem all wrong to you. Keep in mind that she may never before have had a chance to talk about herself without being interrupted or challenged.

Try not to give advice. The purpose of consciousness-raising is not to help you solve your day-to-day problems (e.g., "How can I become less dependent on my boyfriend?") but to help you gain strength through the knowledge that other women share many of your feelings and experiences.

Sum up. After each woman has related her personal experience with the topic, the group should try to find the common element and see what conclusions can be drawn. This is one of the most important parts of consciousness-raising because it is here that we can begin to discover the nature of our oppression.

We have found that eight to twelve women is a good size for a group if everyone is to get a chance to speak. Each member should have the names, addresses, and phone numbers of the other members. A group usually meets once a week and lasts for about three hours. Skipping meetings or perennially coming late can create bad feelings and isn't conducive to ongoing intimacy and growth. By the same token, it is not a good idea to add people after, say, your third or fourth meeting.

Groups usually meet in a different woman's home each week. It is important to create an atmosphere of informality and comfort. It helps to have coffee and something to eat standing by that members can help themselves to during the meeting. Also, the group should have privacy. Husbands, roommates, or parents should be either out of the house or in another room for the duration of the meeting.

Consciousness-raising is different from therapy and encounter groups. Although it is often therapeutic, its purpose is not the solution of personal problems. Some of the means used in therapy to get at "the truth"— confrontation, challenge, acting-out—are all foreign to consciousness-raising. Consciousness-raising is, rather, free space to talk about yourself as a woman.

It is a good idea to periodically devote an entire meeting to reviewing what each member expects from consciousness-raising and how the group can best achieve these goals. In addition, to reevaluate the direction of the group, this kind of meeting might also provide an opportunity to air personal dissatisfactions and group problems. This is best done in the usual consciousness-raising fashion.

We have found that many of the problems that arise within the group are the result of carelessness in using consciousness-raising techniques. Often problems can be eliminated simply by paying particular attention— for the next few meetings at least—to the consciousness-raising format.

Occasionally, a member of the group might have an urgent need to discuss a current personal problem. An effective way of dealing with such a situation is to let her be the first person to speak. Then, when she is finished, try to identify her main emotion or feeling in the situation (e.g., loneliness, anger, dependency) and use this as the topic for the meeting. In this way, the woman who has brought the problem to the attention of the group feels that her problem is shared by each of the other members. This is another way in which we can show support toward one another.

Suggested Topics for Consciousness-Raising

Background Experiences

1. Childhood training for your role as a woman:
   a. Were you treated differently from boys?
   b. What toys did you have? What games did you play?
   c. What activities were encouraged? Discouraged?
   d. What did you think it was going to be like to be a woman?

2. Early childhood sexual experiences:
   a. What experience did you have with children your own age? With adults? How did you feel about these experiences at the time?
   b. Did these experiences affect your view of sex? Did they affect your view of yourself as a woman?

3. Puberty:
   a. How did you feel about your bodily changes? Breasts? Body hair?
   b. What happened the first time you got your period? Were you told what to expect beforehand? Was it a surprise?
   c. What attitudes did you encounter toward your bodily changes from your peers? From adults?

4. Adolescent social life:
   a. How did you spend most of your time? How did your parents feel about how you spent your time?
   b. What sort of relationships did you have with girls? Did you have a best friend? How did you feel about girls your own age? What did you talk about with other girls? What were your activities? Were there older women who you admired and wanted to be like?
   c. What sort of relationship did you have with boys? Did you date? Was there pressure from your peer group to date? What were your parents' attitudes toward dating? How did you get your dates? What kind of boys did you date? What kind of boys did you want to date?
   d. How were your relationships with girls affected by your relationships with boys? Which was more important?
   e. What were your adolescent sexual experiences? Did you "neck," "pet," "make out," "go all the way," etc.? Were you concerned about your "reputation"?

5. First adult sexual experience:
   a. What did/does your virginity mean to you?
   b. Describe the first time you had sex. What did you think it would be like? Did it live up to your expectations? Was it voluntary? Was it planned? Were you raped, seduced, or pressured?
   c. Did you want to do it again?
   d. How did you feel about yourself afterward? Your partner?
   e. Did you tell anyone about it?

6. Education:
   a. What were your parents' attitudes toward education? Did you feel they had the same attitude for girls as they did for boys? What were your parents' academic expectations of you?
   b. What were your teachers'/guidance counselors' expectations of you? Did you feel they had different expectations of female and male students?
   c. What were your own aspirations? Were there courses that you wanted to take but were discouraged from taking? What subjects interested you most? Did these interests change as you went through school?
   d. What kind of student were you? Were you competitive? With whom did you compete?
   e. Were you involved in any extracurricular activities?
   f. Was your education relevant to what you do now?

7. Religion:
   a. What part did religion play in your childhood? Does it play the same part now? What effect did it have on you as a woman? What was your religion's view of women?

Adult Experiences
   1. Masturbation
   a. Have you ever masturbated? If so, when did you begin? What connotations did masturbation have for you?
   b. How often and under what circumstances do you masturbate? How do you masturbate? Do you have an orgasm? Do you fantasize?

   2. Orgasm:
   a. Have you ever had an orgasm? Have you ever faked an orgasm? If so, why?
   b. How do you feel if you don't have an orgasm?
   c. Describe what brings you to orgasm. Can you describe your feelings

and sensations during orgasm? Compare the orgasms you have during sex to those you have during masturbation.

d. To have an orgasm: Are you physically aggressive? Do you communicate to your partner what will bring you to orgasm? Do you depend totally on your partner?

e. Is it necessary for you to have an orgasm in order to enjoy sex? Is it necessary that your partner have an orgasm in order to enjoy sex? Do you feel that your orgasm is as important as your partner's? How important is orgasm, anyway?

f. How do you feel about the following: vaginal orgasm, clitoral orgasm, simultaneous orgasm, frigidity?

3. Contraception: (withdrawal, rhythm, pills, diaphragm, condom, foam, IUD, vasectomy, hysterectomy, tubal ligation, etc.)

a. Do you use contraception? If so, what method? Have you ever used any others? How do you feel about the methods you have used?

b. Do *you* use contraception, or does your partner? Are you satisfied with this arrangment?

4. Abortion

a. Have you ever had an abortion? Describe your experience. How did you feel about it? Would you have another one?

b. If you have never had an abortion, can you imagine yourself in a situation where you would want one? How do you think you would feel?

5. Lesbianism:

a. Have you ever wondered what it would be like to have a sexual relationship with another woman? Have you ever felt sexually attracted to another woman? Have you ever had a homosexual experience?

b. If you are not a lesbian, how do you react when you meet a woman who you know is a lesbian? If you are a lesbian, how do you feel about women who are not?

c. What are socially accepted ways of expressing love for another woman?

6. Rape:

a. Have you ever been raped? By a stranger, a husband, a friend, or by someone you knew? What happened? Did you feel you provoked it in any way? Did you call the police? If so, what was their reaction?

b. Have you ever been coerced into having sex? Have you ever felt pressured to have sex with someone when you didn't want to?

7. Prostitution:
   a. Have you ever had sex in exchange for: money, food, entertainment, gifts, security, approval, etc.?
   b. Have you ever wanted to be a prostitute? What do you imagine it would be like?
   c. Have you ever used your sexuality to get something you wanted?

8. Marriage/Being Single
   a. Are you, or have you been, married or in a marriage-type relationship? Why did you get married? Does/did being married live up to your expectations? How does/did being married affect your self-image? Did/do you find yourself operating within the traditional female/male roles?
   b. If you are single, how do you feel about it? How would being married affect your self-image? Do you feel pressured by your family or society to get married?
   c. Do you feel more important, or different, as part of a couple, or on your own?

9. Housework:
   a. How important is it to you to have a clean home? How is your self-image related to the condition of your home?
   b. If you're living with someone, who does the housework? Is it a shared responsibility? If so, is it because of an agreement, because one person nags the other, or because both feel equally responsible?

10. Pregnancy and Childbirth
   a. Have you ever been pregnant or borne children? How did you feel about yourself during pregnancy? What was the attitude of those around you (i.e., the father of the child, your parents, your employer, other women, men)?
   b. If you have not been pregnant, do you want to bear children? Under what circumstances? How would being pregnant affect your self-image?
   c. If you became pregnant now, what would you do?
   d. How do you feel about giving birth? If you've had a child, was the labor and delivery what you expected? How did you feel about the child when you first saw it?
   e. What are some of the myths of pregnancy and delivery?

11. Motherhood and Child Care
   a. How does, or would, being a mother affect your self-image? How

would you feel if you couldn't have children? How would deciding not to have children affect your self-image?

b. If you are a mother, what is it like? Does being a mother live up to your expectations? Whose decision was it to have children? Is being a mother different from being a father? How did becoming a mother change your life?

c. If you live with someone, do you share child-care responsibilities? If so, is it because of an agreement, because one person nags the other, or because both feel equally responsible?

d. Do you consider child care equal in status to paid work? What is your attitude toward working mothers? Working fathers? Do you, or would you, use day-care facilities?

e. What are some of the myths of motherhood?

12. Divorce:

a. Have you ever been divorced or separated or close to someone who has been? How did you feel about it?

b. If not, how would being a "divorcee" affect your self-image?

c. What is the marital status of most of your friends?

d. If you have been divorced, why did you stay married as long as you did?

13. Employment

a. What were your parents' attitudes toward work? Toward women working?

b. Did your family expect you to get married? To have a career? To get a job and support yourself? Or what?

c. What kinds of jobs have you had, if any? What did you like/dislike about them?

d. Describe your relationships with bosses or employees of lower rank, both male and female. Do you feel you have certain problems or privileges in your job because you're a woman? Do you think your job duties would change if a man were to replace you?

e. How do you feel when people ask you, "What do you do?" What do you say?

f. If you work full-time, do you consider it a "job" or a "career"? Why?

g. What role does your job play in your life?

h. If you are married, or in a marriage-type situation, whose job is considered more important? Who earns more money?

i. If there were a machine that could give you any job, what button would you push?

14. Aging
   a. How old are you? How do you feel about this age?
   b. What age do you consider to be "old"?
   c. What relationships do you have with women who are considerably older than you? Younger?
   d. How do you feel about getting older? Have you noticed any changes in your body?
   e. Are you satisfied with the attentions you receive from men and women of your own age? Older? Younger?
   f. Do you, or have you ever disguised your age? How do you feel when someone mistakes your age?
   g. How do you feel about menopause? What do you know about menopause?

5. Medical/Psychological Care
   a. Psychological Care
      1. Have you ever been in therapy? Was it with a male or a female therapist? Why did you go?
      2. Do you think your therapist has/had any prejudice about women?
      3. Did your therapist ever make sexual advances toward you?
   b. Medical Care
      1. Have you ever been to a gynecologist? Have you ever had a bad experience with a gynecologist—i.e., condescending attitude, inadequate explanations, careless or brutal treatment, sexual advances?
      2. Do you think your doctors understood your problems fully and did you have confidence in their treatment?
      3. If you've ever had a vaginal infection, how did it affect your feeling about yourself?

Contemporary Issues
Here are some questions that concern women. These may be discussed in any order and should be approached both from personal experience and with abstract thought.
   1. How does the media present women?
   2. How do you feel about your body? Fashion? Makeup?
   3. Describe some patterns in your relationships with men.
   4. What is friendship? What is love?
   5. What part has competition played in your life?
   6. What is femininity?
   7. What is your mother like?
   8. What are some of the myths of womanhood (i.e., Prince Charming)?

9. What kind of fantasies do you have?
10. How do you handle street hassles and threats of violence? Do you feel you can defend yourself adequately?
11. What makes you feel secure?
12. How do you manage money? How important are material possessions to you?
13. How do you feel about the following: monogamy, polygamy, communal living, voluntary celibacy, living alone?
14. How do you express anger?
15. What is nonsexist child-rearing?
16. What are your personal goals?

The Liberated Woman
1. What strengths do women have?
2. What is a liberated woman?
3. What are some of the problems/pressures of a liberated woman?
4. What is the best way to deal with a woman who is antagonistic to the women's movement? How do you deal with a man who is antagonistic to the movement?
5. Can a woman with a "raised consciousness" still relate to men?
6. What is equality? Is this what you want?
7. What are the goals of the women's liberation movement? What are the goals of your group?
8. Is consciousness-raising a political action? Is it enough?

For more information: New York Radical Feminists
Box 621, Old Chelsea Station
New York, N.Y. 10011

Appendix III

Pamphlets

A Report on Rape in the Suburbs. " . . . counters the myth that rape occurs mainly in urban high crime areas."
  Ms. Mary Ann Largen, NOW National Coordinator
  Rape Task Force
  5203 Eighth Road South, Apt. 523B
  Arlington, Va. 22204

                                      (single copies free)

How to Start a Rape Crisis Center
  Rape Crisis Center
  P.O. Box 21005
  Washington, D.C. 20009   (single copies $2.00)

Rape: Myth and Fact
  Manhattan Women's Political Caucus
  60 West 13th Street
  New York, New York 10011   (single copies $0.10)

Report of the Public Safety Committee Task Force on Rape
  c/o Councilman Meyers
  District of Columbia City Council
  Washington, D.C. 20004   (single copies free)

Stop Rape
  Women Against Rape
  Women's Resource Center
  18799 Woodward Avenue
  Detroit, Michigan 48203   (single copies $0.90)

Suspected Rape (Technical Bulletin No. 14)
    ACOG Technical Bulletin
    79 Monroe Street
    Chicago, Ill. 60603   (single copies free)

VD Handbook
    Montreal Collective
    P.O. Box 1000, Station "G"
    Montreal, Quebec, Canada   (single copies $0.25)

Video Tape

The Rape Tape (½ inch video tape)
    Women's Interart Center
    549 West 52nd Street
    New York, New York 10019

Newsletter (Reports on rape projects all over the U.S.)

    Rape Crisis Center
    P.O. Box 21005
    Washington, D.C. 20009

*Card Catalogue on Rape (83 Xerox pages, more than
500 annotated references, complete through 5/73: $40.00)*

    Women's History Research Center
    2325 Oak Street
    Berkeley, Calif. 94708

Appendix IV
Suggestions on the Elimination of Rape*

Long-Term Goal to Eliminate Rape

Eliminate sexual roles. The family teaches us our basic attitudes and illustrates male/female divisions. The job market reinforces the subservient position of women in society. Our culture—advertising, major novels, pornography—is based on male consciousness and the objectification of women.

Short-Range Goals to Eliminate Rape

Legal Actions:
1. A law must make it mandatory to render assistance to someone being attacked. Anyone failing to aid becomes an accessory to that crime. This recommendation aims at making an individual, male as well as female, less vulnerable. Many attacks would not be attempted or could not be carried out if the aggressor were not rendered confident by a general apathy for the well-being of others.
2. Charge men who whistle at, comment on, and touch us in the streets with invasion of privacy.
3. Repeal laws that make crimes of sexual activities that do not lead to procreation or to procreation in a socially accepted way, as adultery, anal intercourse, cunnilingus, fellatio, fornication, homosexuality, masturbation, prostitution, statutory rape over fifteen years old. The only provision, in some cases, being that the parties involved consent to the act, be equals, be mentally capable of consent, and involve no physical harm.

*This document was drawn up at the conclusion of the NYRF Conference in 1971 as a guide for future action.

4. Create a classification for rape to indicate its double nature as a hostile aggression using sex; reclassify other crimes with similar characteristics. For instance, the term "sexual aggression" could include: forcible rape of children, forcible rape of women, forcible rape of men, threatened or bribed rape of a child, attempted rape, sexual molestation, etc.

5. Sex offenses should be recorded consistently throughout the U.S. Statistics should note the original charge of rape, not just the plea (often reduced) in court.

6. Psychological or biological rationalizations should not mitigate the sentence.

Psychology:

1. A thorough investigation of the nature of the rapist and his victim should be instituted.

2. Psychiatrists, psychologists, analysts, social workers—both female and male—must have consciousness-raising. Liberated graduates will be certified by a Feminist Committee and be recommended by a Central Medical Bureau.

Education:

1. In order to handle sexual offenses, policemen, detectives, judges, prosecutors must have consciousness-raising.

2. Self-defense courses at all levels for females in schools must begin. Both male and female students should be encouraged to take the same electives, such as Home Economics. No more tracking.

Politics:

1. Support politicians sympathetic to the feminist movement. Encourage feminists to run for public office.

2. Make up a blacklist of hostile chauvinistic legislators; such lists should be distributed to women in the legislator's district during elections.

Procedures to Help Rape Victims:

1. Female detectives, after thorough consciousness-raising, should take the original charge, conduct all interviews with the victim, and handle the investigation.

2. Female judges, after thorough consciousness-raising, should preside over all rape cases involving females.

Living Conditions:

1. Projects should be made safer—for instance, stores to encourage people

into the streets, straight streets, open stairwells, community involvement and patrols, better lighting.
2. Buses should run frequently at night.

Appendix V

Boston Rape Crisis Center (Yellow crisis call form)

CRISIS CENTER, CAN I HELP YOU?
PHONE NUMBER: _____
ARE YOU IN A SAFE PLACE?
IF SO:
ARE YOU HURT?
HOW DO YOU FEEL?

Date:
Time: # _____

IF NOT:
WHERE ARE YOU?_____
_____

Explain what we can do/find out what she wants.

A WOMAN FROM THE CENTER CAN PICK YOU UP, OR I CAN CALL THE POLICE IF YOU WANT.
           Pick up_____
           Police_____

Center_____ Pick up_____
Hospital_____ Don't pick up_____
Police_____ Meet _____
Encourage going to hospital right away for injury or prosecution.

Meet at police station
(Call driver or police.)
       IS COMING TO PICK YOU UP. I'LL STAY ON THE LINE WITH YOU UNTIL SHE (they) COMES.
ARE YOU HURT?
HOW DO YOU FEEL?
WHERE WOULD YOU LIKE TO GO?
Center_____
Hospital_____
Police_____
Other_____

Give information about:
    Hospital procedure
    Medical needs—VD, pregnancy testing

If she doesn't want to go with one of us to hospital, find out if she has a friend she can go with.

Emphasize importance of later testing if she's not going to the hospital.
CAN WE CALL YOU IN A FEW DAYS TO FIND OUT HOW YOU'RE DOING?
Yes _____ No _____ Phone_____
Make sure she feels free to call back and talk.

Referrals:

Hospital:

Police station:

Driver

Who went:

Relief woman:

Staffer:

On back describe (1) how you felt about the call; (2) how you think the caller felt.

SIGNATURE_____

Appendix VI

Boston Rape Crisis Center (Blue general information form)

CRISIS CENTER, CAN I HELP YOU?

DATE: # _____
TIME:

PHONE NUMBER _____ NAME: _____

SERVICES DESIRED:
1. Group discussions _____
2. General counseling _____
3. Referral _____
4. Pick up _____
5. Information about the center _____
6. Other _____

DESCRIPTION OF PROBLEM _____
_____
_____
_____
_____
_____
_____

LIST REFERRALS GIVEN (if any) _____

EVALUATE YOURSELF (What was your reaction to the call? How could you have helped her more? Where did you goof?) _____
_____
_____
_____
_____

PLANS FOR FOLLOW-UP, ADDITIONAL COMMENTS _____
_____
_____

LENGTH OF CALL:
less than 10 minutes _____
10-20 minutes _____
Over 20 minutes _____

SIGNATURE _____

Appendix VII

August 3, 1973

INVITATION TO COVER
Press Conference: AUGUST IS ANTI-RAPE MONTH IN
NEW YORK CITY
Wednesday, August 8, 1973
11:30 A.M.
City Hall Park (between Broadway and Park Row, Chambers and
Park Place)
Subways: BMT—City Hall; Lexington—Brooklyn Bridge; 8th
Ave. IND—Chambers

Press Contact: Roberta Weiner CA 8-9646
              Sally McGee 877-4937

New York—Citing a 19.1 percent increase in rape complaints in the first
six months of 1973 and noting the traditional peak of rape assaults on hot
August weekends, the Manhattan Women's Political Caucus will join the
National Organization of Women, the New York Women Against Rape,
and the New York Radical Feminists in proclaiming August ANTI-RAPE
MONTH in New York City at a press conference in City Hall Park next
Wednesday morning, August 8, at 11:30 A.M.

MWPC member Charlotte Jones, National Community Development
Director for Teleprompter, Inc., and co-chairman of the Negro Ensemble
Company Advisory Board, will chair the conference. Key speakers will
include *Lieutenant Julia Tucker* of the New York Police Department Rape
Investigation and Analysis Unit, *Martha Zelman*, assistant district attorney
in Queens, and *Honorable Karen Burstein*, state senator from Nassau.

Assistant to the Mayor Betsy Hogen will read a prepared statement of
support from *Mayor John Lindsay*, outlining further ways in which wom-
en in the city can protect themselves.

Mayoral candidates and legislative officials from the city have been
invited to attend and to send written statements responding to goals

outlined in the MWPC—NOW—Women Against Rape—Radical Feminists press statement to be issued by Ms. Jones.

A major effort of the caucus in August will be the dissemination through community groups of a self-help brochure, *Rape: Myth and Fact*, published by the MWPC. With information on what to do if you are raped, notes on the existing rape statutes in New York State, and suggestions on how the law could be changed, the brochure is aimed at all women in all districts in the city. It publicizes the police number 577-RAPE for assistance to rape victims.

Appendix VIII

RAPE IS A POLITICAL CRIME AGAINST WOMEN

We've been told

- Don't go out alone after dark

- Don't talk to strangers

- A woman's place is in the home

From 1968 to 1969, rape has increased 46% in big cities!

Women are raped by

- men on the street

- husbands and boyfriends

- psychiatrists

- child molesters

- gang rape

If women don't belong to one man, they're every man's property, and a raped woman is damaged property. RAPE is the logical result of women being told to be submissive to the dominant male.

WOMEN UNITE!   ATTEND A SPEAK-OUT ON RAPE

Let's testify about our experiences.

Sunday, Jan. 24 - 2:30 p.m.

St. Clement's Episcopal Church - 423 W. 46th St., Manhattan
                              (between 9th and 10th Aves)
 Admission: Women Free

          Men, $2.00 (must be accompanied by a woman)

No cameras or tape recorders allowed.

CHILD CARE WILL BE AVAILABLE

Sponsored by New York Radical Feminists, Box 621, Old Chelsea Station

New York, N.Y. 10011

APRIL 17, 1971

9:00 am - 6:00 pm

Washington Irving High School
40 Irving Place
(16th Street West of Third Avenue)
New York, New York

RAPE

CONFERENCE

FOR WOMEN ONLY

SUGGESTED DONATION $1.00

CHILD CARE AVAILABLE

FORUM AND
WORKSHOPS ON:

RAPE AND THE LAW
HEALTH AND MEDICAL ISSUES
RAPE AND PSYCHIATRISTS
SELF-DEFENSE
RAPE AS SOCIAL POLICY
RAPE AND CULTURAL CLIMATE
SEXUALITY AND SENSUALITY
INCEST AND CHILD MOLESTATION
PSYCHOLOGY OF RAPIST AND VICTIM
RAPE, MARRIAGE AND PROSTITUTION
SURVIVAL NOW: COMMUNITY
 RESPONSIBILITY AND IMMEDIATE DEMANDS

SPONSORED BY

NEW YORK RADICAL FEMINISTS

RAPE CONFERENCE

GENERAL MEETING 10:00-12:30

Speakers: Rape victim
           Policeman
           Lawyer
           Psychologist
           Anthropologist
Questions

WORKSHOPS 1:00-4:00

Cultural Climate, Hostility to Women and Rape
Medical Aspects
Legal/Criminal Aspects
Psychology of the Rapist, His Victim and Rape Fantasies
Rape as Social Policy
Incest and Child Molestation
Survival Now, Community Responsibility and Immediate Demands
Self-Defense
Rape, Marriage, and Prostitution
Rape and Psychiatry
Rape, Sensuality, and Sexuality: Claiming the Sex Act

GENERAL MEETING, 4:00-6:00

Workshop Reports
Statement: Redefinition of Rape
            Causes of Rape
            Immediate and Long-Range Actions

SATURDAY, APRIL 17

WASHINGTON IRVING HIGH SCHOOL
16th STREET AND IRVING PLACE
NEW YORK CITY

Contributions   Bring your own lunch
  Women Only   Day Care Provided

                                 New York Radical Feminists

Appendix X
Selected Bibliography

Books

Angelou, Maya. *I Know Why the Caged Bird Sings*. New York: Bantam Books, 1971. (Paperback). Especially Chapters 11, 12, and 13.

Blackstone, William. *Commentaries on the Laws of England. Volume IV, Of Public Wrongs*. Boston: Beacon Press, 1962 (Paperback). Especially Chapter XV.

The Boston Women's Health Book Collective. *Our Bodies Ourselves*. New York: Simon and Schuster, 1973 (Paperback). Especially Chapter 8.

Brownmiller, Susan. *Aspects of Rape*. (Projected title) Soon to be published by Simon and Schuster, New York.

Chesler, Phyllis. *Women and Madness*. New York: Doubleday, 1972.

Cleaver, Eldridge. *Soul on Ice*. New York: A Delta Book, 1968. Especially pp. 14-17, "I became a rapist."

Firestone, Shulamith. *The Dialectic of Sex: The Case for Feminist Revolution*. New York: Bantam Books, 1971. (Paperback)

Flexner, Eleanor. *Century of Struggle*. New York: Atheneum, 1970. (Paperback)

Grimstad, K., and Rennie, S., eds. *The New Woman's Survival Catalog*. New York: Coward, McCann and Geoghegan, 1973 (Paperback), Especially Chapter IV, "Self Defense." Contains names and addresses of rape crisis ccenters and rape projects.

Herschberger, Ruth. *Adam's Rib*. New York: Har/Row Books, 1970. (Paperback)

Lerner, Gerda, ed. *Black Women in White America. A Documentary History*. New York: Vintage Books, 1973. (Paperback)

Mitchell, Juliet. *Women's Estate*. New York: Vintage Books, 1973. (Paperback)

Morgan, Robin, ed., *Sisterhood Is Powerful*. New York: Vintage Books, 1970. (Paperback)

Rowbotham, Sheila. *Women, Resistance & Revolution*. New York: Pantheon Books, 1972.

Ross, Susan C. *The Rights of Women. The Basic ACLU Guide to a Woman's Rights*. New York: Avon Books, 1973. (Paperback) Especially Chapter V.

Slovenko, Ralph, ed. *Sexual Behavior and the Law*. Springfield, Illinois: Charles C Thomas, 1965.

Stambler, Sookie, ed. *Women's Liberation Blueprint for the Future*. New York: Ace Books, 1970. (Paperback)

Vietnam Veterans Against the War. *The Winter Soldier Investigation: An Inquiry Into American War Crimes*. Boston: Beacon Press, 1972. (Paperback) Covers crimes against women, including rape.

Articles

Cohn, Barbara, "Succumbing to Rape?" *The Second Wave*, Vol. 2:2.

Cordell, Sarita. "Self-Confidence/Self-Defense." *The Second Wave*, Vol. 2:4.

Douglas, Carol Ann. "Rape in Literature." *The Second Wave*, Vol. 2:2.

Frankfort, Ellen. "DES: Banned for Cattle and Prescribed for Women." *Village Voice*, 3/22/73, p. 7.

"From Us." *The Second Wave*, Vol. 3:1. The problems of a collective.

Goldstein, Marilyn. "Society Blamed for Sexual Assaults." *Newsday*, 4/19/71, p. 15A Coverage of the NYRF Rape Conference.

Griffin, Susan "Rape: The All-American Crime." *Ramparts*, September, 1971, Vol. 10:3.

Harmetz, Aljeant. "Rape—An Ugly Movie Trend." *The New York Times*, Arts & Leisure, Sunday, September 30, 1973.

Hibey, Richard A. "The Trial of a Rape Case: An Advocate's Analysis of Corroboration, Consent and Character." *The American Criminal Law Review*, Winter 1973, Vol. II:2.

Houstle, Sue. "A Visit to the Police Station." *Cold Day in August*, Issue 10.

Joreen. "The Tyranny of Structurelessness." *The Second Wave*, Vol. 2:1.

Kearon, P., and Mehrhof B. "Rape: An Act of Terror." *Notes from the Third Year*.

Leffler, Ann. "Sisterhood Strikes Again . . ." *Ain't I a Woman?* Vol. 3:5.

Lichtenstein, Grace. "Feminists Hold Rape-Defense Workshop." *The New York Times*, Sunday, April 18, 1971, p. 68. On NYRF Rape Conference.

Lindsey, K., Newman, H., and Taylor, F. "Aspects of Rape." *The Second Wave*, Vol. 2:2.

McNellis, Maryanne, "Rape Victims Tell Libbers What It's Like." *New York Sunday News*, 4/18/71, p. 36. Coverage of NYRF Rape Conference.

Newman, Holly. "Dealing With Rape." *The Second Wave*, Vol. 2:3. Article on rape crisis centers.

"Our Sisters Speak. Rape: The Response." *Women: A Journal of Liberation*, Vol. 3:2.

Price, Colette, "Bringing the Rapist to Trial, A Group Effort." *Women's World*, November-December, 1971. Vol. 1:3.

Sheehy, Gail. "Nice Girls Don't Get Into Trouble." *New York*, 2/15/71. On NYRF Rape Speak-Out.

Walker, Joan. "Consciousness-Raising on Rape and Violence." *Wombat*, February, 1972, Vol. 1:1.

Weiss, Kay. "Afterthoughts on the Morning-After Pill." *Ms.*, November, 1973, Vol. 2:5.

Weisstein, Naomi. "Psychology Constructs the Female; or the Fantasy Life of the Male Psychologist (with some attention to the Fantasies of His Friends, the Male Biologist and the Male Anthropologist)." *Social Education*, April, 1971. Vol. 35:4, pp. 362-373.

———. "Why We Aren't Laughing . . . Any More." *Ms.*, November, 1973, Vol. 2:5.

Williams, Kathy. "What to Do about Rape in a Third World Neighborhood: A White Woman's Self-Criticism." *Ain't I a Woman?*, July 20, 1973, Vol. 3:5.

Resources

Half of the articles listed above are in women's movement magazines and newspapers not included in library periodical collections. The following lists the addresses of these periodicals so that if you are interested in a particular article you can write to request back issues. Another source for women's movement periodicals is the microfilm series "Herstory I & II" published by the Women's History Research Center. The series is available to libraries. If your library does not have these valuable sources for women's studies, ask the librarian to write to the center for information about their library services. We have starred (*) those periodicals available through the microfilm series. Please include a large, stamped, self-addressed envelope when making inquiries about the periodicals or the center.

Because of lack of money, the Women's History Research Center may be forced to close. If you visit or live in Berkelely, please donate time to help microfilm more than 2000 subject files before the funding runs out. Or send contributions to Women's History Research Center, 2325 Oak Street, Berkeley, California 94708.

Ain't I a Woman?
    Box 1169
    Iowa City, Iowa 52240
Cold Day in August *
    Baltimore Women's Center
    101 East 25th Street, Apt. B-2
    Baltimore, Maryland 21218
International Women's History Archive
    Women's History Research Center, Inc.
    2325 Oak Street
    Berkeley, California 94708
Majority Report
    74 Grove Street
    New York, New York 10014
New York Radical Feminists Newsletter
    c/o J. Grove
    80 Thompson Street
    New York, New York 10012
Notes from the Third Year *
    P.O. Box AA
    Old Chelsea Station
    New York, New York 10011
Prime Time * "For the liberation of women in the prime of life . . . "
    c/o M. Collins
    232 East 6th Street, Apt. 5C
    New York, New York 10003
Redstockings Journal: Feminist Revolution Annual
    Box 1284 Peter Stuyvesant Station
    New York, New York 10009
The Second Wave *
    Box 344, Cambridge A
    Cambridge, Maryland 02139
Wombat
    765 Ohayo Mountain Road
    Woodstock, New York 12398
Women: A Journal of Liberation *
    3028 Greenmount Avenue
    Baltimore, Maryland 21218

Women's Rights Law Reporter
    180 University Avenue
    Newark, New Jersey 07102
Women's World*
    Box 1284, Peter Stuyvesant Station
    New York, New York 10009
    (Out-of-print complete set of back issues $2.00)

Notes on the Contributors

Edith Barnett graduated from Barnard College (1964), has an M.S.W. degree from Hunter School of Social Work (1968) and a J.D. from New York University School of Law (1971). During her years at Barnard and Hunter she worked and/or had internships in New York City social agencies including the Department of Welfare. She is the author of "The Hospital Abortion committee as an Administrative Body of the State" which appeared in the *Journal of Family Law*, University of Louisville (1970). Since 1971 she has been an attorney with the Fair Labor Standards Division, Office of the Solicitor, U.S. Department of Labor, Washington, D.C., specializing in litigation under the Equal Pay Act.

Phyllis Chesler is a feminist psychologist, lecturer and Assistant Professor of Psychology at Richmond College of the State University of New York. She is the author of *Women and Madness* and many other scientific articles. She has also published fiction, journalism and poetry. Her work has been published in *Ms., Village Voice, Science, Psychology Today, New York* and *Women in a Sexist Society*. She wrote the preface to *Wonder Woman*, a reissue of the comic book series.

Noreen Connell had the audacity to be born yellow on a Friday the 13th in Mexico City. After graduation from high school in Mexico City where she had seen students gassed in the streets, she came to the U.S. to study sociology. While at college she got a glimpse of U.S. prison life when she taught anthropology, remedial reading and Spanish to women prisoners. Once out of college she headed for Chicago where she worked in a halfway house for ex-mental patients and then went on to New York where she worked as a caseworker. New York City she feels is the perfect place for a manic depressive. She who pooh-poohs astrology, nevertheless follows her Gemini instincts and totally confuses all by taking two masters degrees (in sociology and in film criticism) at two different colleges. Her women's movement activities, especially in the areas of child care and women office workers, has never ceased all through the degrees and work, but her energy was slightly siphoned off by Ms. Wilson who enlisted Noreen's considerable brainpower at that fateful "women and responsibility" meeting toward a project that became this book.—C.W.

Lynne Farrow received a B.A. in Humanities from the New School for Social Research (1969) and an M.A. in Women's Studies from Cambridge Goddard Graduate School (1972). She lobbied for the passage of the Equal Rights Amendment in the U.S. Senate with the National Women's Party and has appeared on radio and television discussing the history and implications of the ERA. She currently edits *Aurora: Prism of Feminism* and is teaching Women's Studies at Ramapo College of the State University of New Jersey.

Linda Fodaski, an early entrant in the women's struggle, participated in both the prostitution conference and the rape conference of NYRF; out of the latter grew her interest in developing the present paper. A graduate of Brooklyn College, she collaborated with a friend to form a non-sexist free-school program for three- and four-year old children which continues to function successfully. Ms. Fodaski will begin graduate training in psychology in the fall of 1974. She lives in Brooklyn's Park Slope with her husband and two children, Kate, 5, and Elizabeth, 3.

Ann Garfinkle and Kristin Glen encouraged and helped their NYU women law students to draft the model rape statute (page 177). She writes, "I am a practicing attorney. I do a great deal of feminist legal work and criminal law. I advise rape victims about what they are up against in pressing a rape charge. I have represented many women who brought civil suits for damages arising out of sexual assaults."

Kristin Glen is "a feminist lawyer, practicing in New York." She founded (with Ann Garfinkle)—and for two years taught at—the New York University Women's Law Clinic. She presently teaches women's studies at New York University Washington Square College. "I am also a closet poet and spend most of my time working to get clear."

Sarah Lydgate is a native New Yorker who has lived and worked in Manhattan most of her adult life. "1970 was the year I became actively involved with the women's movement, most specifically as staff person for the August 26th Women's Strike for Equality. Helped organize the August 26th March for Equality (1970), handled press relations for the strike. Briefly a member of the Boycott Committee after the strike and an executive committee member of NOW. I then joined NYRF, where I helped organize the Medical Issues Committee of the 1971 Rape Conference. During this period my consciousness was raised incredibly, to the point of seeking and holding an executive job (male attitudes remain the same but mine have changed!) and returning to college to finish a B.A. degree and obtain a Master's Degree in Public Administration."

Mary Ann Manhart is a fiery redhead who composes music.—C.W.

Joan Mathews is a painter. A descendant of Susan B. Anthony, she was born and raised in the Midwest. She has lived in New York City since the late 1950's and was active in the antiwar and black liberation movements prior to entering the women's movement in 1969.

Lilia Melani, A.B., M.A., University of Pittsburgh, Ph.D., Indiana University. Lecturer, English Department, Brooklyn College. Feminist activities: New York Radical Feminists, NOW. Founder and Coordinator for City University of New York Women's Coalition wihch filed class actions against CUNY with EEOC and HEW and is going into federal court against CUNY for sex discrimination. Officer at Large of Professional Staff Congress/CUNY (union).

Florence Rush has been a psychiatric social worker for over twenty years. She is a member of NOW and NYRF. She is presently writing a book about children to be published by Richard W. Baron.

Cassandra Wilson was born by the Newport, R.I., seashore, and then she was kidnapped by her parents and taken to Rockland County, N.Y., where she lived twenty-one years. She studied modern dance at Juilliard and Sarah Lawrence and then traveled around the country for eight years in search of a meaningful B.A. Her odyssey was interrupted by short stints as a vacuum cleaner saleswoman, a long-distance operator, a lawyers' representative in the Supreme Court of New York, and a price marker for a gigantic discount store in San Jose. She was present at such historic occasions as the Los Angeles dam break and the New York blackout, both of which served as material for sociology papers. She was going to embark on another odyssey, this time a meaningful M.A., but became involved in feminism and film production work and now spends her time going to meetings and calling up her answering service. During a heated debate on "responsibility and the women's movement," she raised her hand in a moment of passion and stated that she would undertake the job of making a pamphlet out of a collection of papers from the NYRF conference. She was handed a Bloomingdale's shopping bag filled with handwritten notes, partially erased tapes, lists of names of women who had long since left New York, and pages upon pages of statistics without any references cited. Another odyssey began.—N.C.

Pamela Lakes Wood is currently a third-year student at Georgetown University Law Center, where she is an editor on the *American Criminal Law Review* and a member of the Women's Rights Collective. Her involvement with the rape issue has included participation in a panel discussion before the Washington, D.C., chapter of the National Lawyer's Guild. Originally from New York City, Ms. Wood is currently living in Bethesda, Maryland, and plans to practice law in the D.C. area after her graduation from law school. Her interests include photography, sailing, painting, and bridge.